Josette Baer

Seven Czech Women

Portraits of Courage, Humanism, and Enlightenment

Josette Baer

SEVEN CZECH WOMEN

Portraits of Courage, Humanism, and Enlightenment

ibidem-Verlag
Stuttgart

Bibliografische Information der Deutschen Nationalbibliothek
Die Deutsche Nationalbibliothek verzeichnet diese Publikation in der
Deutschen Nationalbibliografie; detaillierte bibliografische Daten sind im
Internet über http://dnb.d-nb.de abrufbar.

Bibliographic information published by the Deutsche Nationalbibliothek
Die Deutsche Nationalbibliothek lists this publication in the Deutsche Nationalbibliografie;
detailed bibliographic data are available in the Internet at http://dnb.d-nb.de.

Cover picture: Evžen a Eva, 1939. © Ladislav Sitenský.
                 Reprint with kind permission.

∞

Gedruckt auf alterungsbeständigem, säurefreien Papier
Printed on acid-free paper

ISBN-13: 978-3-8382-0640-0

© *ibidem*-Verlag
Stuttgart 2015

Alle Rechte vorbehalten

Das Werk einschließlich aller seiner Teile ist urheberrechtlich geschützt. Jede Verwertung außerhalb der engen Grenzen des Urheberrechtsgesetzes ist ohne Zustimmung des Verlages unzulässig und strafbar. Dies gilt insbesondere für Vervielfältigungen, Übersetzungen, Mikroverfilmungen und elektronische Speicherformen sowie die Einspeicherung und Verarbeitung in elektronischen Systemen.

All rights reserved. No part of this publication may be reproduced, stored in or introduced into a retrieval system, or transmitted, in any form, or by any means (electronic, mechanical, photocopying, recording or otherwise) without the prior written permission of the publisher. Any person who does any unauthorized act in relation to this publication may be liable to criminal prosecution and civil claims for damages.

Printed in the EU

Dedication

In memoriam Eva 'Mimi' Jiránková (1921–2015)

This study is dedicated to Czech women in particular and women in general, wherever they live. Two of them are particularly dear to me: Marta Neracher taught me Czech in the late 1980s and sent me off to study at the *letní škola* (Summer School of Bohemian Studies) at Charles University – a summer month in Prague in 1991 that would crucially determine my life as a scholar specializing in Czechoslovak history. Thanks to my knowledge of Czech, I eventually met Mimi. Every day, I miss Mimi's optimism, straightforwardness and black humour, her happy and energetic voice. We used to talk about Czech and world politics on the phone at least once a week. When we spent time together walking in Prague, Mimi used to explain to me how that particular house or that particular corner looked in Masaryk's Republic and how it changed during the German occupation. Her witty and enlightened comments about what was happening *doma* taught me a lot about Czech politics in the 20th and 21st centuries. Dearest Marta, thankfully we will still meet up for our traditional cup of tea and talk about Czech literature and our lives as scholars at the university. Dearest Mimi – we all follow.

Table of Contents

Foreword XI

Acknowledgements XIII

X. Introduction 1
    X. 1   Criteria of selection 2
    X. 2   The portraits 6
    X. 3   The method 7
    X. 4   A brief word on gender studies in Central Europe 10

I. Ema Destinn (1878–1930) – a Bohemian in New York 17
    I. 1   The historical context 17
    I. 2   Emmy or Ema? Destinn's success, work for independence and decline 20
    I. 3   Conclusion 33

II. Alice Garrigue Masaryková (1879–1966) – the First Czech feminist? 35
    II. 1   The historical context 35
    II. 2   Imprisoned for being a daughter 56
    II. 3   The Czechoslovak Red Cross as the fulfilment of "small works" (*drobná práce*) 65
    II. 4   Conclusion 82

III. Eva 'Mimi' Jiránková (1921–2015) – a witness of Democracy and Nazism (OHI) 87

IV. Milada Horáková (1901–1950) – executed for her belief in Democracy 99
    IV. 1   Historical context 99
    IV. 2   Milada Horáková – a democrat and feminist 111
    IV. 3   The propaganda campaign creating the Socialist Citizen 131
    IV. 4   Conclusion 156

V. Věra Čáslavská (*1942) – an Olympic champion punished with silence 158
   V. 1   The historical context 173
   V. 2   From Olympic stardom to social isolation 185
   V. 3   Conclusion 198

VI. Nataša Lišková (*1949) – a Czechoslovak citizen (OHI) 201

VII. Tereza Maxová (*1971) – Beauty and the care of children (OHI) 207

Conclusion 213

Appendix

Chronology 221

Bibliography 247

Index 263

Abbreviations

CC	Central Committee of the Communist Party
CSCE	Commission for Security and Cooperation in Europe
ČNB	Česká Národní Banka – Czech National Bank
ČSČK	Československý Červený Kříž – Czechoslovak Red Cross
ČSNS	Československá Strana Národně Socialistická – Czechoslovak National Socialist Party
ČSS	Československá Strana Socialistická – Czechoslovak Socialist Party
ČSTV	Československý Svaz Tělesné Výchovy a Sportu – Czechoslovak Association for Physical Education and Sport
FTVS	Fakulta Telesné Výchovy a Sportu – Faculty of Physical Education and Sport
HZDS	Hnutie Za Demokratické Slovensko – Movement For a Democratic Slovakia
KSČ	Kommunistická Strana Československá – Czechoslovak Communist Party
KSS	Kommunistická Strana Slovenska – Slovak Communist Party
MNV	Místní národní výbor – local branch of the Czechoslovak National Council
NAM	Non-Alignment Movement

NBČS	Národní Banka Československá – Czechoslovak National Bank
ODS	Občanská Demokratická Strana – Civic Democratic Party
OF	Občanské Forum – Civic Forum
OSS	Office of Strategic Services
OSCE	Organization for Security and Cooperation in Europe
SAV	Slovenská Akadémie Vied – Slovak Academy of Sciences
SBČS	Státní Banky Československé – Czechoslovak state banks
SNK	Slovenská Národná Knižnica, Martin – The Slovak National Library, Martin, Slovak Republic
SNR	Slovenská Národná Ráda – Slovak National Council
SNP	Slovenské Národné Povstanie – Slovak National Uprising
StB	Státní Bezpečnost – State Security Service
ÚV KSČ	Ústřední výbor Kommunistické Strany Československá – Central Committee of the Czechoslovak Communist Party
VPN	Verejnosť Proti Násilie – Society Against Violence
ŽNR	Ženská Národní Ráda – Czechoslovak National Women's Council

Foreword

Josette Baer's book is a very interesting undertaking, which offers an insight into the volatile history of the 20th century, through to the present day, in the Czech lands and, in a wider context, also in Europe and the world, through the fates and activities of seven women. The author set herself the difficult task of presenting women of various professions, who originated from different backgrounds and distinguished themselves also in their significance in the international context. What they all have in common, though, are their humanism and attempts to promote these values. Also, the women portrayed do not let themselves get carried away by the historical events, but try to influence them, each one in her own particular way.

Josette Baer is an experienced author, her book is most readable and informative. I am no friend of lengthy forewords and explicatory comments. Readers should form their own opinions. In any case, I recommend reading this book carefully and I thank the author for her admirable work. Reading it is very inspiring, offering a deep insight into the subject matter.

Karel Borůvka
Ambassador of the Czech Republic to Switzerland
Bern, Switzerland, July 2015

Acknowledgements

This volume is the second of a two volume project of Czech and Slovak History seen through the eyes of women. The first volume *Seven Slovak Women* was published in April 2015.

This volume *Seven Czech Women* is a study in its own right, focussing on Czech women's life histories. Owing to the peculiar history of the Czech lands before and after the Czechoslovak Republic (1918–1992), the seven portraits explain the specific political circumstances Czech women were facing from the late 19th century to the present day. *Seven Czech Women* and *Seven Slovak Women* provide the reader with a comprehensive picture of women's lives in Central Europe; the volumes can explain, to some extent, the disparate development and political and cultural identity of Czech and Slovak women.

My thanks. I am greatly indebted to my colleagues and friends for their interest in my research and willingness to discuss specific issues with me. My thanks, in alphabetical order, go to Zdeněk V. David, Markéta Doležalová, Blanka Hajnová, Kristina Larischová, Radka Handlová, Vladimír Handl, Thomas Hardmeier, Adis Merdzanovic, Slavomír Michálek, Miroslav Michela, Daniel E. Miller, Marta Neracher, Marie Neudorflová, Libora Oates-Indruchová, Francis D. Raška, Nikola Todorović and Martin Vadas. The ladies at the Prague National Library Clementinum were very professional and went to great lengths to help me with finding the source material crucial for this volume.

Karel Borůvka, the Ambassador of the Czech Republic to Switzerland, supported this book from the start, and I am honoured that he agreed to write the preface. Valerie Lange at ibidem publishers in Stuttgart is an exceptionally patient, effective and supportive editor. Peter Thomas Hill proofread the manuscript, perennially soldiering on with the demanding task of teaching me English that is up to his own high standards.

I would like to express my gratitude and respect to the ladies who agreed to participate in my oral history interviews, which, to some, meant going back in history to remember painful events. Nataša Lišková, Tereza Maxová, and Terezie Sverdlínová, your esprit, commitment, modesty, beauty, honesty and intellect are inspiring – you are in a league of your own. Sadly, Eva 'Mimi' Jiránková, my great friend, can no more witness the publication of this volume. Mimi passed away peacefully on 26 April 2015 at the age of 93 at her Devon home, surrounded by her loving family.

The errors and shortcomings in this volume are my own.

Josette Baer
Zurich, Switzerland, and Prague, Czech Republic, August 2015

X. Introduction

This book[1] is the second volume of my project *Slovak and Czech History from a female perspective.* I became interested in the history of Slovak and Czech women because of the superb study my friend and colleague Gabriela Dudeková published in 2011.[2] As a political scientist focussing on the history of political thought in Slavic Central and Eastern Europe, and a careful student of Czech, Czechoslovak and Slovak political history, I admired Gabriela's study; in a *tour de force* reaching from the 19th to the 21st centuries, she and her fellow authors analysed the political situation of Austrian, Czech, Hungarian and Slovak women, providing copious historical analysis based on archive material in four languages.

Neither the first[3] nor this second volume is a contribution to theories of gender or nationalism studies. I would like to present to the Western reader the history of the Czech lands seen through the eyes of seven women who lived through one hundred and fifty years of the often cruel political waves so characteristic of Central European history. If an interest in women's lives and a distinct curiosity about how women fared in history is considered a feminist

---

[1] All translations from Czech, German and Slovak into English are mine, if not referred to otherwise.
[2] Gabriela Dudeková, *Na ceste k modernej žene. Kapitoly z dejín rodových vzťahov na Slovensku* (Bratislava: Veda, 2011). See also Johanna Gehmacher and Natascha Vittorelli (eds.), *Wie Frauenbewegung geschrieben wird. Historiographie, Dokumentation, Stellungnahmen, Bibliographien* (Wien: Erhart Locker, 2009); Edith Saurer, Margareth Lanzinger and Elisabeth Frysak (eds.), *Women's Movements. Networks and Debates in Post-communist Countries in the 19th and 20th Centuries* (Köln: Böhlau, 2006).
[3] Josette Baer, *Seven Slovak Women. Portraits of Courage, Humanism and Enlightenment* (Stuttgart: ibidem, 2015).

approach – then this volume has a feminist focus and should be considered a modest contribution to feminist historiography with a focus on Czech women.

X. 1 Criteria of selection

I selected the seven women on subjective grounds since, in my opinion, they represent the spirit and reality of *seven distinct historical eras* of Czech and Czechoslovak history. My *three criteria* for selection are: all of them have a *Czech cultural and political identity*; second, their *visibility* in the Czech, Czechoslovak and international public eye; and third, their *physical presence* in the Czech lands.

Compared with the volume on Slovak women, I have made three exceptions for this book with respect to *visibility* and *physical presence*. First, although she emigrated in 1948 after the Communist coup d'état, Eva 'Mimi' Jiránková's story (chapter III) is a lively account of the liberties Czech women enjoyed in the First Republic (1918–1938) and how their lives changed with the beginning of the German occupation in March 1939. She was most probably the only woman in history whose husband was arrested by the Gestapo on her wedding night. Second, Nataša Lišková (chapter VI) is what one would call an ordinary citizen, that is, without ties to the Communist Party or influential relatives; she is not a celebrity. Yet, her personal account of the normalization provides us with a vivid picture how Czech women experienced the liberties of the Prague Spring and the post-68 tightening of the political screw dictated by Moscow. Bringing up children in the harsh political and economic realities of the Husák[4] regime was a daily ordeal. Third, as a world-famous top

---

[4] See the excellent biography of Husák: Slavomír Michálek, Miroslav Londák a kol., *Gustáv Husák. Moc politiky. Politik moci* (Bratislava: Veda, 2013). For a review of Michálek and Londák in English see my "A Man

model, Tereza Maxová is highly visible in the Czech and international public sphere; she is not a resident of the Czech Republic, but frequently travels to Prague to support the activities of her foundation.

Thus, given that the Western reader is much more familiar with the names of famous Czech (-born) women such as Madeleine Albright, Olga Havlová, Marta Kubišová, Martina Navratilova, Božena Němcová,[5] Petra Kvitová and Ivana Trump, I took the liberty to make the exceptions mentioned above: Mrs Jiránková emigrated and she is not a celebrity. Mrs Lišková stayed in Czechoslovakia, and she is not a celebrity either, and Mrs Maxová is a celebrity who lives abroad.

Each woman can be seen as a symbol of her times representing *the spirit and reality of the historical era* in which she lives and acts. All seven women share their belief in women's equality with men, political liberty and participation in a rule-of-law state and fraternity. They share the idea that caring for others in the sense of *res publica*, that which is common to all, is the social glue that keeps state, nation and government together. They share also a crucially important legacy of the Enlightenment: *tolerance*. Only tolerance as the civilized lack of interest in what others, my neighbour, my friend or my colleague, believes in allows for pluralism, which is the principal element of a democratic civil society.

Motivated by Power", *New Eastern Europe 4*, no. 5 (2014): 156-160. See also my attempt at a psychological interpretation of Husák in "Vertrauen ist nichts, Macht ist alles. Gustáv Husák (1913–1991) und die tschechoslowakische Normalisierung. Versuch eines politischen Psychogramms", forthcoming in *Vertrauen* (Basel: Schwabe, 2015).

[5] For short biographies of Prague women, among them the famous writer, see Wilma A. Iggers, *Women of Prague. Ethnic Diversity and Social Change from the Eighteenth Century to the Present* (New York: Berghahn, 1995).

My selection is *not representative* – and I don't claim that it is. Furthermore, it is far from my intention to belittle or ignore the effort millions of Czech women made in the Austrian monarchy, during the two world wars, under the German protectorate and Communism to bring up their families. On top of scarce resources, they had to deal with an immense bureaucracy and a patronizing state that treated the citizens as children, depriving them of the most basic civil rights, such as the right to leave one's country. After 1989, citizens had to deal with the harsh transformation of the economic system; Capitalism, with its often inhuman face, did not acknowledge a right to work.

It is far from my intention to make a moral judgement about those who emigrated; nobody who has not experienced daily life in a non-democratic political system, be it a monarchy run by the aristocracy and the clergy or a workers' paradise governed by the Communist Party, should be judgemental of those who leave in the hope of finding a better life for themselves and their families. My focus is on the seven Czech women who can teach us a lot about courage and commitment; they voice, through their activities, what millions of unknown Czech women were and are concerned with, sharing with them the often brutal experience of Czech and Czechoslovak politics.

Before I present the portraits, a brief note about the historical epochs dealt with in this volume: my principal aim was to avoid repetition. My selection of portraits should thus be understood as a deliberate choice designed to throw light on specific political events and realities that affected each nation and its history in their own particular way. Therefore, I do not deal with the Munich Agreement of 1938, Hitler's dissolution of Czechoslovakia in 1939 and WWII in this volume, since I have dedicated chapter III of the Slovak volume to this period. Chapter IV of this volume is dedicated to the Communist Party's assumption of power in February 1948 and the early years of Czechoslovak Stalinism, because I have not dealt with these years in the Slovak volume. The political liberalization starting in the 1960s and culminating in January 1968 with Alexander Dubček's (1921–1992) election to First Secretary of the KSČ, the Prague Spring, the invasion and the normalization are presented extensively in chapter IV of the Slovak volume. Yet, the normalization affected the Czechs in a different way than the Slovaks; therefore, I present a brief summary of the normalization in the Czech part in chapter V, focussing on two specific aspects of those years.

The years following the separation of Czechoslovakia in 1993 are not dealt with in this volume, since I presented them in my oral history interviews with the Czechoslovak diplomat and Slovak politician Magdaléna Vášáryová (*1948) and former Slovak Prime Minister Iveta Radičová (*1957).[6] The interviews introduce the reader to the difficult years from 1994 to 1998 when Vladimír Mečiar (*1942) was Prime Minister of the young Slovak Republic. By contrast, there was no threat of a relapse into communist-style authoritarianism in the young Czech Republic. Western political orientation and the democratic and market-orientated spirit of the Czech government with the late Václav Havel (1936–2011) elected Czech President in 1993 dominated the years after 1993.

Naturally, the seven Czech women I chose are of the same singular importance for the Czech lands as their Slovak counterparts were for their nation. The two volumes are separate entities in their own right and complement each other with respect to the historical contexts presented in both volumes; the two together should be perceived as *companion books*, providing the reader with a comprehensive picture of women's lives in the Czech lands and

---

[6] "Magdaléna Vášáryová (*1948) – actress, diplomat and politician", in *Seven Slovak Women*, 133-142; "Iveta Radičová (*1957) – the first female Prime Minister", in *Seven Slovak Women*, 143-154.

Slovakia, stressing the distinct political circumstances Slovak and Czech women had to cope with.

X. 2 The portraits

In the last decades of the 19th century, Ema Destinn (1878–1930) was a famous opera singer whose international career peaked when she got a contract with the New York Metropolitan Opera. Destinn was a Czech patriot and supported the movement for an independent Czechoslovakia.

Alice Garrigue Masaryková (1879–1966), the future president's daughter, studied history and philosophy at Charles-Ferdinand University in Prague and worked as teacher at a high school for girls. She was the chairwoman of the Czechoslovak Red Cross and died in US exile.

Eva 'Mimi' Jiránková (1921–2015) was a witness to the democracy of the First Republic and the protectorate under Nazi occupation. She was born in Prague and fled Czechoslovakia with her husband Miloš and their little daughter Martina in 1948. After she retired from her work as fashion consultant for Liberty's in Great Britain, Mimi and Miloš moved to Devon. Until her death in April 2015, Mimi regularly visited her native Prague.

Milada Horáková (1901–1950), a lawyer and politician, member of the Czechoslovak National Socialist Party (ČSNS) and close to President Edvard Beneš (1884–1948), was accused in the Stalinist show trial of 1950 as a traitor. The Communist government executed her. During WWII she had been active in the Czech resistance movement.

Věra Čáslavská (*1942), a gymnast, became known to the world when she won Olympic gold in Mexico City in 1968, just two months after Warsaw Pact troops had occupied her country. She is the most successful female athlete in Czech history.

Nataša Lišková (*1948) was born in Prague and brought up her children in the difficult years of the normalization. Nataša is a retired freelance journalist and spends her time with her grandchildren in the countryside.

Tereza Maxová (*1971) is a world-famous top model and one of the first Czechoslovaks who conquered the world of fashion and beauty in the early 1990s. She is the founder of the Tereza Maxová Foundation for children that changed Czech society's perception of neglected and homeless children. Her foundation is a crucially important contribution to Czech civil society, the self-organization of citizens.

X. 3   The method

In methodological terms this volume is *eclectic*. Chapters I, II, IV and V are in the form of essay; I describe the four women's lives based on source material in Czech, using *traditional historical analysis*. A short introduction at the beginning of each of the essay chapters introduces the reader to the historical context.

In chapters III, VI and VII I use the method of the *oral history interview* (OHI). This method has a considerable advantage for the author and the reader alike – it is history rendered vibrant through the individual expression, description of events and memory of a person involved in the historical context subject to investigation.

The main research questions of this volume are: how did and do women deal with political, social and economic issues? How did the rights of Czech women change from the 19th to the 21st centuries and what are they concerned with today?

From the last decades of the 19th century to the first decade of the 21st, Czech women lived through *seven political regimes*:

1. The Austro-Hungarian empire (1867–1918);
2. Czechoslovakia (ČSR, the First Republic, 1918–1938);
3. The Protectorate of Bohemia and Moravia (1939–1945);
4. Post-war Czechoslovakia (ČSR, the Second Republic, 1945–1948);
5. Communist Czechoslovakia (ČSR, 1948–1989, after the federation of 1970 referred to as ČSSR);
6. The democratic Czechoslovak Federation (ČSFR, 1990–1992);
7. The Czech Republic (1993–) after the Velvet Divorce.[7]

---

[7] For a superb analysis of the separation see Jan Rychlík, *Rozdělení Česko-Slovenska 1989–1992* (Praha: Vyšehrad, 2012). Summarizing Rychlík's analysis to the best of my understanding, I think that there was one principal reason for the separation: the lack of political will on both parts to keep the state together. This absence of common interest was largely based on the different views about economic transformation, but it was also underpinned by historical prejudices and animosities. One could generalize the Czech viewpoint as follows: 'The Slovaks collaborated with Hitler and betrayed the common state. They never understood democracy and now they want to keep the communist-style economic infrastructure, because they have no clue about market economy.' The Slovak perspective could be generalized as follows: 'The Czechs have never respected us as a nation with our own language and way of life. They blamed us for the separation of the state in 1939, which was dictated by Hitler. They always wanted to dominate us with their centralism – and now, they want to do it again, with a policy of economic transformation that will catapult our citizens into poverty.' A further important factor that led to the negotiating parties' decision to divide the state was the territorial issue: the Czech political elites were no longer interested in keeping Slovakia, since a corridor to the East, as Masaryk had projected it prior to WWI, was obsolete. With the *odsun*, the expulsion of the Germans after WWII, and the fall of Communism in 1989, the Eastern half of the state was in fact more of a burden, as Slovakia's economic structure was different from the Czech one. The Czech part would have to finance the privatization and transformation of Slovakia's economy, which the Czech centre-right politicians wanted to avoid, literally, at all costs; Rychlík, *Rozdělení* ..., 314. See also the

Of these political regimes, the First Republic, post-war Czechoslovakia from 1945 to 1948 governed by the National Front, the Czechoslovak government established after the Velvet Revolution (*Sametová revoluce*) of 1989 and the Czech Republic after the Velvet Divorce (*Sametový rozchod*) of 1993 were legitimate in democratic terms.

Czech Prime Minister Václav Klaus (*1941) and Slovak Premier Vladimír Mečiar could not find common ground to set a course for economic privatization. In the summer of 1992, they agreed to divide the state, popularly referred to as the Velvet Divorce, in analogy to the Velvet Revolution that began on 17 November 1989.[8] In legal terms, the agreement to separate was a violation of the Czechoslovak Federal Constitution that required a plebiscite.[9]

2012 yearbook of the Czecho-Slovak / Slovako-Czech Commission of Historians dedicated to the relations of Czechs and Slovaks from 1993 to 2012: *Češi a Slováci 1993–2012. Minulost je bitevním polem současníků*, (Bratislava: Veda, 2013).

[8] For a chronology of the revolutionary events of November 1989 see *Deset pražských dnů. 17.–27. listopad 1989* (Praha: Academia, 1990).

[9] Karel Vodička, "Wie der Koalitionsbeschluss zur Auflösung der ČSFR zustande kam", *Osteuropa 45*, no. 2 (1994): 175-186; 182. In a survey from 1990, only 9.6% of Slovaks and 5.3% of Czechs were in favour of the separation; in 1991, 11% of Slovaks and 6% of Czechs supported the dissolution of the federation. The separation prompted Czechoslovak President Václav Havel to resign in protest; Vodička, 181. Because of the different structures of the Slovak and Czech economies, the transformation hit the Slovaks much harder than the Czechs: the unemployment rate in the first half of 1992 was 2.7% in the Czech lands and 11.3% in Slovakia; Jiří Kosta, "Systemwandel in der Tschechoslowakei. Ökonomische und politische Aspekte", *Osteuropa 41*, no. 9 (1990): 802-818; 993.

In October 1992, some twenty Czech and Slovak citizens submitted a letter to the General Secretary of the United Nations Mr Boutros Boutros-Ghali, protesting against the separation: "The representatives of the political parties who won the latest parliamentary elections failed

On 1 January 1993, the Czech and Slovak Republics came into being, internationally recognized as sovereign states. The international community was occupied with the war in former Yugoslavia and the political situation in Russia; hence the peaceful, apparently democratic and negotiated separation was no burning issue. The Czech Republic achieved NATO membership in 1999 and became a member of the EU in 2004. The citizens of the small Central European state experienced the rule of the Habsburg dynasty, two world wars, the First Republic, German occupation, Communism and, eventually, the post-1989 harshness of the economic transformation from a planned central economy to a free market economy with the concomitant economic and social problems.

X. 4   A brief word on gender studies in Central Europe

Western historians have been working on gender issues for decades; little is known, however, about the history of women in Central Europe. In the 19th century, Czech women found themselves in a difficult situation. On the one hand, they were eager to engage in what we call gender issues today, for example, to found educational institutions for girls. On the other, they shared men's views that the Czech national movement opposing Austrian rule required the nation's united resistance.

---

to enter into a political dialogue with each other, which resulted in the decision to break up our state ... According to constitutional law no. 327/1991, the citizens have the right to a referendum on fundamental issues concerning the form of state and government." Dokument no. 37, "Bratislava, 1992, 22 října. Protest iniciativy 'Za spoločný štát' proti dohodě o rozdělení Československa zaslaný generálnímu tajemníkovi OSN Butrusovi Butrusovi Ghálímu", in *Češi a Slováci ve 20. století. Československé vztahy 1945–1992* (Bratislava, Praha: AEP, ústav T. G. Masaryka, 1998), 533-534; 533, further referred to as *Češi a Slováci II.*

Female emancipation in the Western understanding of the freedom to choose how to spend one's life would have meant fighting a battle on two fronts: first, against the domination of men, and second, against political oppression. Of crucial importance to women in the Habsburg monarchy in the 19th century was the *opening up of the public sphere*, contextualizing women's public appearance in the national and cultural *spolky*[10] (associations, clubs) such as choirs and reading circles. The main activities of women were traditional female activities: social care, charity, literature, and the teaching of cooking and sewing. The education of girls was not a burning issue since a labour market for women did not yet exist, save, of course, for the lowest class, the servants. Farmers' girls from the countryside sought to improve their families' income with employment in the city. Few women of social standing engaged in the international women's movement; the majority still adhered to the conservative view that women represented the values of faith, modesty, industriousness and, above all, passivity and obedience to men.

In general, the liberation and self-liberation of women in Europe began around 1900. In this regard, Switzerland, one of the oldest democracies, holds a sad record: Swiss women achieved the vote only in 1971[11] – yet on the grounds of a referendum, that is, Swiss women fought for their political equality, convincing the men to vote for their future right to vote. In terms of procedural ethics, the Swiss women's vote was achieved in a democratic fashion following the rules of the Swiss constitution; female and male citizens fought for female political equality, it was not bestowed on them.

---

[10] Elena Mannová, "Mužské a ženské svety v spolkoch", in *Na ceste ...*, 175-195.
[11] "Women's right to vote" on http://history-switzerland.geschichte-schweiz.ch/chronology-womens-right-vote-switzerland.html; accessed 31 January 2015.

Regardless of their national identity, European women had to face the same prejudices of the male-dominated societies, which ascribed to them only a limited space: charity and the family. For the purpose of this volume, I would like to specify what I consider the *five most important aspects* of female emancipation in Europe:

1. The conquest of the public space = being visible in society, clubs, associations and organisations; second half of the 19th century;
2. The right to higher education = the access to high schools and universities; after WWI, early 20th century;
3. The right to political participation = the right to vote and run for office; after WWI, early 20th century;
4. The right to work and earn one's salary = financial independence; early 20th century;
5. The right to prevent pregnancy with the contraceptive pill and the right to legal abortion = autonomy of the female body; 1960s and 1970s.

In WWI and WWII women had replaced the men in the work force and contributed to the war effort; after the war they were increasingly demanding equal status. The fourteen women portrayed in my two volumes were and are active in crucial areas of a modern European society. Their life stories illustrate how much women and the progressive men who supported them achieved in the last hundred and fifty years in their fight for gender equality in all spheres of society:

1. Literature: Elena Maróthy-Šoltesová (1855–1939), Slovakia in Upper Hungary;
2. Music: Ema Destinn (1878–1930), the Czech lands in the Austrian part of the Habsburg Empire and Czechoslovakia;

3. Politics: the Czechs Eva 'Mimi' Jiránková (*1921) and Nataša Lišková (*1949) as historical witnesses; the Slovaks Magdaléna Vášáryová (*1948) and Iveta Radičová (*1956) as politicians;
4. Political resistance: Chaviva Reiková (1914–1944), the Slovak state; Milada Horáková (1901–1950), Czechoslovakia;
5. Science: Mária Bellová (1885–1973); Slovakia in Upper Hungary and Czechoslovakia;
6. Social care, NGO, media: Alice Garrigue Masaryková (1879–1966), Czechoslovakia; Tereza Maxová (*1971), Czech Republic; Adela Banášová (*1980), Slovak Republic;
7. Sports: Vera Čáslavská (*1942), Czechoslovakia.

Unlike Slovak women, Czech women enjoyed a much more liberal atmosphere in the last decades of the 19th century, as their language was not threatened. The Czechs had their own journals, newspapers and a market for books in Czech; this was the reason why the Czech national movement could successfully negotiate the establishment of a Czech section of the Charles-Ferdinand University in Prague. From 1882 on, Czech and also Slovak students, who did not speak German or Hungarian, could get a university degree in Prague. The physician Vavro Šrobár (1867–1950) and the astronomer and general of the French Army Milan Rastislav Štefánik (1880–1919), two Slovak adherents of Masaryk's, had graduated at Charles-Ferdinand University and became principal figures in the building of the Czechoslovak Republic.[12]

---

[12] Josette Baer, *A Life dedicated to the Republic. Vavro Šrobár's Slovak Czechoslovakism* (Stuttgart: ibidem, 2014); Peter Macho, *Milan Rastislav Štefánik v hlavach a v srdciach. Fenomén národného hrdinu v historickej pamäti* (Bratislava: HU Prodama, 2011).

Under Communism, Czechoslovak women enjoyed constitutionally granted equality with men. Because of the duty to work under Socialism, women liberated the men from the role of the principal nurturer of the family. Yet, society still conceived of their role as the traditional one of mother and wife. Women were occupied with family matters during their entire lives; after retirement, they took care of their grandchildren.

In the first two decades of its rule, the Communist Party was eager to mobilize women; since the Party identified the concept of 'feminism' with Western Capitalism and the 'bourgeois' women's movement in the First Republic, it invented the concept "working among women (*práce mezi ženami*)" in its mobilizing effort.[13] "Feminism" was not a popular term among critically minded intellectuals either, since the Socialist regime was not popular, in particular after the invasion of August 1968 and the politics of normalization. Václav Havel, the most prominent dissident of *Charter 77*, explained in 1985 that Czechoslovak women considered feminism as "dada, the fear of becoming unintentionally ridiculous when publicly addressing women's oppression by men".[14] In a political system that oppressed the civil and political rights of all, women's issues were neither interesting nor of vital importance.

The political change of 1989 affected women who were being marginalized by the new democratic and economic spirit.[15]

---

[13] Denisa Nečasová, *Buduj vlast – posílíš mír! Ženské hnutí v českých zemích 1945–1955* (Brno: Matice moravská, 2011), 380.

[14] Václav Havel, "Anatomie jedné zdrženlivosti (duben 1985)", in *Do různých stran* (Praha: Lidové Noviny, 1989), 65-91; 78-79. See also Veronika Wöhrer, "Som feministka, no a čo? Versuche mit einem Schimpfwort politische Arbeit zu machen?" in *Women's Movements ...*, 179-196.

[15] Barbara Einhorn, "Where Have All the Women Gone? Women and the Women's Movement in East Central Europe," *Feminist Review XXXIX* (1991): 16-36; Georgina Waylen, "Women and Democratization:

They were the first to lose their jobs when the privatization of the large state-owned enterprises began in the 1990s. Besides criminality, pornography, greed, and asocial behaviour, the hitherto unknown phenomenon of sexism wormed its way into the post-Communist societies: a sad consequence of the regime change is the trafficking of young women who apply for a job in the rich states of the West and often land in brothels where they are forced into prostitution.[16]

For political reasons, Czech and Slovak scholars started only in the mid-1990s to investigate women's roles and functions in society.[17] In the years after the Velvet Revolution of 1989, Czech

---

Conceptualizing Gender Relations in Transition Politics," *World Politics XLVI* (1994): 327-354.

[16] See Siddharth Kara, *Sex Trafficking: Inside the Business of Modern Slavery* (New York: Columbia University Press, 2010).

[17] Libora Oates-Indruchová, "The Local and the Global in Czech Gender Studies", *ASEEES Newsnet 53*, no. 4 (2013): 1-3; 1. I am indebted to Libora Oates-Indruchová, who kindly provided me with a list of titles about Czech gender studies. A selection in chronological order: Alena Heitlinger, "Framing Feminism in Post-Communist Czech Republic", *Communist and Post-Communist Studies 29*, no. 2 (1996): 77-93; Jiřina Šiklová, "Feminism and the Roots of Apathy in the Czech Republic", *Social Research 64*, no. 2 (1997): 258-280; Vera Sokolová, "Getting the Words Right: Transformations of Feminism in Czech Society", *The New Presence 2*, summer (2000): 31-32; Karen Kapusta-Pofahl, "Who Would Create a Czech Feminism? Challenging Assumptions in Process of Creating Relevant Feminisms in the Czech Republic", *The Anthropology of East Europe Review 20*, no. 2 (2002): 61-68; Marianne A. Ferber and Phyllis Hutton Raabe, "Women in the Czech Republic: Feminism, Czech Style", *International Journal of Politics, Culture, and Society 16*, no. 3 (2003): 407-430; Angela Argent, "Hatching Feminisms: Czech Feminist Aspirations in the 1990s", *Gender & History 20*, no. 1 (2008): 86-104; Hana Havelková, "Dreifache Enteignung und eine unterbrochene Chance: Der 'Prager Frühling' und die Frauen- und Geschlechterdiskussion in der Tschechoslowakei", *L'Homme: Europäische Zeitschrift für feministische Geschichtswissenschaft 20*, no. 2

citizens allegedly rejected feminism; pioneers of gender studies, such as the former dissident Jiřina Šiklová and Hana Havelková did not reject feminism but explained why Czech women rejected a feminist view.[18] Also, as Oates-Indruchová points out, the assertion that Czech women rejected feminism has never been critically analysed by empirical research. The media, publishers and academic institutions of the post-socialist state played a major role in demonizing gender studies in the early 1990s; there was no funding available, the interest of the universities to offer feminist topics in the curricula was very low, and some institutions expressed their doubts about the scientific legitimacy of the field. Since then, much has changed in the academic landscape of the Czech Republic, and a second generation of gender scholars is at work.

(2009): 31-49; Megan R. Martin, "The growth of Czech feminism: analyzing resistance activities through a gendered lens, 1968–1993", *Gender, rovné příležitosti, výzkum 10*, no. 1 (2009): 37-44; Hana Hašková, "The Origins, Institutionalization, and Framing of Gender Studies in the Czech Republic", in *Travelling Gender Studies: Grenzüberschreitende Wissens- und Institutionentransfers* (Münster: Westfälisches Dampfboot, 2011), 132-146; Libora Oates-Indruchová (ed.), *Tvrdošíjnost myšlenky: od feministické kriminologie k teorii genderu (Publikace na počest Prof. Gerlindy Šmausové)* (Praha: Sociologické nakladatelství, 2011); Hana Havelková and Libora Oates-Indruchová (eds.), *The Politics of Gender Culture under State Socialism: An Expropriated Voice* (London: Routledge, 2014).

[18] Oates-Indruchová, "The Local ...", 1.

I. Ema Destinn (1878–1930) – a Bohemian in New York

"What Czech Would Not Love Music."[19]

I. 1 The historical context

On 26 February 1878, when Emilie Kittlová (later Ema Destinn) was born in Prague, Tomáš Masaryk (1850–1937),[20] a young Doctor of

---

[19] František Fürbach, *Ema Destinnová a Bedřich Smetana* (Praha: Nadace pro dějiny ve střední Evrope, Association for Central European Cultural Studies, 2011), 25. The epigraph is an elegantly worded version of the popular and traditional Czech saying 'Co Čech, to muzikant' – 'Every Czech is a musician'. I thank Francis D. Raška for his advice on this translation. The Czech popular saying goes back to Smetana's opera Dalibor: *"Který pak Čech by hudbu neměl rád"*; Fürbach, 25. The Emmy Destinn Foundation in the UK is a good Internet source for basic information about the diva: http://www.destinn.com/aims/4523141 301; accessed 25 May 2015.

[20] A selection of studies about Masaryk in chronological order: Otakar Funda, *Thomas Garrigue Masaryk. Sein philosophisches, religiöses und politisches Denken* (Bern: Peter Lang, 1978); Roland J. Hoffmann, *Thomas G. Masaryk und die tschechische Frage* (München: Oldenbourg, 1988); Jozef Novák (ed.), *On Masaryk. Texts in English and German* (Amsterdam: Rodopi, 1988); Stanley B. Winters (ed.), *T. G. Masaryk (1850–1937). Thinker and Politician* (Basingstoke: MacMillan, SSEES, University of London, 1989); Robert B. Pynsent (ed.), *T. G. Masaryk (1850–1937). Thinker and Critic* (Basingstoke: MacMillan, SSEES, University of London, 1989, 1990); Harry Hanák (ed.), *T. G. Masaryk (1850–1937). Statesman and Cultural Force* (Basingstoke: MacMillan, SSEES, University of London, 1990); Jaroslav Opat, *Filozof a politik T. G. Masaryk, 1882–1893* (Praha: Melantrich, 1990); *Masaryk a myšlenka evropské jednoty* (Praha: Filosofická Fakulta Univerzity Karlovy FFUK, 1992); Zwi Batscha, *Eine Philosophie der Demokratie. Thomas G.*

Philosophy, was on the way to New York to join his fiancée Charlotte Garrigue (1850–1923), who was recovering from an accident. They had met in Leipzig in 1877, where he had been enrolled in postdoctoral studies in economics and philosophy. The young American woman from a protestant family, which was progressive with regard to women's rights, was a talented pianist. Her family was wealthy, and Charlotte had enrolled at the Leipzig Conservatory, planning to train as a concert pianist.[21] She would give up her career plans to be the wife of the Czech philosopher, with whom she shared common views about religion, social issues, and politics. On 15 March 1878 Charlie, as her parents called her, and Tomáš married in New York. They returned to Vienna, where Masaryk began to write his second post-doctoral thesis. He had submitted his first one shortly before he learnt about Charlie's accident. He had rushed to the USA and could not attend his post-doctoral thesis' defence, therefore, his first thesis had become invalid. Little did Vienna University and the Austrian authorities know that the philosopher from a working-class background who was teaching at high schools for a low salary would lead the Czechs and Slovaks to sovereignty in a common state called Czechoslovakia, ending five centuries of Habsburg rule in Central Europe in 1918.

The career and life of the talented Emilie Kittlová are a good illustration of the professional opportunities open to Czech women in the last decades of the 19th century, in particular with respect to

---

Masaryks Begründung einer neuzeitlichen Demokratie (Frankfurt a. Main: Suhrkamp, 1994); Dalibor Truhlar, *Thomas G. Masaryk. Philosophie der Demokratie* (Frankfurt a. Main: Peter Lang, 1994); Josette Baer, *Politik als praktizierte Sittlichkeit. Zum Demokratiebegriff von Thomas G. Masaryk und Václav Havel* (Sinzheim: Pro Universitate, 1998) and Radan Hain, *Staatstheorie und Staatsrecht in T. G. Masaryks Ideenwelt* (Zürich: Schulthess, 1999).

[21] Funda, 25.

social mobility. Emilie's family was of modest means: they were comfortable, but not rich; her talent would make her a millionairess.

Czech delegates to the Austrian *Reichsrat* were trying to push through political rights to counteract the dominance of the German minority in the Czech lands; they were demanding a status of autonomy and self-government within the monarchy's political framework. In the last two decades of the 19th century, mass parties were emerging in the Czech lands that would later compete with each other in the first free elections in 1907. Naturally, women did not yet have the vote; they would gain access to higher education and political participation only in the 20th century.

Girls and women from the lower social classes received compulsory primary education and then would find jobs as housemaids, seamstresses, shop assistants, cleaners and cooks – in brief, the usual female occupations in the service of others. Daughters of the aristocracy and girls from families that had achieved some wealth and formed the social stratum of the entrepreneurial middle class were focussed on the two events that would determine their lives: marriage and motherhood. Girls were taught how to instruct the personnel, oversee a respectable household, bring up children and be faithful and supportive wives. To marry well, that is, find a wealthy husband, secured the social and financial standing of the bride and groom's families. Besides the family, charity was another area where respectable society ladies could engage in helping the poor in the spirit of Christian love. Thanks to her father, the young Emilie would be able to choose a different life for herself.

Who was Ema Destinn? In this chapter, I will focus on her career as an opera singer, which peaked when she signed a contract with the prestigious Metropolitan Opera in New York in 1908. A further important aspect of her life was her patriotic activities during WWI. After 1918, the authorities of the new state, whose creation she had continuously and courageously supported, ignored her, causing a slow and painful decline in her health and mental wellbeing. Ema's sad life in the Czechoslovak Republic demonstrates how badly Czech society treated the diva who had made the 'mistake' of beginning her career under the old monarchy.

I. 2 Emmy or Ema? Destinn's success, work for independence and decline

Emilie's father was successful in the mining business and, with hard work and astute financial investments, had acquired some wealth. Emanuel Kittl supported his first-born child in her extraordinary talent for music and literature; he made no difference between girls and boys.

Emilie Kittlová was pretty, with a shock of dark brown hair, matching dark brown eyes and perfect fair skin. Her voice was strong yet light, sensitive but also dramatic. She could sing anything; her extraordinary soprano mastered the heavy and lyrical Wagnerian parts as well as the lighter Italian operas of Giuseppe Verdi (1813–1901) and Giacomo Puccini (1858–1924). Her interpretation of the roles, acting ability and absolute dedication to the music would endear her to the members of the international aristocracy and the wealthy American public attending her performances. She would rise to international stardom under the name of Emmy Destinn.

Ema would translate Italian and German libretti into Czech, and Bedřich Smetana (1824–1884) and Antonín Dvořák's (1841–1904) libretti into German, introducing the music of the most famous Czech composers to an international audience. This was an extraordinary accomplishment since, in the eyes of international opera fans, the Czech lands were but an Austrian province. A laird in Scotland or a millionaire in Oregon knew the Austrian Empire from the map, but had no idea about the Czechs as a nation. To them, the Czech lands were some territory in Central Europe governed by Austria.

Wolfgang Amadeus Mozart (1756–1791) had experienced, in the 18th century, that the Czechs were his most accomplished and educated public. Like Ema, Mozart achieved success abroad, not in his native Salzburg and not at court in Vienna, but in Prague, the province of the Austrian monarchy. He deeply appreciated the Czechs' dedication to music and allegedly said "My people, the citizens of Prague, understand me" (*Meine Prager verstehen mich*) after the première of his Don Giovanni at the *Ständetheater* (*stavovské divadlo*) in Prague in 1787; when Mozart was in the Bohemian capital, he used to stay at the Villa Bertrámka, a mansion on the left bank of the Vltava.[22]

Ema would write poetry, plays, fairy tales and memoirs, buy a castle in southern Bohemia, sing Smetana's Libuše for President Masaryk and eventually die alone and impoverished at the age of 51, a month short of her 52nd birthday.

Young Emilie gave her first performance in public at the age of eight: she played the violin. Music was how the little girl expressed herself. When she signed her first international contract with the Court Opera House in Dresden, Saxony, in 1896, she was 18 years old and had accomplished five years of education in piano, violin, languages and voice. That same year she had attended an audition at the Czech National Theatre in Prague; she was not hired – apparently she was not good enough. Yet, young Ema was determined; she knew that she was extraordinarily talented and did not give up. She

---

[22] Villa Bertrámka Mozart museum on http://www.bertramka.eu; accessed 5 June 2015. See the lovely novella by Eduard Mörike (1804–1875), *Mozart's Journey to Prague* (*Mozart auf der Reise nach Prag*) (London: John Calder Limited, 1957); on http://www.almaclassics.com/excerpts/mozartsjourney.pdf; accessed 6 June 2015.

received no role while in Dresden, but would make her stage debut a year later at the Court Opera House in Berlin.

The Czech opera houses' refusal to offer her a contract in the early stages of her career was painful, but steeled her and strengthened her resilience, a quality that would prompt her to try her luck abroad. Ignored at home, Ema would become *prima donna assoluta* at the Royal Opera House Covent Garden in London. She would perform at the *Národní Divadlo* (National Theatre) in Prague for the first time in 1901, after her great successes in Wilhelminian Germany.

She was particularly indebted to her teacher Marie Loewe, whose stage name was Destinn, a short form of the English destiny, fate. The fact that Ema adopted Destinn as her stage name[23] proves her life-long friendship with Marie and Thomas Loewe. When Ema learnt about Thomas Loewe's death in June 1921, she immediately sent Marie a large sum to see her over the first difficult months,[24] although she was in dire financial straits herself. Two of Ema's characteristic qualities were generosity and loyalty. Whenever a friend in need asked her for help, she did not think twice.

Ema's lifestyle conformed to the cliché of the archetypal artist: emotional, impulsive, enthusiastic, caring only for art, completely impractical and absolutely indifferent to money. Money was to her but a means of gaining freedom, of being herself, of enjoying life without any further thought.

At the peak of her career, from 1908 to 1916, Ema was unmarried; she didn't have children and earned fantastic fees, but this did not mean that she was a suitable candidate for marriage. She was rich, but no respectable gentleman would have thought of marrying her. Only her colleagues and friends from the theatre,

---

[23] Marie Bajerová, *O Emě Destinnové* (Praha: Vyšehrad, 1979), 136;
[24] Miloslav Pospíšil, *Ema Destinnová. Česká pěvecká legenda* (Praha: Nakladatelství Brána, 2008), 283.

fellow artistes, were realistic and suitable candidates for marriage. In the late 19th century, European society still regarded artists, and female artists in particular, as fair game. Certainly, Ema was admired and praised. European aristocrats would have love affairs with actresses and singers, but they were not suitable partners for marriage. The democratic Americans had no home-grown aristocracy and thus were more liberal in this regard, but there is no record of a marriage proposal being made to Ema by an American citizen.

Ema spent her money as she liked, she knew that she would never receive a marriage proposal from an aristocrat – but then it seems she was not bothered. When she was earning most, at the peak of her career, she spent it on clothes, antique furniture and her collection of Napoleon memorabilia. She had admired Napoleon since her childhood, so she told the young pianist Arthur Rubinstein (1887–1982), who would become a close friend[25] and later a Chopin virtuoso. Her wealth allowed her to entertain friends at her castle, Stráž, in southern Bohemia. Ema was reckless with money; she could not be bothered to exercise financial discipline and was incapable of long-term financial planning. An example: in 1912, her household spending amounted to USD 2311 in January and USD 3278 in February.[26]

In 1908, Emperor Wilhelm II honoured her with the prestigious accolade of *Kammersängerin* of Prussia, an honorary title for female singers.[27] Ema's success catapulted her to international stardom. Her favourite place was the Royal Opera House Covent

---

[25] Pospíšil, 154.
[26] Pospíšil, 277. I have no means to estimate how much USD 2311 would be today, but considering how steep a sum USD 2311 still is today, Ema's expenses were astronomical. Nikola Todorović, a banker and economist, gave me a rough estimate: 2311 USD would today amount to 56365 USD.
[27] Pospíšil, 265; Bajerová, 138.

Garden in London, where she sang 17 roles and performed from 1904 to 1914. In the winter season of 1908, she gave her stage debut at the Metropolitan Opera in New York, singing Verdi's Aida with Enrico Caruso (1873–1921), directed by Arturo Toscanini (1867–1957). She would perform at the Met for eight years in 21 roles, and the New York public adored her:

> "Her popularity with the public, favourable reviews and fantastic emoluments showed her at the height of her career. Thanks to her exceptional voice, her dramatic acting and the care she took to 'live' every role, her performances were incomparable. Not only did she put her whole soul into every part, but she drew the rest of the cast with her. ... In New York, Emmy Destinn enjoyed a phenomenal success ... but at the cost of endless rehearsals, exhausting performances, concerts, guest appearances in other American cities (Boston, Chicago, Philadelphia and elsewhere), recording sessions, performances for Czech-American patriotic societies as well as for American millionaires..."[28]

One event in Ema's young life before she conquered the world is shrouded in mystery: on 4 April 1899, she attempted suicide in her Prague apartment and returned to Berlin that same night.[29] In 1897, her first love with Jindřich Vodílek had ended. This is not that tragic, rather the norm for us in the 21st century. Many first loves do not have a happy end; thank God, one might add with hindsight.

But in the last decades of the 19th century, courtship that did not end in marriage and children was still a stigma, for the woman, of course. To have several relationships before one ties the knot was unheard of back then; the norm was a decent and parent-approved courtship, engagement and then marriage and children. Catholic Austrian society did not accept divorce. A marriage was forever; all

---

[28] Fürbach, 16.
[29] Pospíšil, 265.

the more important, therefore, to find the perfect match for daughters.

Ema kept her private life to herself, and little is known about her relationships. Her long-term companion Marie Martínková, who acted as her *garderobière*, her wardrobe lady who took care of her stage costumes, was her closest friend and confidante. Marie was in her service from 1909 to 1922.[30] For 13 years, Ema and Marie lived together: for the winter season at the Met they would travel to New York and return to Europe in the spring, where Ema performed mainly at Covent Garden in London and in Paris. In 1923, a couple of months after Marie had left Stráž, Ema married the much younger air force officer Josef Halsbach – her only marriage proved a perfect mismatch.

The British pianist Harold Samuel (1879–1937), a specialist in Bach, had made a formal proposal of marriage to Ema in 1917;[31] his intention was to give her shelter, to protect her from the Austrian authorities. From 1916 until the end of the war, she was confined at Stráž for her activities on behalf of the *maffie*, the underground Bohemian resistance that was in steady contact with Masaryk's exile lobby. Her contract with the Met was cancelled and her American income with it.

With the rational decision to accept Samuel's proposal and move to Great Britain, Ema could have made her life a lot easier; as Mrs Samuel, she would have received British citizenship. She could have spent the war in London and actively supported the Allies' cause with performances at Covent Garden and concert tours in Great Britain and America. She could have used her celebrity status to support the Czechoslovak exile *odboj* and the Czech and Slovak

---

[30] Bajerová, 138, 140.
[31] Pospíšil, 280.

patriotic associations in America; American and British opera fans were besotted with her.

Back in the spring of 1911, Ema had sung Verdi's Aida at the coronation of King George V (1865–1936). Queen Mary (1867–1953) had thanked her for her splendid performance:

> "Certainly, I am queen, but only one of many. You, my dear, are the queen of music in the entire world."[32]

After the war, Ema could have returned to Stráž with Samuel and used her personal network, acquired in Great Britain and the USA, to promote Masaryk's Czechoslovakia. She could have had an important say in rebuilding institutions, in particular, promoting education in the country's music academies. She might even have been given a position at the Ministry of Education or a professorship at the Prague Conservatory. As a Czech patriot, having worked abroad for independence like Masaryk, Beneš, Štefánik and the *legia*, she could have used her celebrity status to strengthen Czechoslovakia's position in international relations. As a symbol of Czech music and the embodiment of the Republic's democratic values, she would have been an excellent cultural ambassadress.

Yet, Ema was an impulsive artist; she was no rational actor and made her decisions from the heart. WWI and her activities for the *maffie* prompted her house arrest at Stráž; her irrational refusal to marry Samuel would cause the end of her career.

Halsbach wormed his way into her affections in 1922, approaching her with an offer to take aerial pictures of her castle; the 44-year-old diva fell for his smooth talk and good looks.[33] The marriage would not be a happy one. Halsbach, whom she used to call Joe, thoroughly enjoyed the wealth of his wife and was often in Prague, spending her money, while Ema was trying to solve her

---

[32] Pospíšil, 166.
[33] Pospíšil, 238.

financial problems by selling her furniture, her collection of antiques and her beloved Napoleon memorabilia – items of high value that were still in her possession because Joe had not yet sold them.

Joe was bored in Stráž, bored to spend time with his wife, and Ema missed him whenever he left for Prague; she was incapable of standing up to him. She could have cut his spending by taking control of her finances, or rather, file for divorce once she noticed that he had married her only for her wealth. Yet, she was not a practical person and most probably thought that the maintenance of her husband's expensive lifestyle and penchant for flashy cars was the duty of a wife, her responsibility. Divorce was no option for her.

In April 1926 she wrote to her friend Ema Mečírová from the Prague mansion of her sister Jindřiška, called Jitta:

> "I am here without a penny ... I did not spend those 100 crowns that I received for the antique plate, Joe took them to pay for his fuel."[34]

In a letter from October 1926, she told Ema that she was on her own at Stráž; doubtlessly, Joe was having a good time in Prague. He had taken the wallet with him, and she was on tenterhooks, with no cash left in the house.[35]

I deem it interesting that Ema's longest relationship was the one with Marie, her wardrobe lady; they lived together for thirteen years, but when Ema met Halsbach, Marie left the castle for good. Ema's attempt at suicide at the age of 21, her long relationship with Marie and her late marriage to a younger man who was obviously interested only in her money, seem to hint at her sexual orientation: was she a lesbian and, shocked by that insight at a young age, tried to commit suicide and then hide it for the rest of her life, making sure she was always surrounded by attractive male friends such as

---

[34] Pospíšil, 256.
[35] Pospíšil, 256.

Caruso, Rubinstein and the French baritone Dinh Gilly (1877–1940), with whom she bought Stráž Castle?

Did she think it was preferable to have people gossiping about her many lovers than finding out about her true sexual orientation? Back in those years, this would have been reasonable behaviour for a lesbian and an artist; homosexuality was as much a social stigma as having a child out of wedlock. Or was she bisexual, anxious to hide it and thus, when the dashing young officer stepped into her life, thought that marrying him would make her a respectable woman in the eyes of society? Or was she a heterosexual, and the rumours about her many lovers true? Did she fall head over heels in love with Halsbach, accepting him the way he was?

In 1923, when Ema married Joe, her international career was practically finished; the financial problems accelerated her health problems and deep disappointment with people. Alone in her castle, when Joe was away in Prague, Ema occupied herself with fishing and mushroom hunting.[36] Her doctor warned her: she had high blood pressure and was suffering from arteriosclerosis. She should eat less and live a healthy lifestyle, follow a strict diet and avoid the sun.

But Ema loved the heavy Bohemian cuisine that consists of meat, potatoes, deep-fried vegetables and sweet and savoury pastry; she saw no point in depriving herself of one of the few joys that were left to her. She simply ignored her physician's advice. She used to spend her days at the lakes on her domain, sitting in the sun for hours to catch fish. In the evenings, she met friends in the village to discuss art, music and angling. After she had run out of money, she would often find refuge at her sister's mansion in Prague Vysočany; Jitta had married a wealthy aristocrat and was always helping her out with cash.

---

[36] Pospíšil, 204.

Hoping that she would get a position or a contract at the National Theatre in her native Prague, Ema could not afford a scandal. Did she think that if she had to keep up appearances she might as well marry a young and handsome man instead of a man her age? Why did she ignore Samuel's friendly proposal? Samuel was not only her age, but had the same passion for music. She had nothing in common with Halsbach. Did Marie, her wardrobe lady, leave Stráž in protest, because she was at the end of her tether, having warned Ema in vain of Halsbach's hidden intentions? We can't possibly know. Apparently, in the 1920s, Ema was feeling lonely, and the young officer knew his way around with her. Did she perhaps miss a child? Was Joe a kind of Ersatz son to her, the child she never had?

My thoughts about Ema's unhappy marriage and mysterious love life are, of course, speculation; speculation is no substitute for facts, but it can point the way to possible explanations. What we can say for sure is that Ema was capable of a long relationship, but was easily fooled by flattery and good looks. She was not capable of seeing through Joe's intentions and ignored Samuel's friendly proposal.

The short biography on the Emmy Destinn Foundation website states that the singer had various lovers, among them her stage partner Enrico Caruso, the young pianist Arthur Rubinstein, and her director at the Met Arturo Toscanini.[37] Ema's biographer Miloslav Pospíšil, however, describes her relationships with the three men as amicable, based on mutual respect and admiration.

Not every hug or show of affection extended to one's partner on stage at the end of a performance is necessarily a sign of a love affair. Neither does natural human curiosity imply sexual interest. Ema met Rubinstein in Paris. The pianist fondly remembered her:

---

[37] http://www.destinn.com/life/4523141317; accessed 1 June 2015.

"The Czech Ema Destinn's Salome was, in my opinion, the greatest character of her times. I was helping out during rehearsals, as a coach for the ensemble and soloists. Destinn herself asked me, the youngster, to rehearse the highlights of the opera with her. After the performance, she invited me to the Hotel Regina, where she was staying with her sister. The ladies changed into their house dresses, and we had a little snack with champagne. ... Later, I travelled to Berlin, following the divine Ema. I was going through a crisis, and meeting up with Ema was the best medicine for my melancholia. ... I had had many friends. All of them died, leaving a painful void. Ema Destinn was one of my best friends."[38]

Ema's patriotism would prompt her confinement at her castle, Stráž, in 1916. The authorities searched her when she entered Austria, returning back home from New York. In mid-July 1916, they took away her passport. House arrest was quite a lenient sentence in view of the fact that Ema was, according to Austrian law, a traitor. From 1915 on, she had been smuggling messages from the US *odboj* to Bohemia, supporting the *maffie*. She had the messages sewn into her stage costumes.[39] Ema knew perfectly well what she was doing: she was a Czech patriot and, after 1914, refused to sing in Wilhelminian Germany. The Austrian authorities could have her executed for high treason. She was as reckless in her patriotic endeavours as she was with money.

When Czechoslovak independence was declared on 28 October 1918, Ema put up the flag of the Republic on the tower of her castle and changed her name from the English/American Emmy Destinn to the Czech Ema Destinnová.[40] She was hoping that she could continue her career in the new state, but the rejection and lack of respect she encountered hurt her deeply.

---

[38] Pospíšil, 155.
[39] Pospíšil, 247.
[40] Pospíšil, 225.

Ema's last years were a slow, sad decline. Her health was deteriorating, accelerated by mental problems. She was in dire need of money and agreed to go on three concert tours in the USA, in 1919, 1920 and 1921.[41] The tours were exhausting, some of the hotels she had to stay in were cheap and dirty, but more painful was the ignorance she met at home. The diva was treated abominably. She wrote to a friend, describing what had happened when she had had part of her antique collection valued by a state agency in Prague before it went to auction:

> "The way 'our' authorities treat us... 'You lied to Austria, but you won't fool us!' – 'I have never lied to anybody and have never hidden anything, I am no capitalist, I have more debts than hair on my head."[42]

Wherever she applied for a position, the doors were closed and the posts were given to younger persons. Nobody wanted to hire her, and the famous diva, whose voice had enchanted emperors, queens and the audience at the New York Met, saw herself forced to give singing lessons. She did have offers to teach in the USA and would have earned a high salary, but she wanted to stay in Czechoslovakia.[43] The new government could have thanked her for her patriotic activities during the war with a professorship at the Prague Conservatory.

A professorship for voice had yet to be established; the Conservatory's curriculum offered violin, piano, conducting, cello and organ.[44] Eager careerists at the Interior Ministry instigated intrigues, and the procedure to establish the professorship was deliberately prolonged. Some thought that being an excellent singer did not necessarily qualify her as a teacher; the civil servant

---

[41] Bajerová, 140.
[42] Pospíšil, 248.
[43] Pospíšil, 243.
[44] Pospíšil, 252.

responsible for Ema's future professorship was also in charge of the Conservatory's finances. After learning of her death, he allegedly said that she had died just in time, as this affair would cause only problems.[45] Ema had a few students and was teaching them at her sister's mansion in Vysočany. Her mental state was close to depression.

On 22 November 1929 she wrote to her friend Adolf Wenig (1874–1940):

> "For three days I have not been outside, it is cold and windy. I am sitting here quietly, thinking about the futility of everything ... My old sorrows are putting a strain on me, draining and exhausting me, that's why I am keeping to myself, not seeing anybody. ... Lately, I caught a fish; it was 9kg ... I found some mushrooms in the forest, and my little salon now looks like a glasshouse ... What do you expect from someone who is retired from life itself?"[46]

In an interview she gave to the *Národní Listy* (*National News*) that was published after her death on 1 February 1930, Ema had said:

> "No, I don't trust people, I don't like them. How much more beautiful are water, the sun, trees and animals!"[47]

Ema withdrew to her castle, increasingly avoiding the public. The only contact she had with the world were her letters; she wrote to the few true friends she had. A sad and humiliating event on 8 May 1929 illustrates how far the once famous singer had fallen, the fall caused by envy and jealousy, but also in part by her decision to marry Halsbach, who was responsible for her debts. In the break between two films, she performed songs by Dvořák at a Prague cinema.

A women's magazine interviewed her: how did the Republic appreciate her efforts to promote the young state and Czech music

---

[45] Pospíšil, 252.
[46] Pospíšil, 248.
[47] Pospíšil, 248.

abroad? Ema had a bitter smile on her lips and, averting her eyes, replied:

> "I am paying taxes on my Stráž domain, like everybody else. Otherwise, the Republic doesn't know me…"[48]

On 28 January 1930, Dr Slavík was called to Stráž; besides problems with her eyes, Ema's blood pressure was 240 and she was rushed to the hospital in České Budějovice. Suddenly, she stopped talking, and the doctors found that she had suffered a stroke. The left side of her brain had lesions. At 10.10 pm she died.[49]

She was buried on 3 February. The funeral procession passed the National Theatre and went up to Vyšehrad. The diva, who had done so much for the independence movement, always generously supported young musicians and composers, and introduced the music of Dvořák and Smetana to an international audience, was buried in the Slavín National Cemetery. Shunned while she was alive, Czech society made her a legend, praising her as a patriot. The news of her death prompted many letters, telegrams and last wishes from her public. The composer Richard Strauss (1864–1949), whose Salome she had sung, wrote:

> "The royal Kammersängerin Ema Destinn, one of the greatest singers and one of the most beautiful sopranos of the century, has left this world."[50]

I.3 Conclusion

I am no specialist in opera and certainly not qualified to pass judgement on Ema Destinnová's voice. Yet, listening to Ema's Tosca

---

[48] Pospíšil, 254.
[49] Pospíšil, 259.
[50] Pospíšil, 260.

and Aida on YouTube, I must say that her voice reminds me of the divine Maria Callas (1923–1977).

Ema lived the life of an artist – she was an artist. She conquered the world with her voice and was the highest paid soprano of her times. She sang for kings and queens and her voice enchanted her public. The sad years of her decline began with her confinement at her castle, Stráž. The Austrian authorities put her under house arrest because of her patriotic activities.

Alone and feeling lonely, with a young husband who was spending her money in Prague, she had to face up to the cruel reality of her lost career. She was feeling desperate; the young Republic she had so courageously supported with her activities for the *maffie*, did not acknowledge her. The times had changed in Prague in 1918, and it was changing Czech society.

Now, all of a sudden, citizens were democrats. There was no place left for the singer; younger persons and eager careerists were occupying governmental positions that granted a steady income, a means of survival.

President Masaryk was decent enough to receive the elderly diva at Prague Castle, but he was not that interested in helping her. He could have used his immense influence to secure her a professorship at the Prague Conservatory, but he did not. I think that Masaryk, although he clearly admired her, made a strategic decision – to enforce the people's belief in the Republic. To him, and to the Republic, Ema Destinnová was a relic from the old days of the Austrian monarchy. Ema was a symbol of the old Austria. Austria was dead. Czechoslovakia needed new, younger people.

II. Alice Garrigue Masaryková (1879–1966) – the First Czech feminist?

"We Czechoslovaks have the linden tree as our national symbol. What does it mean? What is its significance? If we look at the leaves of the linden, we see hearts. The linden tree ... consists of an infinite number of tiny hearts. All of us are fresh leaves, we are the heart of the nation, and nobody feels ashamed to acknowledge that one is completely committed to the common good of all."[51]

II. 1   The historical context

Alice Garrigue Masaryková was born on 3 May 1879 in Vienna to parents who considered girls equal to boys. She grew up in a family that held high the values of the Enlightenment and was progressive in political, ethical and social issues. Her parents were Protestants, religious, but not dogmatic. A further unusual fact, given the limited mobility of women in the second half of the 19th century, was her mother Charlotte's American origins. Alice and her siblings were educated to become critical and independent minds, and democracy as a political system was not alien to them since they had relatives in the USA, whom they visited. The Masaryk children spoke English and Czech, and were taught by their mother how US democracy worked, and by their father why Austrian absolutism did not.

In terms of the emerging women's movement in Europe that was pushing forward women's equality with men, Alice was a feminist; she graduated from Minerva, the first high school for girls in Prague, achieved a doctorate in history and philosophy from

---

[51] Radovan Lovčí, *Alice Garrigue Masaryk. Život ve stínu slavného otce* (Praha: Opera Facultatis philosophicae Universitatis Carolinae Pragensis, 2007), 439.

Charles-Ferdinand University, worked all her life and was financially independent, yet never wealthy. She committed herself to teaching, and it was thanks to her efforts that the Czechoslovak Red Cross came into being. Alice did not have a private life of her own, at least not one she wanted to talk about, as she was always meticulously discreet. She never married and died childless. Due to her mother's illness, Alice replaced her in the role as First Lady of the Czechoslovak Republic and accompanied her father on official state visits and receptions. In this chapter, I focus on two principal epochs in Alice's life: the years of WWI and the First Republic, since the years after 1939 are dealt with in chapter III. For the details of Alice's life after 1939, when she left what the Germans cynically called the Protectorate of Bohemia and Moravia, I refer the reader to the chronology in the appendix.

As the first child of the future founder of the Czechoslovak Republic, Alice's life and her career decisions are intrinsically linked to her father's political thought, efforts, and achievements. In his superb biography, Radovan Lovčí describes her in the subtitle as having led "a life in the shadows of the famous father". Therefore, I present the historical context in this subchapter with a focus on Masaryk's activities that give us an insight into the intellectual atmosphere in Prague prior to WWI.

Alice was seven years old, hence capable of reading and writing, when her father was fiercely attacked in the controversy surrounding the Old Czech manuscripts in 1886; she was twenty, when the Hilsner affair broke in 1899; and twenty-six, when her father published his famous *The Czech Question* in 1905. Thus, when Masaryk went into exile in December 1914, his 35-year-old daughter was familiar with his plan for an independent state based on his theory of Czechoslovakism.

Until the outbreak of WWI, Tomáš Garrigue Masaryk was swimming against the currents of Czech politics.[52] Like many Czech intellectuals, he had been educated at Vienna University, but it was rather unusual to enrol at Leipzig University in protestant Saxony for postgraduate studies.[53] This facet of internationality or cosmopolitanism did not chime well with the provincial, uncritical, aggressive and often also antisemitic Czech nationalism dominant in Prague. With his approach of *Realism*[54] Masaryk tried to inculcate scientific rationalism into the emotional tone of the political debates in the Czech lands under Austrian rule. Two controversies illustrate not only the nationalist atmosphere, but also the hatred and concomitant social apartheid Masaryk and his associates had to endure for their critical views: first, the controversy of the manuscripts (*boj o rukopisy*)[55] in 1886 and, second, the Hilsner affair (*Hilsneriáda*) in 1899/1900.

In 1817 and 1818, manuscripts had been found in Königinhof (*Dvůr*) and Grünberg (*Zelenohorský*), which contained

---

[52] Gordon H. Skilling, *T. G. Masaryk proti proudu (1882–1914)* (Praha: Práh, 1995).

[53] See Richard G. Plaschka, and Karlheinz Mack (eds.), *Wegenetz europäischen Geistes I. Wissenschaftszentren und geistige Wechselbeziehungen zwischen Mittel- und Südosteuropa vom Ende des 18. Jahrhunderts bis zum ersten Weltkrieg* (Wien: Verlag für Geschichte und Politik, 1983); and Richard G. Plaschka, and Karlheinz Mack (eds.), *Wegenetz europäischen Geistes II. Universitäten und Studenten. Die Bedeutung studentischer Migrationen in Mittel- und Südosteuropa vom 18. bis zum 20. Jahrhundert* (München: Oldenbourg, 1987).

[54] On Masaryk's Realism see Eva Schmidt-Hartmann, *Thomas G. Masaryk's Realism* (München: Oldenbourg, 1984) and *Masarykova praktická filosofie. Sborník z přednáškového cyklu* (Praha: Masarykova společnost, 1993).

[55] Excellent on the controversy are Hoffmann, 79-88; Opat, 136-177; and Milan Otáhal, "Význam bojů o rukopisy", in *Masarykův Sborník VII* (Praha: Academia, 1992), 40-71.

epic and lyric poetry; one poem had allegedly been composed by Libuše, the ancestress of the Premyslide dynasty that had ruled Bohemia in the Middle Ages (approximately from 895 to 1306). The ferocious anti-German tone of the manuscripts had raised immediate suspicions, and Joseph Dobrovský (1753–1829), the father of Slavonic linguistics, had identified them as forgeries in 1818.

Forgeries were widespread in Europe at the turn of the 19th century, the first originating from the Scottish poet James Macpherson (1736–1796), who had published a collection of poems and songs translated allegedly from ancient Gaelic, among them *Ossian*, that seemed to originate in the 2nd century.[56] As expressions of Romantic thought that embraced cultural diversity and rejected the rationalism and universalism of the French Enlightenment, forgeries were fabricated to legitimate an alleged grand medieval past of the nations in formation; in this regard, Bohemian fabrications did not differ from their Russian, Bulgarian, Scottish or English counterparts.[57]

What was unusual in Bohemia, however, was the vehemence with which the controversy was kept alive for almost a century, separating the Czechs practically into two camps, the defenders of the manuscripts and the critics. Anybody who dared to doubt the authenticity of the "holy documents of Czech obrození nationalism"[58] had to bear the scorn and contempt of the Czech press, led by the dominant *Národní Listy* (*National News*), which

---

[56] Otáhal, 40.
[57] Otáhal, 42.
[58] "... sakrosankte Dokumente des tschechischen Obrození-Nationalismus"; Hoffmann, 79. On the intellectual and religious origins of the Czech Renaissance (National Awakening, *národní obrození*), see the seminal study by Zdeněk V. David, *Realism, Tolerance and Liberalism in the Czech National Awakening* (Washington D.C.: Woodrow Wilson Press, 2010).

used smear campaigns and personal attacks, mostly because of its lack of expertise and scientific arguments. Not only the press, but also experts of serious academic and artistic standing, such as the historian and erstwhile leader of the Old Czechs, František Palacký (1798–1876), and the poet Jan Neruda (1843–1891), believed that the manuscripts were evidence of a great Czech medieval past.[59]

Masaryk publicly defended the philologist Jan Gebauer (1883–1907), an adherent of Dobrovský's assessment, who was a Prague German. The public scolded Masaryk, a few like-minded colleagues from the university, and critical journalists who had taken his side, as traitors to the national cause. The philosopher was excluded from academic and educational projects he had initiated, such as the foundation of a Czech scientific encyclopedia, modelled on the *Encyclopaedia Britannica*. Intrigues in the academic senate would postpone his tenure until 1896.[60]

A positive result of the controversy, however, was the formation of a small group of critically minded scholars, students, journalists and intellectuals who supported Masaryk. They called themselves the *Realists*, being much more the *nucleus* of a civic movement than a political party; their main tenet was Masaryk's Realism. Considering themselves a unifying group that was trying to bridge the gap between the conservative Old Czechs and the progressive Young Czechs, they aimed to create a new style of politics: to use scientific principles in politics to de-emotionalize national issues. In Masaryk's view, Czech nationalism as a collective positive self-identification did not have much to offer for the future if values such as truth, tolerance and critical thought counted less than provincial and semi-educated hooray patriotism based on

---

[59] Otáhal, 47ff.
[60] Hoffmann, 88.

polemic, lies and forgeries.⁶¹ Masaryk and his associates would found the *Czech People's Party the Realists* (*Česká strana lidová realistická* – ČSL r) in 1900 and in 1906 the *Czech Progressive Party* (*Česká strana pokroková*, ČSP), for which he would receive a mandate in the Imperial Council (*Reichsrat*).

Alice's father had the public against him a second time when he engaged in the Hilsner affair. From 1867 to 1914, twelve trials of alleged Jewish ritual murders occurred in the empire, providing a vivid picture of antisemitism in the Habsburg monarchy.⁶² Masaryk defended the homeless Jew Leopold Hilsner who had been accused

---

61 As president, Masaryk would time and again stress how important education, training and expert knowledge were for a functioning democracy – and what danger semi-educated citizens posed to the democratic procedure: in the First Republic, he initiated institutions for continuing education, which was the logical continuation of an enterprise he had started in the 1880s with the journals *Athenäum* and *Naši Doba*; see Baer, *Politik als ...*, 86-189; Tomáš G. Masaryk, "Několik poznámek k problému vychování dorostlých", in *Cesta demokracie III. Projevy, články, rozhovory 1924–1928* (Praha: Ústav T. G. Masaryka, 1994), 214-217.

62 Petra Rybářová, "Chiméra rituálnej vraždy. Údajné zločiny Židov v Rakúsko-Uhorsku a ich ohlas na Slovensku", in *Storočie Procesov. Súdy, Politika, a Spločnosť v moderných Dejinách Slovenska* (Bratislava: Veda, 2013), 25-39. Rybářová focuses on how the Slovak conservatives used the Hilsneriáda to attack Masaryk and his Slovak associates of the journal *Hlas*. The conservative Slovak patriots interpreted any critique of the Hilsner trial as treason of the Slovak national movement and an act of loyalty to the liberal government in Budapest that, in their antisemitic view, was under the spell of Hungarian Jewry; Rybářová, 35. The deeply felt opposition to Hungarian liberalism should be understood as the Slovak defence against Magyar assimilation; liberalism in Hungary promoted liberal thought in its economic and anti-Habsburg aspects, but it was not at all liberal with regard to the claims of the cultural and language rights of the non-Magyars. The bad experience with Hungary's liberalism is but one of many historical reasons why liberalism was never successful in Slovakia.

of the ritual murder of the 19-year-old Anežka Hrůzová. Her body had been found in March 1899 in a forest close to the little Moravian town of Polná. According to the blood libel, an antisemitic myth originating in the Middle Ages, Jews needed the blood of Christians, preferably young females, to bake their matzos for Pessah. Eyewitnesses had spotted Hilsner in the vicinity at the estimated time of Hrůzová's murder. The court in Kutná Hora (Kuttenberg) sentenced Hilsner to death.

With the help of experts in criminology and pathology, Masaryk analysed the case and published his results in *Čas*, the only newspaper critical of Hilsner's death sentence.[63] His strongest arguments against the ritual murder were, that first, the neck of the girl had been stabbed, not sliced. According to the myth of the blood libel, slicing allowed the Jews to collect the blood of the murdered Christians the practise being similar to kosher slaughtering that kills the animal by letting it bleed to death. Second, pathologists at the medical faculty of Prague University determined the date of Anežka's death after the Pessah festivities.

Masaryk's efforts led to a second trial in October 1900; the court revised the version of ritual murder and spared Hilsner's life, but sentenced him to life in prison. As in the controversy over the manuscripts, the press scolded Masaryk again; he was called a 'traitor' and 'slave of the Jews'. His condemnation of the blood libel as antisemitic fairy tale[64] led to massive protests by radical

---

[63] Steven Beller, "The Hilsner Affair: Nationalism, Antisemitism and the Individual in the Habsburg Monarchy at the Turn of the Century", in *T. G. Masaryk (1850–1937). Thinker and Critic* (London: SSEES, 1990), 52-76; 54. See also Jiří Kovtun, "Masaryk proti radikalismu a antisemitismu na přelomu století", in *Masarykův sborník VIII* (Praha: Ústav T. G. Masaryka, 1993), 83-88.

[64] Masaryk had told his biographer Emil Ludwig (1881–1948) that his principal motivation to engage in the cause had not been to prove Hilsner innocent, but to reveal the phoniness of the superstitions of

nationalist student groups who disturbed his lectures. The students' rallies got so much out of hand that the university had to place him on a two-week leave of absence. Emperor Karl I (1887–1922) released Hilsner in the war amnesty of 1916. Shortly before he died in 1969, Anežka's brother confessed that he had murdered his sister in 1899.[65]

In his famous conversation with Karel Čapek, Masaryk explained why he had got involved in the *Hilsneriáda*.[66] As a little boy, he had been raised in the Catholic faith and was afraid of Jews; he believed in the myth of Jewish ritual murder. After he had seen a Jew at prayer, he was deeply touched by his religiosity and decided to fight antisemitism. The revision of the death sentence was thus a cultural victory to him: science had defeated superstition.[67]

Masaryk had to endure years of defamation and smear campaigns in Prague, but he was the only Czech politician who presented the Allies with a plan for the organization of post-war Central Europe and post-Habsburg rule alike. Czech politicians, among them his former associate in the Party of the Realists, the lawyer Karel Kramář (1860–1937), hoped that Tsarist Russia would liberate the Austrian Slavs – more a utopian reverie than a political

---

antisemitism; Emil Luwig, *Gespräche mit Masaryk* (Amsterdam: Querido Verlag, 1935), 124.

[65] Funda, 37.

[66] Karel Čapek, *Hovory s T. G. Masarykem* (Praha: František Borovy, 1946), 12. Karel Čapek (1890–1938) was a Czech writer and journalist and a close confidant of Masaryk. See the excellent biography of Čapek by Ivan Klíma, *Karel Čapek, Life and Work* (North Haven, CT: Catbird Press, 2002).

[67] Beller, 59.

concept, let alone a plan or a programme.[68] Masaryk, ever the Realist, set his hopes on the Allies and the military might of the USA.

Masaryk contested both Austrian and Hungarian rule, which he considered illegitimate, since it did not respect the equality of nations and the people as the only legitimate sovereign. By 1913, he had opted for a nation-state of the Czechs and Slovaks. His state-building theory of Czechoslovakism included the historic rights of the Bohemian crown as the historical unity of Bohemia, Moravia and Silesia on the one hand, and natural law argumentation to justify Czechoslovak independence, on the other. He was the principal Czech intellectual to support and inspire Slovak students in Prague with his thoughts about a common state.[69] In exile, Masaryk would lay the international grounds for the state-building process. His view of politics as the realm of positive, constructive agency set him apart not only from Czech but also Slovak politicians: because of the Austrian absolutist system, the unconstructive Czech politics focusing on petty negotiations about language rights in Bohemia got

---

[68] See Jan Bílek and Luboš Velek (eds.), *Karel Kramář (1860–1937). Život a dílo* (Praha: Masarykův ústav a Archiv Akademie věd ČR, Historický ústav AV ČR, 2009).

[69] On Masaryk's role in the foundation of the Slovak *Hlas* movement I recommend Zdeněk Urban, "K Masarykovu vztahu ke Slovensku před první světovou válkou", in *Masaryk a Slovensko (soubor statí)* (Praha: Masarykova společnost a Ústav T. G. Masaryka, 1992), 68-89; Dušan Kováč, *Slováci. Češi. Dejiny* (Bratislava: Academic Electronic Press AEP, 1997), 59-63, and Tomas D. Marzík, "The Slovakophile Relationship of T. G. Masaryk and Karel Kálal prior to 1914", in *T. G. Masaryk (1850–1937), Thinker and Politician* (London: SSEES, 1989), 191-209. Masaryk's political expertise and advice was crucial to the Slovak student club *Detvan*, as its members lacked a political perspective for Slovakia. Prague at the turn of the 20th century offered a liberal atmosphere where the Slovak students could gather freely for political and cultural discussions in their mother tongue, activities the laws of the Hungarian kingdom punished.

them nowhere, while the conservative leaders of the Slovak national movement defending themselves against the Magyar proto-totalitarian[70] assimilation were equally unsuccessful in their utopian hopes for a liberation by Russia. Save for him, nobody thought of the war as a geopolitical opportunity for independence.

Masaryk's political thought was as eclectic as it was impressive in its blend of Western and Czech political thought: American constitutionalism based on John Locke (1632–1704); empiricism and rational analysis of the international situation according to the scientific positivism of Auguste Comte (1798–1857). Masaryk was a master of statecraft thinking in bold terms and anticipating the future of the 20th century; as a Realist, he detested the realism of Machiavelli (1469–1527), whose political principles he considered not only historically obsolete but also deeply immoral. Power was an intrinsic element of politics, even more so in a state where the people were sovereign, but power should never overrule justice; the people's sovereignty and the rule-of-law state were inseparable political principles. Democratic power without the rule-of law state was unthinkable, a philosophical and political contradiction in terms. In Masaryk's view, politics as morality in the

---

[70] By the term 'proto-totalitarian' I mean the mechanism and institutions of control the Hungarian government exercised on the non-Magyar citizens of the Hungarian kingdom. Naturally, Budapest did not exert totalitarian control, since totalitarianism was a form of governmental control that required the technology of the 20th century, that is, state-controlled broadcast, the technological means to control the press and the supervision of the citizens' movements exercised either by a state secret domestic service or, in our times, CCTV. But an early form of overarching government control of the non-Magyar citizens was visible in the way the press reported non-Magyar national movements and the application of laws fighting language rights. For a definition of totalitarianism, I refer the reader to Hannah Arendt, *The Origins of Totalitarianism* (San Diego, New York, London: Harcourt Brace & Company, 1973).

practice of the 20th century had nothing to do with the Machiavellian principles of statecraft the Florentine thinker had formulated in the chaotic conditions of the Italian peninsula in the early 16th century.[71] Masaryk's eclectic thought and philosophical experience allowed him to formulate a Czech nation-building theory, his *The Czech Question* (*Česká otázka*) in 1905.[72]

Masaryk was not all too keen to promote Johann Gottfried Herder (1744–1803) and Ján Kollár's (1793–1852) romanticist view of the Slavs. Zdeněk V. David (*1931) explains this particular aversion to romanticism as fundamental in preparing resistance against "the subsequent appeal of German idealism in general and Hegelianism in particular".[73] Masaryk generally objected to German idealism but was open to be inspired by Herder's concept of *Humanität* (Humanity) as the goal of his philosophy of history and Jan Hus' medieval humanism. While *liberté* and *égalité* could be realized only in a democracy, *fraternité* as the third value of the French Revolution and Enlightenment needed clarification and definition in the Czech national context: to Masaryk, the French appeal to *fraternité* was identical with Herder's *Humanität*, which played a distinct and important role for the Czech future:

---

[71] Machiavelli, *The Prince* on http://www.constitution.org/mac/prince.pdf; accessed 1 March 2015.

[72] Tomáš G. Masaryk, *Česká otázka* (Praha: Svoboda, 1990); for his plans to create a sovereign Czechoslovak democracy see Thomas G. Masaryk, *The Problem of Small Nations in the European Crisis* (London: Athlone Press, 1966); for details of his state-building theory see my *Slavic Thinkers or the Creation of Polities. On Intellectual History and Political Thought in Central Europe and the Balkans in the 19th century* (Washington, D.C.: New Academia Publishing, 2007), 15-42.

[73] Zdeněk V. David, *Johann Gottfried Herder and the Czech National Awakening: A Reassessment* (Pittsburgh, PA: The Carl Beck Papers in Russian & East European Studies, no. 1807, University of Pittsburgh, 2007), 32.

> "Humanity is our final national and historical goal, humanity is the Czech program."[74]

After thorough study of Bohemia's history and Czech thought in the 1890s, Masaryk developed his theory of Czech nation-building, creating a blueprint for the nation's characteristic features. His central tenet, inspired by the Hegelian world spirit (*Weltgeist*) was the *democratizing spirit* that had been prevailing and moving forward in Czech history. His theory of a historical process was identical to Herder's philosophy of history, conveying the idea that humanity is the starting point of a continuous historical development and its advancement through the history of mankind. Masaryk combined Herder's historical process of Humanity with the Hegelian theory of a world spirit that is moving toward the final goal of a constitutionally granted liberty, adding to this Hus' Protestant resistance against Catholicism, and lastly, his own belief in democracy. He thus delivered a philosophically eclectic theory of Czech nation-building which he conceived as legitimate in moral, historical and political terms.

In Masaryk's perception of Czech history, four "national awakeners" had created, shaped, reformed and defined the essentially Czech idea of democracy, determining a process of continuous democratization as the philosophical sense of Czech

---

[74] Masaryk, *Česká otázka*, 186.

history:[75] Jan Hus (1369–1415)[76] fought against the power of Rome for the freedom of religion and conscience in the 14th century, anticipating the linguistic awakening Joseph Dobrovský would initiate in the 18th century. Ján Kollár[77] created the idea of a Slavic nation and its cultural individuality, identifying the Czechoslovak

---

[75] Mainly historians, the most prominent ones being Jozef Pekař (1870–1937) and Jaroslav Goll (1846–1929), objected to Masaryk's *Czech Question*, criticizing his text and method of inquiry inadequate. They failed to understand, however, that Masaryk's principal goal was to deliver a theory of Czech history that would serve as the programme of Czech nation-building to fight the Austro-Hungarian empire, not a historical analysis based on dry dates and facts. A detailed summary of the historical debate can be found in Miloš Havelka, *Spor o smyslu Českých dějin 1895–1938* (Praha: Torst, 1995). The Czech philosopher Jan Patočka (1907–1977), one of the initiators of the dissident group *Charter 77*, described Masaryk's *Česká otázka* as "a failed attempt to create a national philosophy", since it lacked an elaborate concept of metaphysics and was too focused on the current political situation; Jan Patočka, "Pokus o českou národní filosofii a jeho nezdar", in *Tři studie o Masarykovi* (Praha: Váhy, mladá fronta, 1991), 21-52, 40-41. Neither historians nor philosophers who analyzed Masaryk's thoughts from a perspective of pure theory respected the essence of his eclecticism and pragmatism.

[76] See the superb biographical novel by Eva Kantůrková, *Jan Hus. Příspěvek k národní identitě* (Praha: Melantrich, 1991).

[77] A selection of studies on Kollár: Tibor Pichler, "Obavy z politiky: Ján Kollár a myšlienka slovanskej vzájomnosti", in *Národovci a občania. O slovenskom politickom myslení v 19. storočí* (Bratislava: Veda, 1998), 15-30; Tatiana Ivantyšynová (ed.), *Ján Kollár a slovanská vzájomnosť. Genéza nacionalizmu v strednej Európe* (Bratislava: SDK SVE, 2006); for an English translation of parts of Kollár's *Über die literarische Wechselseitigkeit der zwischen den verschiedenen Stämmen und Mundarten der slawischen Nation* see Josette Baer, "Ján (Johann) Kollár (1793–1852)", in *Preparing Liberty in Central Europe. Political Texts from the Spring of Nations 1848 to the Spring of Prague 1968* (Stuttgart: ibidem, 2006), 20-57.

branch of the Slavic nation. The historian František Palacký[78] took this branch to a higher level of development; his *Geschichte von Böhmen* and Kremsier draft constitution of 1849 gave the nation the features of its historical and political identity. Masaryk considered the journalist Karel Havlíček (1821–1856)[79] the fourth "awakener"; he was the first to defend the interests of the excluded lower classes of the industrial workers and peasants, raise awareness about social misery and address the corruption reigning in the absolutist Austrian system.

All four awakeners had fought for liberty and equality and against discriminatory power monopolies. The next phase of the nation's historical development towards humanity was the one initiated by Masaryk himself. By declaring that the nation's next phase would necessarily involve *a constitutional solution*, he put himself at the end of the historical process of democratization – which was his own assessment of Czech history. The next phase was, according to the intrinsic elements of democracy and humanity, a modern democracy in a Czech sovereign nation-state. Czech nation-building hence was legitimate according to natural law that promoted the equality of nations, and the final goal of that process would be a product of positive law and public international law: the *democratic Czechoslovak constitution*.

---

[78] A selection of studies on Palacký: Jiří Kořalka, *František Palacký (1798–1876): Životopis* (Praha: Argo, 1998); Jiří Štaif, *František Palacký. Život, dílo, mýtus* (Praha: Vyšehrad, 2009).

[79] A selection of studies on Havlíček: Barbara K. Reinfeld, *Karel Havlíček (1821–1856). A National Liberation Leader of the Czech Renascence* (New York, NY, Boulder, CO: Columbia University Press, 1982); Ilona Bažantová, "Zapomenutý ekonom Karel Havlíček Borovský", *Politická Ekonomie 5*, no. 2 (1999): 621-629; Marie L. Neudorflová, "Karel Havlíček, T. G. Masaryk a demokracie", in *Spisovatelé, společnost a noviny v promínách doby* (Praha: Literární Archiv Národného Písemnictví, 2006), 11-28;

In a pragmatic step, Masaryk reformulated his Czech nation-building theory into his Czechoslovak state-building theory to convince the Allies that, on the grounds of natural law,[80] the *Czechoslovak nation* deserved sovereignty as much as Poland. He conceived of the Slovaks as kin who spoke a kind of Eastern Czech dialect – which was clearly not the case as Slovak had been a written language since 1843,[81] though it was not internationally recognized. Masaryk conveniently ignored the efforts of the Slovak patriots for their language. By declaring the Czechs and Slovaks one nation – and in this, the Czech and Slovak exile communities in the USA supported

---

[80] On the significance of natural law and positive law in the Czech lands and Slovakia see my "The Genesis of Czechoslovakism. An Interdisciplinary Inquiry into the Influence of Rousseau's Réligion Civile", in *East European Faces of Law and Society: Values and Practices* (Leiden: Brill Nijhoff, 2014), 307-345.

[81] The Slovak patriots and national awakeners Ľudovít Štúr (1815–1856)), Michal Miloslav Hodža (1811–1870) and Jozef Miloslav Hurban (1817–1888) coined the Slovak written language in 1843, based on the central Slovak dialect, which was more a political decision than one based on linguistic details. Masaryk wrote in the first volume of his study about Russian philosophy and thought in 1913: "The Slovaks lack a language of their own, and the political conditions [they were subject to in the Hungarian kingdom, add. JB] led to the fact that the Slovak dialect vanished as a literary language"; T. G. Masaryk, "Slavjanofilství. Mesianismus právoslavné teokracie. Slavjanofilství a Panslavismus", in *Rusko a Evropa. Studie o dúchovních proudech v Rusku*, vol. I (Praha: Ústav T. G. Masaryka, 1995), 181-246; 225. This was a pragmatic lie; Masaryk knew the situation in Slovakia very well, since he was in steady contact with the Hlasists. I think one has to understand this quote not only with regard to his independence plans, but also in the context of his self-defence: he was fighting his Slovak enemies, the conservative Martinists led by Svetozár Hurban Vajanský, who were attacking him and his associates for their modern views. For a summary of Masaryk's dispute with Vajanský that ended their friendship see my "Thomas G. Masaryk and Svetozár Hurban Vajanský. A Czecho-Slovak friendship?" *KOSMAS Czechoslovak and Central European Journal 26*, no. 2 (2013): 50-62.

him by signing the Pittsburgh Agreement in May 1918 – he created a historically incorrect yet politically successful portrait of the Czechs and Slovaks. Back in 1905 he had written:

> "Just think how we consider Bohemia, Moravia, Silesia and, finally, Slovakia as separate units! Two million Czechs [*dva miliony Čechů*] live in the Hungarian kingdom! ... We won't give up *a third of our nation*."[82]

In the decade before the war, Masaryk had pragmatically blended the historic rights of the Bohemian crown with the natural law demand for the Czechoslovak nation.[83] He was a pragmatist. With natural law, he justified to the Allies the equality of the Czechoslovak nation and its right to a sovereign nation state; with the historic rights of the Bohemian Crown he legitimated the sovereignty of the Czechoslovak nation over the territory of the Czech lands with a large German minority and Slovakia with a large Hungarian minority.

From Masaryk's point of view, the Czechoslovak state would have a three-fold legitimacy: first, in ethical terms, since the people would be the sovereign in a democracy and rule-of-law state that embodied the values of liberty, equality and fraternity. Second, it would be legitimate in terms of public international law, since the victorious Allies would dictate the terms and conditions of the forthcoming peace negotiations and reward the Czechoslovaks for their military support with their recognition of the Republic. Third, the state would be legitimate because of the consent of the Czech and Slovak émigré communities in the USA who had emigrated from Austria-Hungary exactly because of the non-democratic political system and its oppression of cultural and civil rights.

---

[82] Tomáš G. Masaryk, "Proststředky národa malého", in *Ideály humanitní* (Praha: Melantrich, 1991), 85-88; 87; italics by me.
[83] Anton Štefánek, *Masaryk a Slovensko* (Praha: Náklad spisovatelový, 1931), 34.

The distinguished Czech historian Jan Rychlík about Czechoslovakism:

> "To pretend that the Czechs and Slovaks were one nation was generally accepted. While many Czechs truly believed that Czechs and Slovaks formed one nation, the Slovaks considered the Czechoslovak nation as a strategic construct that should be given up once the goal [the international recognition of the Czechoslovak state, add. JB] had been achieved. From a Czech perspective, the idea of one nation should form the continuing basis of the state's existence. ... Yet in that phase of development one should not understand the concept of so-called Czechoslovakism in a negative fashion, since, without it, there would have been no Czechoslovakia at all."[84]

The distinguished Slovak historian Dušan Kováč about the building of the state:

> "Czech politicians often said that the Slovaks would get everything they wished for. The majority of the Slovaks accepted the idea that, in the first phase, in the interest of international recognition and a smooth separation from the Hungarian administration, the centralist model of the state would be the best solution. All forces concentrated on achieving that basic goal – a plan that not too long ago had been referred to as the crazy ideas of an ageing Prague professor. ..."[85]

---

[84] Jan Rychlík, *Češi a Slováci ve 20. století. Česko-Slovenské vztahy 1914–1945* (Bratislava: Veda, 1997), 54-55.

[85] Dušan Kováč, *Slováci. Češi. Dejiny* (Bratislava: AEP, 1997), 66-67. Mentioning "the crazy ideas of an ageing Prague professor", Kováč refers to the Czech journalist Ferdinand Peroutka (1895–1978), a close confidant of Masaryk's, who published a book about the foundation of the state in 1927. Peroutka, the best friend of Eva 'Mimi' Jiránková's husband Miloš Jiránek (1909–1989), criticized the Prague politicians, who, during WWI, conceived of Masaryk as a "dangerous nut" since he planned to break up the Austro-Hungarian empire; Ferdinand Peroutka, "O účasti na revoluci" (1924), in *Kdo nás osvobodil?* (Praha: Náklad Svazu národního osvobození, Tisk 'Pokrok', 1927), 5-25.

Was the foundation of Czechoslovakia on 28 October 1918 legitimate in democratic terms? Yes, for three reasons: first, the independent wish to form a state with the Czechs expressed by the Slovak National Council (SNR) on 30 October 1918;[86] second, the negotiations with Czech politicians in Geneva in October 1918;[87] and

---

[86] The Martin Declaration signed on 30 October 1918 was the independent expression of the Slovak National Council's (SNR) wish to leave the Hungarian kingdom and form a common state with the Czechs, while the Prague Declaration of 28 October included Slovakia as a part of the common state. Because of war censorship, the signatories in Martin did not know about the events in Prague when they agreed on the contents and formulation of the declaration. Milan Hodža (1878–1944) informed them when he reached Martin in the evening hours of 30 October. Vavro Šrobár (1867–1950) had signed the Prague Declaration representing the SNR; Márian Hronský and Miroslav Pekník, *Martinská deklarácia. Cesta slovenskej politiky k vzniku Česko-Slovenska* (Bratislava: Veda, 2008), 264. See also Jörg K. Hoensch, *Geschichte der Tschechoslowakei* (Stuttgart, Berlin, Köln: Kohlhammer, 1992 (3)), 39, and Jan B. Kozák, *T. G. Masaryk a vznik Washingtonské deklarace v říjnu 1918* (Praha: Melantrich, 1968), 27. Hoensch and Kozák consider the Slovak radicals' claims for autonomy of the 1920s and 1930s as unsubstantial; their questioning of the legitimacy of the Pittsburgh Agreement and the Prague Declaration had no legal grounds, as no government of the nations at war had officially recognized the SNR. The council emerged as a result of a pragmatic *ad hoc decision* of the patriots convening in Martin to validate their subsequent declaration. The foundation of the SNR and the Martin declaration have to be understood as an immediate reaction to Austro-Hungarian foreign minister Gyula Andrassy's (1823–1890) receipt of President Wilson's (1856–1924) note on the conditions for signing a peace agreement on 27 October 1918. Hronský and Pekník stress that the Martin Declaration did not create a "new nation, but a new state", 281.

[87] In mid-October, Beneš met with delegates from the Czech National Council in Geneva to negotiate further proceedings: they agreed on the political system of a republic and the composition of the first provisional government, with Masaryk as president. Karel Kramář (1860–1937) was the first prime minister, Beneš kept the Ministry of Foreign Affairs, Antonín Švehla (1873–1933) led the Ministry of Internal Affairs, Alois

third, the consent of the émigré communities of Czechs and Slovaks in the USA who had signed the Pittsburgh Agreement on 31 May 1918.

Certainly, the *zeitgeist* was friendly to democracy and the nation state, but without the lobbying of the exile troika in France, Britain and the USA, the Allies would not have recognized Czechoslovakia at the peace conferences in Versailles and Trianon. A further important factor was the *legia*, the Czechoslovak army that Slovak and Czech soldiers deserting from the Hungarian and Austrian armies had formed during the war. The *legia* had practically and pragmatically proven the wish for independence of what the Allies came to perceive as the Czechoslovaks who were fighting at their sides. A third reason for the Allies' recognition of Czechoslovakia's territorial borders was the *fait accompli* in Slovakia: Czechoslovak troops had secured the state's borders at the Danube by November 1918. Masaryk's associates in Slovakia began replacing the Hungarian administration in early November and by the summer of 1920, when the Trianon peace negotiations with Hungary started, Czechoslovak rule was firmly established in Slovakia.

Thanks to Masaryk's concept of the Czechoslovak state and the continuous efforts of Milan R. Štefánik, Edvard Beneš[88] and Vavro Šrobár in Slovakia, the Republic came into being. According to Masaryk's thinking, the last phase of the historical democratization

---

Rašin (1867–1923) the Ministry of Finance and František Soukup (1871–1940) the Ministry of Justice. Václav Klofáč (1868–1942) was the Minister of Defence and Štefánik the Minister of War. On 28 October, the Revolutionary National Assembly (*Revoluční Národní Shromáždění*) declared the independence of the sovereign Czechoslovak Republic in Prague; the first Czechoslovak government was established the same day.

[88] The latest critical edition of Beneš's memoirs is Edvard Beneš, *Paměti II. Od Mnichova k nové válce a k novému vítezství* (Praha: Academia, 2008).

process had begun with the foundation of the sovereign state. From now on, there was only one goal the Czechoslovaks had to concentrate on: to secure the state and its institutions through the citizens' continuous improvement of their social, economic and political life.

Masaryk achieved what no philosopher before him had: he had created a state with the people as the sovereign. He was the *spiritus rector* of Czechoslovak sovereignty, following his admired Plato in the imperative that philosophers should be kings, by virtue of their ethical acumen. However, an inherent problem of the state that Hitler would use to carve up the Republic was Masaryk's *constitutional construct of the Czechoslovak nation*, which was interpreted from the Czech side also as a political nation. In the interwar years, radical Slovak nationalists became increasingly critical towards Prague, whose centralism they misinterpreted as the denial of their own status as a nation. Also, they rejected the idea of the political nation, because they had had only the worst memories of the concept 'political nation': the Magyar interpretation of a united Hungarian nation had been a pretence to oppress the non-Magyar national groups with a harsh assimilation.[89] Yet Masaryk did not see the Slovak criticism as a problem:

> "Masaryk's personal origins made it difficult for him to understand an issue that was no problem to him. ... he felt a Czechoslovak in the truest sense of the word, that is, as Czech and Slovak in one person."[90]

The Czechs and Slovaks running the country had to face immense problems in the first years: the building of new institutions, the defence of Slovakia's territory against Hungarian troops in March

---

[89] Kováč, *Slováci. Česi. Dejiny*, 123.
[90] Hain, 225. Masaryk's father was a Slovak coachman and his mother a Moravian cook who spoke German; he grew up in the Eastern Moravian Hodonín, a village close to the Slovak border.

1920, the lack of trained personnel to run and govern Slovakia and the economic crisis in the 1930s. Yet Czechoslovakia was the only democracy in Central Europe in the inter-war period; had it not been for Hitler in 1938, the state would have prospered, and, perhaps, sometime in the 1940s or 1950s, changed its constitution through a referendum to a Czecho-Slovak Federation. These are but speculations, but the majority of Slovaks supported the common state, even in 1938 with the Munich Agreement hanging over the Republic like the sword of Damocles.[91] On the occasion of the tenth anniversary of the Republic on 18 October 1928, Masaryk's warning was a chilling portent:

> "The foreign policy of our state … will require caution and a clear understanding of the changing political situation in Europe … On several occasions I have called your attention to the fact that we have to face a renewed and strong, not a defeated Germany."[92]

---

[91] The autonomist block of HSĽS and SNS had won the parliamentary elections in 1935 in Slovakia; they wanted a change of constitution that would put Slovakia on an equal footing with the Czech lands in a federation. In May 1938, however, HSĽS was no longer the strongest party: "HSĽS intensified its push for autonomy, but concerns about the international threat soon strengthened the position of the centralist parties, confirmed by the course and results of the community elections of May 1938. … 1452 communities held elections. Slovenska Jednota [an electoral association of Agrarians, Social Democrats, the Slovak National Party and further small parties, add. JB] received most votes with 43.93%, followed by HSĽS with 26.93% and KSČ with 7.4%. … The results of these elections were never published, but they confirm that the Slovak citizens were not only aware of the threat against but also in support of the Republic;" Kováč, *Dejiny Slovenska*, 209.

[92] Tomáš G. Masaryk, "Projev prezidenta Republiky", in *Cesta demokracie III. Projevy, články, rozhovory 1924–28* (Praha: Ústav T. G. Masaryka, 1994), 237–240; 239.

II. 2   Imprisoned for being a daughter

The war did not spare the Masaryk family from fateful blows.[93] Masaryk, under suspicion of high treason that could lead to immediate arrest, trial and a death sentence, left Prague in December 1914 under the pretence of accompanying his youngest daughter Olga abroad where she would get medical treatment.[94] Charlotte suffered from heart ailments and mental problems; Jan was recruited into the Austrian army and sent to the eastern front, and Herbert, Alice's closest sibling and beloved little brother, died of typhus on 15 March 1915. The financial difficulties, the lack of information about the father and sister in exile and the brother at the front, the illness of her mother and Herbert's large debts – all this was on Alice's shoulders. To Charlotte, Alice was the only family member she could rely on; the servant Marie Blahová was loyal to the family and stayed with them without pay.[95] The university, under pressure from the Austrian authorities, had to suspend Masaryk's professorship, including salary and pension; Alice's meagre income that she earned as a teacher at the Holešovice high school for girls saw them through the first half of the war.

To the Austrian authorities, the fact that Masaryk, who was warned by members of the Czech resistance movement *maffie*[96], did

---

[93] A recommendable study about WWI in the Czech lands is Ivan Šedivý, *Češi, České Země a Velká Válka 1914–1918* (Praha: Nakladatelství Lidové Noviny, 2001).

[94] Lovčí, 139. In fact, Olga was not physically ill, but suffered from mental problems and was psychologically unstable after her divorce; POLÁK, STANISLAV: *Charlotta Garrigue Masaryková*. Praha, Mladá fronta, 1992, s. 34, quoted from Lovčí, 139.

[95] Lovčí, 149.

[96] Recommendable about the origins, development and activities of the *maffie* is Milada Paulová, *Dějiny Maffie. Odboj Čechů a jihoslovanů za světové války 1914–1918* (Praha: Československá grafická unie, 1937). According to Paulová, it was Masaryk's political adversary from the

not attend Herbert's funeral in Prague, was clear proof of his anti-Austrian activities; they increased the secret observation of the family. Apart from her teaching, Alice was active in the Austrian Red Cross and published under a male pen name a portrait of her American friend, the deaf-blind writer and socialist Helen Keller (1880–1968).[97] She was most impressed by Helen's courage, optimism, mental strength and dedication to social issues.

In the summer holidays of 1915, Alice volunteered as assistant nurse in a war-front hospital in Pardubice that was taking care of the wounded from the Russian front. In her diary, she wrote that the principal decision to volunteer was her eagerness to learn what the war really looked like, to critically examine what the Austrian War propaganda was hiding from the citizens.[98] While she was attending to the wounded, the authorities searched their apartment on 30 September, looking for anti-Austrian documents.

Masaryk had hidden his writings, leaving behind only a letter informing the authorities that they would find nothing.[99] The police interrogated Alice when she was back in Prague after the summer holidays, but they were unsuccessful for the second time, because Alice knew nothing. She was not that interested in politics anyway and had always concentrated her efforts on social welfare. She was not politically active in the *maffie,* but she knew, of course, the

---

struggle of the manuscripts Julius Grégr (1831–1896), who coined the term *maffie*, comparing Masaryk and the Realists to a criminal organization.

[97] Lovčí, 146.
[98] Lovčí, 147.
[99] Lovčí, 148. Alice remembered the wording of the letter as follows: "Before he left he hid his political documents and left a letter in his library: 'Gentlemen, I have hidden my political papers, the family doesn't know where they are.' Mother gave this letter to the police while they were searching the apartment;" "Foreword by Dr. A. G. Masaryková", in *Listy do Vězení* (Praha: Vladimír Žikeš, 1947), 7.

association's Prague members, as well as a daughter knows her father's social life.

When a female courier, supposed to deliver news from the *odboj* (resistance) in exile to agents of the *odboj* in the Czech homeland, was mistakenly identified as an Austrian police agent and handed over to the authorities, it triggered a wave of arrests, many among them members of the *maffie*.[100] Alice was arrested and accused of anti-state activities.[101] She didn't take the arrest seriously and freely admitted in the interrogation that she had given Dr. Beneš papers from her father, but they had been of a scientific, not a political nature. Charlotte knew nothing about her husband's activities abroad, because Masaryk protected his family by not contacting them. They would be safest if they knew nothing. Charlotte, supportive and understanding of her husband's every decision, took Alice's arrest with calm, poise and pragmatism:

> "I was arrested on 28 October 1915. We didn't expect that they would keep me in custody at police headquarters, that's why I called home to inform my mother. 'Do you need anything? Are you there for the entire day?' I can still hear this truthful voice – without pathos and so infinitely touching."[102]

Conditions in the Prague prison were not as bad as those that would await her in Vienna. The interrogators, policemen and prison personnel treated her in a decent fashion, and with some of them the still energetic Alice was on friendly terms:

---

[100] Lovčí, 150; the tragic incident is referred to in the literature as the so-called Knoflík affair.
[101] Lovčí, 150.
[102] "Foreword by Dr. A. G. Masaryková", 6-7.

"I was in good humour, I kept asking them about their handicrafts and hobbies; one traded in pictures, another collected stamps, a third was a musician."[103]

Jan Satranský, the director of the girl's high school and her boss, acted very kindly by letting her know that he had given her unlimited leave of absence[104] – which meant that he would keep her position open and she would have an income once she came back to teaching. In the school's annual report of the year 1914/15 he mentioned Dr. Alice Masaryková's remarkable contribution to the Austrian war effort; she had initiated and organized collections of humanitarian goods for the soldiers. Little did Satranský, Charlotte and Alice know that she would never return to the school. The prison authorities informed Alice about her transfer to Vienna at the end of November 1915.

The Austrian authorities made no distinction between political prisoners and common criminals – the usual practice of every non-democratic state that does not respect basic human rights. Charged with high treason, the personnel treated Alice as they treated prostitutes, thieves and murderesses; they thought she was a dangerous spy.[105] The nine months she would be imprisoned in cell no. 207 at the Landesgerichtliches Gefangenenhaus[106] would affect her physical and psychological health.

The hygienic conditions were so terrible that she wrote in her diary that the clean world of her home now appeared an abnormality.[107] Several prisoners had to share a non-functioning

---

[103] *Dráha mama/dear Alice. Korespondence Alice a Charlotty Masarykových 1915–1916.* Hájková, Dagmara – Soukup, Jaroslav (ed.). Praha, Masarykův ústav AV ČR 2001, s. 184-185, quoted from Lovčí, 153.

[104] Lovčí, 156.

[105] Lovčí, 162.

[106] Lovčí, 160.

[107] Lovčí, 163.

latrine that stank abominably; toilet paper was available only when one was prepared to negotiate at length with the personnel, and to open the window for fresh air only led to disputes with the other prisoners. The diet lacked vitamins, sugar and dairy produce and only worsened the inmates' fragile health, already undermined by a lack of fresh air and movement.

Alice began to suffer from anaemia and heart problems, but the worst was the lack of quiet and seclusion she needed for her reading and writing. After many sleepless nights, she developed signs of mood changes and had difficulties distinguishing day from night.[108] Her optimism vanished once she understood the gravity of her situation.

What kept her going were the letters from her mother. Charlotte and Alice established lines of communication immediately. They wrote to each other in German. I deem it safe to assume that they wanted to shorten any delay caused by the censors if they were to write in English, the language of the enemy. Letters in Czech would have made the authorities very suspicious; they would have assumed that the two women were exchanging information about Masaryk and the Czech *odboj*. Their closeness bordered on a symbiotic relationship; it seems to me that mother and daughter were psychologically connected to the extent that they almost shared one personality, or a virtual cloud, enabling them to communicate with each other without words. Each anticipated what the other thought and felt. When Charlotte sensed from Alice's letters that her mental state was worsening, she encouraged her to stay strong, sent her books, told her news about relatives and friends and mentioned happy times, making Alice remember her family before the war. Charlotte sounded very positive and optimistic and

---

[108] Lovćí, 163.

avoided talking about her own fragile health. Her pragmatism and care were a great comfort to Alice:

> "I have sent you your books about practical sociology ... you are saying that it's not easy to concentrate with many people around. Not everybody is capable of doing this, and I am happy that you are. I am thinking about you all the time. Did you get the 200 crowns that I sent on 30 November? ... Just tell me what you need and I'll send it immediately."[109]

Charlotte gave her practical advice on how to organize their correspondence: Alice should always date her letters, always reply to all her questions, confirm receipt of the money she had received and take care of her health. She should buy light food, such as fruit, drink fresh milk and try to get as much fresh air as possible.[110] Also, Alice should not be concerned with Charlotte's health; she was fine and following the instructions of her physician Professor Syllaba. Fresh air and water were the best medication.[111] Charlotte's advice on learning that Alice had difficulty falling asleep is very touching. In her letter of 2 January 1916 Charlotte wrote:

> "I wish you a happy New Year. The first thing I did yesterday morning was to write to you. I think often of you and love you very much. My heart is too full that I could waste words. ... But I am telling you this: if you can't sleep, imagine that you are a child again – which you actually are – and that I am sitting at your bedside, just as I did every night for many many years, telling you about our garden and the dear people I knew. And then you close your dear eyes and sleep a refreshing sleep with the most beautiful dreams."[112]

---

[109] Charlotta G. Masaryková, *Listy do Vězení* (Praha: Vladimír Žikeš, 1947), 9.
[110] Charlotta G. Masaryková, 13.
[111] Charlotta G. Masaryková, 15.
[112] Charlotta G. Masaryková, 17-18. There is no indication what garden and people Charlotte was referring to, but I deem it very possible that she spoke of their holiday home in Bystrička, since she knew how much

Once Charlotte learnt that Alice would be released soon, the tone and contents of her letters changed. I think that she kept herself strong and optimistic to make sure that Alice would not get depressed, to keep her daughter in good spirits; after all, Alice was accused of high treason and could be sentenced to death at any moment. Charlotte must have been exhausted with writing letters almost every day. On 11 May 1916 she described for the first time her physical and mental state:

> "You are asking about my health. I am not really well, my heart is weak and I tire very quickly. I have to save my strength. If only you were here, you could do so much for me. When I passed the care of the household on to you in 1914, I did so only because I couldn't do it any longer, and in the last two years I have not gained in strength. ... My whole life I spent at home and my entire happiness was the wellbeing and prosperity of my children. And, in one moment – all is gone. ... You know, I have to lie down all the time. Often, I rest the whole day and when I feel a bit of strength, I get up and go for a short walk, and once I am back home, I lie down again. ... In brief: I feel completely incapable. ... Just come quickly! Your faithful mother."[113]

Apart from her physical illness, Charlotte also suffered from a congenital mental illness, most probably depression. Alice inherited that depression, as did her siblings Olga and Jan. The grave conditions of the prison accelerated Alice's mental problems. Yet, her mother's letters starting from May must have put her on alert: her mother needed her, she had to be the strong one again in the relationship, the principal carer. A further interesting fact, but a logical one given their situation, is their caution: they often mentioned Herbert, and other relatives and acquaintances in

---

Alice loved the Slovak countryside and the Slovak people. The somewhat odd wording of Charlotte's 'the dear people I knew' is, I think, a reference to Tomáš. The emphasis on people Charlotte knew, and not Alice, was most probably a smoke screen intended for the censor.

[113] Charlotta G. Masaryková, 84-85.

Prague, but never Tomáš. Obviously, they did not want to risk drawing more attention to Alice. On 2 July 1916 Charlotte sent a telegram to Vienna with the brief message that she was saving her strength. On 3 July 1916, Alice was released and returned to Prague.

At first glance, Alice's arrest and release seem a paradox: she was arrested and charged because of her father's anti-Austrian activities abroad, but it was thanks to the international pressure of his associates and Alice's friends in the USA that she was eventually released. Thus, the reason of arrest and release was the same: being the daughter of Professor Masaryk, who was engaging in anti-Austrian activities.

On 20 August 1916 the Austrian Consul General in the USA, Alexander von Nuber, confirmed Alice Masaryk's release.[114] Since her arrest, Masaryk's main American associate Charles R. Crane and representatives of the Czech exile communities had been contacting US diplomats and representatives, explaining to them Austria's injustice in imprisoning the daughter of a well-respected academic and intellectual: the kin liability Austria applied in Alice's case was a clear punishment of her father. Their activities presented Alice as the innocent victim of a rogue state the Czechs wanted to leave anyway, linking Alice's fate to the Czech independence movement.

Alice's American friends, among them Miss McDowell, Dr. Julia Lathorp, Jane Addams and many other prominent women organized a campaign on her behalf; the University of Chicago Settlement Woman's Club, the Bohemian Woman's Medical Club, the Fabian Club of Boston, the Women's Peace Party and many other Women's organizations urged their members to send letters of

---

[114] *New York Times*, Aug. 20, 1916. The *Christian Science Monitor*, Aug. 21, 1916, reported that she was freed on July 3, quoted from Betty M. Unterberger, "The Arrest of Alice Masaryk", *Slavic Review 33*, no. 1 (1974): 91-106; 105.

appeal to the US State Department.[115] The organizations of Czechs and Slovaks in the USA joined forces with the American Women's associations and their efforts prompted a great success: *Denní Hlasatel* (*The Daily Herald*) was the largest Czech-American newspaper; it reported on 21 July that the campaign organized by Miss McDowell had resulted in forty thousand letters sent to Vienna.[116]

A further paradox, related to what became known in the USA as the 'Alice Masaryk Affair', was the goal of the campaigners, diplomats and protesters. While it was quite clear that Masaryk and his daughter Olga feared for Alice's life, interpreting her arrest as an attempt to silence the professor, the women's organizations looked at Alice's case from the perspective of the women's peace movement and female emancipation.[117] The feminist campaigners protested against the injustice of arresting a young doctor of history who had committed no crime; they criticized Austria's kin liability as gender-biased discrimination. The women's peace movement's principal goal was peace, not Bohemia's independence. They wanted to save Alice's life, end the war as quickly as possible and avoid an American involvement. The Czech independence movement, on the other hand, sought to get the USA involved with the Allies, since only the USA with her military might and moral pressure could promote the cause of a free Czechoslovakia.

The pressure of so many US citizens, mainly of Czech and Slovak origins, and appeals by US diplomats eventually led to Alice's release. The Austrian government most probably considered that executing Alice on charges of treason would have three negative consequences.

---

[115] Unterberger, 103-104.
[116] Unterberger, 102.
[117] Unterberger, 106.

First, Alice Masaryková's execution would considerably strengthen and unify the American Czechs' independence movement, with concomitant pressure on the US government. Second, Alice's death would provoke her father who was already very well connected with US diplomats and influential persons into stepping up his anti-Austrian activities, encouraging him in his leadership. Third, executing a young woman would be a dangerous damage to Austria's international image and war propaganda. Thus, from an Austrian point of view, there was nothing to gain but much to loose from Alice's death. First, her release might help to weaken the American Czechs' anti-Austrian attitude by taking the wind out of their sails that is, rendering an issue obsolete that was unifying them in their protests. Second, Alice's release might be interpreted as a gesture of Austria's good will and, with regard to Germany, Austria's vital interest in keeping up separate diplomatic relations with the USA.

II. 3 The Czechoslovak Red Cross as the fulfilment of "small works" (*drobná práce*)

By 3 July 1916, Alice and Charlotte were together again, but in the last one and a half years of the war they faced immense financial problems that were so grave that they often did not have enough to eat.[118] They received financial support from members of the *maffie* and associates, among them the future Czechoslovak chancellor Přemysl Šámal (1867–1941).[119] Alice was not idle: she gave private lessons in English; as the daughter of a traitor she had lost her teaching position at the Holešovice high school. The authorities tried

---

[118] Lovćí, 186.
[119] Lovćí, 186.

to suppress the increasing anti-Austrian attitude simmering in the Czech educational institutions.

After the US declaration of war on Germany in April 1917, a declaration of war on Austria-Hungary was to be expected – which must have fuelled the *maffie* in Prague with hope of liberation and independence. On 12 July 1917, the governor of Bohemia count Max Coudenhove wrote to k.k. Minister President Ernst Seidler von Feuchtenegg and k.k. Minister of internal affairs Count Friedrich Toggenburg:

> "Your Excellency! In view of the recent political developments in Bohemia, I consider it my duty to submit a report to your Excellency's attention, concerning the present rather disquieting situation. ... Everywhere, anti-Austrian tendencies are being expressed in open fashion ... two anonymous publications, recently discovered, spoke in drastic terms of the 'death throws of Austria' ... reports about the war, especially in the *Narodni Listy*, give the impression that Bohemia does not belong to Austria, and the friendliness towards the Entente ... is being concealed less and less ... the current thinking of the decisive political circles of the Czech nation ... must therefore be considered revolutionary."[120]

The Austrian government opted for a separate peace with the Allies on 27 October 1918, offering the Empire's nationalities political participation in vague terms, yet it was too late. With his programme of 14 points, US President Wilson had set the conditions for peace. Emperor Karl I offered a separate peace to the USA on 27 October 1918, which prompted the Czechoslovak Declaration of Independence on 28 October 1918 in Prague.

Alice's life changed immediately with the inception of Czechoslovak rule: she was freed from the responsibility of being the single carer of her mother and could rely on personnel; her father

---

[120] Quoted from Zdeněk Šolle (ed.), *Masaryk a Beneš ve svých dopisech z doby pařížských mírových jednání v roce 1919*, vol. I (Praha: Archiv AV ČR, 1993), pozn. 52, 85, 88, 89.

and sister Olga returned to Prague in December 1918. Also, the financial difficulties were gone, since the president and his family moved to Lány, the presidential residence outside Prague. Nurses now took care of Charlotte, but she was not capable of serving as First Lady at the side of her husband and her health was quickly deteriorating.

Olga, the youngest daughter, acted as First Lady at the side of her father for two short years, but when she got married to the Swiss physician Henri Revilliod and moved to Geneva in 1920,[121] Alice had to step in, representational tasks being an activity she did not like much. Charlotte died on 13 May 1923, which deeply affected Alice and her brother Jan. The two fixated themselves on Hana Benešová, who would become a replacement for Charlotte, a close confidante and kind of surrogate mother.

Already in November 1918, Alice contacted two social institutions: she offered to volunteer for the "Czech Commission for the Protection of Children and Care of the Youth" (*Česká zemská komise pro ochranu dítek a péči o mládež*) and was co-opted to the executive board of the charity association "Czech Heart" (*České srdce)*.[122] I deem it safe to assume that Alice had two crucial principles she followed in all her activities: the Christian principle of love thy neighbour and her father's principle of the "small works" (*drobná práce*).

Masaryk's "small works"[123] projected the daily, ethical and unspectacular efforts of every individual to lead a self-determined

---

[121] Lovćí, 207.

[122] Lovćí, 245.

[123] "… our people enjoy a considerable extent of liberty in our imperfect constitution that it has no reason to embark on violent tactics. That's why the call to the small works is justified – let us do our best. Let's not wait for the Vienna government and others to do this work for us [in our interests, add. JB] and on our behalf;" T. G. Masaryk, *Česká otázka*, 136-137. "… we acknowledge that revolution is the symptom and basis for

and moral life: continuous self-education, activities for the nation and the exercise of tolerance and critical thinking were required to transform the Czechs and Slovaks into enlightened citizens who would be capable of acting as the sovereign of their future independent state. The "small works", first mentioned in 1895, was a stroke of genius from Masaryk, as he rightly saw that Czech party politics were stuck because of unrealistic goals and blocked by the intransigence of Vienna. Therefore, a non-political movement, a movement concentrating not on party politics but on the daily improvement of society through science and education, and dealing with social issues and cultural questions should unite the citizens. The "small works" were a part of his Czech nation-building theory and the pragmatic and practical principle that would create civic discipline, individual responsibility and social cohesion. If the citizens wished for self-government in a sovereign state, they had to learn, to work; idle waiting and complaining would not bring about political change. The "small works" were a practical and, in terms of national identity, political guideline on how to realize the basic principle of the Enlightenment under the conditions of absolutist rule and the absence of general franchise: to use one's critical reason, to overcome superstition and slave mentality and develop inner strength against the rule of the clergy and the aristocracy.

Masaryk had an ambivalent relationship with Kantian philosophy, since, in his perception, Kant had put too much emphasis on reason. With his *Categorical Imperative* Kant, so Masaryk thought, considered morality an iron duty, but neglected the crucial psychological facet of humanity: individuals are selfish, but not only

---

further problems and are thus calling for work, continuous, systematic and considerate work. Politics for the people is a never-ending and uninterrupted process of reform – politics for the people is dedicated to work, it is work;" T. G. Masaryk, "Naše nynejší krize", in *Česká otázka*, 191-345; 225.

and not always – they also have a natural capability to act in a non-selfish manner, to take care of others like Jesus did. If he considered Kant's philosophy on ethics too idealistic, Masaryk certainly shared with the great philosopher from Königsberg one crucial idea:

> "Enlightenment is man's emergence from his self-imposed nonage."[124]

Enlightenment thus meant to Alice not only continuous self-education, discipline and critical thinking but also activities on behalf of those who could not yet liberate themselves. The Republic had to develop institutions that took care of the poor, and help them, first, to improve their lives and, second, help them with education. The "small works" were therefore also pragmatic help to self-help, embodying the ideas of scientific progress, life-long learning and instruction of the citizens in science, economics, social issues and politics to inculcate their intellectual emancipation from the servant mentality of the past.

In January 1919, the Czechoslovak Red Cross (ČSČK) was built from the Czech and Slovak sections of the former Austrian and Hungarian Red Cross.[125] From her former activities on behalf of the Austrian Red Cross and her stay in the USA in 1904 to 1905, Alice was experienced in the organization and planning of social work; she was eager to build the new organization from scratch and give it a national Czechoslovak mission and face. The Austrian Red Cross had reflected the aristocratic rule with ladies of the Czech nobility

---

[124] The original quote in German: "Aufklärung ist der Ausgang des Menschen aus seiner selbstverschuldeten Unmündigkeit." Kant's essay *Beantwortung der Frage: Was ist Aufklärung?* from 1784 on http://www.gutenberg.org/files/30821/30821-h/30821-h.htm; accessed 27 February 2015. The English translation of Immanuel Kant's *What is Enlightenment?* on http://www.columbia.edu/acis/ets/CCREAD/etscc/kant.html; accessed 27 February 2015.

[125] Lovčí, 245.

presiding over the Prague section who considered the organization a charity, a kind of hobby; it had had only a few thousand members. The Czechoslovak Red Cross would be a professional mass organization, based on expert assessment, the latest results of medical research and linked to the Red Cross network that was emerging in 1919 as the International Federation of Red Cross Societies.[126] It was thanks to Alice's principal influence that the humanitarian aid the Czechoslovak Red Cross provided applied modern international standards and was effective.

The bad hygienic conditions in the young Republic called for concerted and, above all, swift action: in her speech at the preparatory meeting in the Prague Municipal House (*Obecný Dům*) on 1 January 1919,[127] Alice listed the most pressing problems. The war had brought about contagious diseases such as tuberculosis and typhus; in many regions, particular in the Eastern part of the country, people suffered from hunger. The Red Cross had not only to build sanatoria and modern hospitals but also concern itself with the prevention of diseases and epidemics. A further issue were the orphans; many children, especially in Slovakia and the Sub-Carpathian Rus had lost both parents in the war. In those regions, the social network was not as developed as in the Czech lands and a public healthcare system worthy of the name was virtually non-existent. As a result of the meeting that social workers, physicians, members of the army and artists attended, the board adopted the statutes of the new organization and elected Alice chairwoman. The president confirmed her election; always thinking in terms of international relations aimed at integrating the young Republic into post-war Europe, he gave her a political task: she should establish

---

[126] See the history of the IFRC on http://www.ifrc.org/en/who-we-are/history/; accessed 2 March 2015.
[127] Lovčí, 246.

contacts to foreign Red Cross organisations on the basis of the Geneva Convention.[128]

Alice's election was a provisional solution to grant a smooth transition of the Austrian and Hungarian branches to the new Czechoslovak mass organization, yet she would step down from the chair only in 1939 with the Nazi German occupation of her country. Former Austrian and German members of the board protested in fear of loosing their positions, but to no avail: already in February 1919, the government established a special commission, whose task was to liquidate the former Austrian sections, provide them with Czech names, appoint Czech chairpersons and confiscate the property of the Hungarian Red Cross in Slovakia.[129] The government's official recognition followed in June 1919, defining the Czechoslovak Red Cross in legal terms as the only national institution representing the Red Cross's mission and values on the Republic's territory.

Under Alice's leadership, swift changes occurred that connected Slovakia to the Czech lands by respecting the young state's internal borders based on language: according to the Czechoslovak constitution, the languages of the ČSČK's local and regional branches were Czech and Slovak.[130] The Red Cross was divided into four regional divisions: the Czech, the Moravian-Silesian, the Slovak and the Sub-Carpathian Rus, with headquarters in Prague, Brno, Martin and Mukačevo respectively. Each division had its own board and regional director. The organization's main decision-making board was the Prague headquarters with Alice as chairwoman; it had an executive committee at its disposal. For the first few months, Alice had to have the board members convene in her own flat in Prague Castle until the government gave the

---

[128] Lovčí, 247.
[129] Lovčí, 247-248.
[130] Lovčí, 248.

organization a palace in the city centre that became its official headquarters.[131]

The booklet *What the Czechoslovak Red Cross needs: compiled from official reports* which the Bohemian National Alliance in Chicago published in 1919 provides interesting information that illustrates the dire need for aid and know-how: money to build quarantine stations for patients with contagious diseases; clothing; food, especially fresh milk; linen and soap for the hospitals; technical equipment and cinemas for instruction about the importance of hygiene.[132] In spite of the abysmal situation in the hospitals, the high child mortality, the orphans living in the streets and the general lack of food and clothing, the text shows the optimistic spirit and professional rationality of the headquarter's employees. Asking the American Red Cross for help, listing the seven most pressing needs, the Czechoslovak Red Cross wrote:

> "We want to have our state placed on a firm basis of expert, scientific work, no dilettantism or 'goody-goody' enthusiasm; we believe in clear business-like idealism for the transition period. This idealism will never leave Czechoslovakia – but now we need all hands on deck to save many thousands of lives."[133]

I deem it safe to assume that Alice had a crucial influence on the text's composition; it is very likely that she wrote the entire booklet herself: the text was written by a person experienced in writing in English, presenting facts and figures gathered from the four regional divisions. Only a board member had an overview of the situation in all four regions.

---

[131] Lovčí, 249.
[132] *"What the Czechoslovak Red Cross needs: compiled from official reports"* on https://archive.org/stream/5926299upenn/5926299#page/n3/mode/2up;accessed 3 March 2015. The booklet has 16 pages.
[133] *"What the Czechoslovak Red Cross needs: compiled from official reports"* on https://archive.org/stream/5926299upenn/5926299#page/n3/mode/2up;accessed 3 March 2015, 15.

Tirelessly, Alice worked for the Red Cross: as she was very popular, hundreds of citizens literally overwhelmed her with demands and claims. Some tried to curry favour with her to receive a government position; others asked her to be the godmother to a baby – which would, or so they must have thought, ensure the protection and welfare of their offspring.[134] This behaviour was what Masaryk, the government and his daughter were fighting against: the old means of securing one's existence by relations to powerful persons that gave way to nepotism and corruption. The citizens were used to this way of life under the conditions of Austrian absolutism, when personal connections used to improve one's existential security and financial and social status. Since the board members could not deal with the massive influx of demands, they had to reorganize: the ČSČK's press office issued a printed form with Alice's signature the citizens were asked to fill out. They were then directed to the regional division responsible for the village or town they lived in.[135]

Alice travelled the country to inspect the situation in the regional divisions; she instructed the personnel and held uncountable lectures advertising the new Red Cross. In her very limited spare time, she studied pathology and learnt from specialists about tuberculosis; her mother's physician, Professor Ladislav Syllaba and the physicians Dr Kamil Henner and Professor Rudolf Jedlička were at her side and often gave her private instruction.[136] Yet not everybody admired her popularity, leadership and energy; active and successful persons often encounter the envy of those who are not as capable, and their leadership provokes rejection and criticism.

---

[134] Lovčí, 249.
[135] Lovčí, 249.
[136] Lovčí, 251.

Already in the early days of ČSČK in 1919, a group of ladies refused to work with her on the board, reproaching Alice that she wanted to employ a Prague lady who had allegedly been too sympathetic towards the Austrian government during the war. A further conflict arose when Naděžda Kramářová, the wife of Masaryk's adversary Karel Kramář, repeatedly rejected Alice's invitation to join the board; Alice's intention was to employ society ladies who, owing to their social status, would be role models advertising the Red Cross and gathering a large following, especially among women.[137] After Naděžda's husband was voted out of the premiership in the summer of 1920, his wife started to pester Alice with petty reproaches that were directed against the president. Alice's love of her father, but also her temper and lack of diplomacy, is visible in her answer to Naděžda, whose reproaches she called

> "the product of the psychology of a slave, the petty-mindedness and envy that springs from comparing one's own successes and lack thereof with those of others. ... As every honest Czechoslovak, I'd readily give my life for my nation, more eagerly I give my inspiring work. I would feel embarrassed to speak about my love of the noble Czech nation. Dr Kramář has chosen a misguided path. Flattery and self-love are clouding his judgement."[138]

Naděžda never forgave Alice, but the president's daughter had other worries than to brood on Mrs Kramářová's hurt feelings. Between 1919 and 1921, she went on several trips to the USA, France and Switzerland to advertise the Czechoslovak Red Cross and raise funds. Czech physicians criticised her for seeking help abroad by inviting foreign specialists to Czechoslovakia.[139] She could not

---

[137] Lovčí, 257.
[138] AMÚ AV ČR, fond A. G. Masaryková, karton 4, jednotka 21, složka: Korespondence - opis dopisu A. Masarykové Naděždě Kramářové z 26. 8. 1920, quoted from Lovčí, 254-255.
[139] Lovčí, 263.

understand their hurt pride; to her such thoughts were proof of a distinct provincial short-sightedness. Alice reacted straightforwardly again in a communiqué:

> "People look at the foreign specialists who come to us either with infinite admiration, which is uncritical, or then coldly, which lacks objectivity. ... We have well-known economists, talented specialists. Often we are better educated, with respect to theory. Yet, we lack the attributes that are internationally acknowledged as [professional, add. JB] qualities: precision, punctuality, the answering of letters and questions and, above all, tolerance. If the maturity of foreigners sometime differs from ours – with regard to tolerance we can learn from them."[140]

In spite of her successful fund-raising at home and abroad and her hard work, the president's daughter was financially completely dependent on her father – she received no salary from the Red Cross.[141] In her undated diary she wrote that the chairman of Prague's Chamber of Commerce once offered her 100,000 crowns per annum if she came to work in his shop: he had seen her at work.[142] She knew that her work was irreplaceable, but wished she had funds of her own for her retirement. Yet, it would be mistaken to assume that Alice was poor; I think that what she disliked as a feminist was the fact that her work was not paid like a regular job, that social welfare was still considered charity, hence a branch of female activity. Charity, in its original sense of Christian care for others was expected to be for free; getting paid for charity work was seen as unchristian. The president was generous though; at the end of the 1920s Alice had, according to her own words, two million

---

[140] AMÚ AV ČR, fond A. G. Masaryková, karton 2, jednotka 9, Literární činnost, Poznámky převážné sociologické, přednášky, zápisy, quoted from Lovčí, 264.

[141] Lovčí, 264.

[142] Lovčí, 264-265.

crowns at her disposal.[143] The boulevard press kept reproaching her that she was enriching herself at the cost of the tax-payers in the particularly difficult situation of the world economic crisis of the 1930s, and the principal question of how the president obtained these large sums was legitimate.

Masaryk often helped associates from the former *maffie* or friends when they were in debt;[144] donations from Jaroslav Preiss, the chairman of the Živnobanka, managers of the Legiobanka but also the president's own salary allowed him to be generous. The lack of transparency about the president's funds was considered proof of corruption – which it most probably was, yet Alice didn't see it that way: the funds received from her father were legitimate because they were financing a humanitarian organization, hence spent for the benefit of society.[145] Alice was never interested in designer fashion, flashy restaurants or fancy cars; she had no expensive hobbies and, as an intellectual, preferred a frugal and sober lifestyle. The only luxury she allowed herself a couple of years later was her house in Slovakia.

In the early 1920s, the situation in the Sub-Carpathian Rus in the North East of the country bordering on Poland and the Ukrainian SSR demanded her full attention. Several epidemics were decimating

---

[143] Lovčí, 265.

[144] An example: in 1930, the president helped Vavro Šrobár, the principal Hlasist at the turn of the 20th century and former Czechoslovak governor of Slovakia (1918–1922) by paying off his large debt incurred by the purchase of a collection of faked paintings; the debt amounted to 750'000 crowns, with a murderous interest rate at 10% that raised the sum well over a million crowns in a few months. To avoid a public scandal, Masaryk provided 1 million crowns from the presidential funds, but it has never been sufficiently explained who else was involved in helping Šrobár, who was on the brink of suicide; for details of the 'affair of the forged paintings' see my *A Life Dedicated to the Republic*, 157-163.

[145] Lovčí, 265.

the population and could not be brought under control because of a painful lack of physicians and funds. Attempts at preventing the spreading of infectious diseases by improving general hygienic standards failed, since 90% of the population was illiterate, rendering the Red Cross's leaflet campaign largely ineffective.[146] Alice asked the Rockefeller Foundation and the American Red Cross for help; the Czechoslovak Red Cross sent specialists in epidemiology to the region, while the Americans contributed a special train equipped with diagnostic machines, beds for the patients, a kitchen and a surgery unit.[147]

Alice inspected the situation on several trips. She was not successful in gathering support in the Rusin communities and thus contacted in 1924 an old friend, the Protestant clergyman František Urbánek, who ran a home for orphans in Prague; he sent immediate financial support and personnel. To improve literacy among the Rusin children, the ČSČK started "operation pupils" (*žákovská akce*).[148] According to the Red Cross's investigations, the way to school in the mountainous region was too long for the children to attend school on a regular basis; the distance was miles and particularly dangerous in winter, since the children were poorly dressed and their shoes unfit to protect them from the icy temperatures. They used to sleep in sheds and stables in the countryside to avoid the tiresome journey back and forth. The Red

---

[146] Kárník, Zdeněk: *České země v éře první republiky / 1918–1938 /. Díl druhý. Československo a České země v krizi a ohrožení (1930–1935)*. Praha, Libri 2002, s. 237, quoted from Lovčí, 281. As if the situation was not bad enough, the few inhabitants who could read and write were divided by language and identity issues: those who did not regard themselves as members of the Rusin nationality, refused to acknowledge the medical instructions in Ruthenian, insisting that they should be printed in Ukrainian or Russian.

[147] Lovčí, 281-282.

[148] Lovčí, 282.

Cross established boarding houses in the schools where the children could live during termtime; the homes provided food, shelter and medical care.

The Red Cross was also the principal initiator of an important reform of the school curricula in the Sub-Carpathian region: the schools offered new courses, training the pupils in diverse professions, granting the children a new future. In the past, they had to work in the fields with their families and lacked the basic education that allowed them to take up vocational training. They literally had only a future that repeated the miserable cycle of their parents and grandparents; Under Hungarian rule, there was no way out from the cycle of poverty: the state's dictate of Hungarian as language of instruction caused illiteracy, which in turn caused poverty and despair, resulting in alcoholism that generated a new cycle of poverty, lack of education and more alcoholism. Thanks to the ČSČK's reform, the children could learn various professions and apply for apprenticeships in the Czech lands.

Lady Muriel Paget was a British friend of Alice and her father; thanks to her and her associates' efforts, hospitals, children's homes, children's hospitals and soup kitchens were built in Slovakia with funds collected in Great Britain.[149] The émigré communities in the USA were not idle either: American Slovaks and the ČSČK initiated the project and contributed the funds for the first college of nursing that opened in 1926 in Turčiansky Sv. Martin in North Central Slovakia.

Alice's relationship with Elena Maróthy-Šoltésova (1855–1939),[150] the chairwoman of the Slovak Women's association *Živena*, and representatives of the cultural association *Matica Slovenská* was fruitful and successful: she went on inspection tours through

---

[149] Lovčí, 282.
[150] For the first biographical portrait of Elena Maróthy-Šoltésová in English see chapter I of my *Seven Slovak Women*, 17-42.

Slovakia, accompanied by members of the two associations. The women organized courses, lectures and published regularly in the journal edited by *Živena*; the members were so grateful to Alice and the efforts of the Czechoslovak Red Cross that they elected the president's daughter honorary chairwoman.[151] To them, the financial and logistical support of the Czechoslovak government was a godsend. The gratitude of *Živena's* board members was based on experience: in the past, *Živena* had had to tread carefully in order not to arouse the suspicions of the Hungarian government. The official recognition of the Czechoslovak government, which Alice embodied, gave the association a boost and cemented its loyalty to the Republic.

Alice had known Slovakia since childhood and loved Slovak folklore; she spent her holidays and spare time in Bystrička. The president's favourite place was Lány Castle. In the 1930s, when he was already suffering the illnesses of old age, he stayed a couple of times in Topoľčianky, where the family had spent summer holidays prior to the war. Alice's many tours of inspection to Slovakia led her to the idea of making Slovakia her permanent home: in the 1930s, she bought, with the financial support of her father, a plot of land in Bystrička, a small village close to Martin. The construction work for her house began.[152]

In the economically difficult years of the 1930s, the boulevard press attacked her again; Antonín Zápotocký (1884–1957), the future Communist Prime Minister under President Klement Gottwald, excelled in his defamations. He wrote that the cost of Alice's house amounted to three million crowns, because the government had paid for a new highway that led to the house in timeswhen thousands of workers lived in the poorest conditions.[153] Others wrote that Alice had built herself a castle, which was proof of

---

[151] Lovčí, 285-286.
[152] Lovčí, 287.
[153] Lovčí, 288.

a new nobility to emerge; the poor people in the Slovak countryside would see with their own eyes the difference between the liberators and the liberated.[154] If Alice was hurt by these defamations, she did not show it; she thought that she deserved the house after years of unpaid work for the Red Cross. Government-friendly journalists from the *Lidové Noviny* came to her defence. They published the real figures: the costs for the construction of the highway amounted to two hundred thousand crowns; the president had paid one million crowns from his personal funds to build the house.[155]

If a free press, including the defamations and slandering of the boulevard press, is a pillar of a functioning democracy, the Republic's political system functioned like a charm: the press campaign over Alice's house prompted an attack on Kramář by journalists close to the Castle. They rejected the mistaken allegations about Alice's house with facts: she had employed a Czech architect, while a German and a Polish architect had designed Kramářs' villa, the "Anti-Castle".[156] Employing Czechs and Slovaks was considered an act of loyalty to the Republic, an act of Czechoslovak patriotism.

Alice was very proud of her house and happy to finally show it to her family: in August 1931, she invited her relatives to Bystrička. She had furnished it with pieces from their former Prague flat and had a special surprise prepared for her father: she had reconstructed in detail his old study. The room looked exactly like Masaryk had left it when he went into exile in December 1914.[157] The house was a refuge for Alice; it was her home, where she could retreat, relax and do whatever she wanted: read, play piano, listen to music, write. The

---

[154] Lovčí, 288.
[155] Lovčí, 289. The term "Anti-Castle" (*protihrad*) has a political meaning, since *hrad* connoted the Prague Castle, the centre of the government, hence the president and his associates.
[156] Lovčí, 289-290.
[157] Lovčí, 290.

52-year-old woman, in the sexist terms of those years an old spinster, had put the wellbeing of others first for decades. Now, she could finally find peace and seclusion and escape the attacks of the boulevard press.

If Alice looked forward to her retirement in her Slovak home, the megalomaniac plans of a half-educated private and evil-minded Austrian narcissist elected in 1933 to govern Germany would deal a cruel blow to Czechoslovakia. The president with his foresight and knowledge of psychology had warned the parliament of Hitler already in 1928;[158] yet, no European state could have foreseen to what ends Hitler would go. Advised by his personal physician, Masaryk stepped down from the presidency on 14 December 1935. Already in 1920, he had made sure that Beneš would be eligible as his successor by lowering the minimum age of the candidates from forty-five to thirty-five; Beneš was thirty-six years old in 1920.[159]

Masaryk's health was deteriorating and Alice, the dutiful and loving daughter, took care of her father; she travelled with him to his beloved Lány, acted as his personal assistant and oversaw and instructed the nurses. On top of her heavy workload, she organized help for the refugees from Hitler's Germany, which again prompted the criticism of the press.[160] Masaryk died on 14 September 1937. Little did Alice know that her home, the state her father had created and to which the Masaryk family and many others had dedicated their lives, would be destroyed by the Munich Agreement of 1938.

---

[158] Masaryk had published a review of Hitler's *Mein Kampf* in 1923; as so many times before, he was spot on with his assessment: Hitler was a fanatic and warmonger, whose creed would achieve the status of a religion of the German people; Lovčí, 310, footnote 10.

[159] Helmuth Slapnicka, "Die Rechtsstellung des Präsidenten der Republik in der Verfassungsurkunde und in der politischen Wirklichkeit", in *Die Burg. Einflussreiche politische Kräfte um Masaryk und Beneš. Band II* (München, Wien: Oldenbourg, 1974), 9-29; 13.

[160] Lovčí, 312.

She was devastated, but Masaryk's death resulted in reconciliation with her brother Jan. On 30 November 1937 she wrote to her friend Pavla Horváthová in perfect Slovak:

> "So many years I lived happily with my father … he used to tell me: 'The Masaryks won't give in'. And so I know, with a clear mind, that I have devoted my life to the Red Cross and still have work to do, that I have to finish the tasks I received from my father's hands. Thus, everybody has his own personal fate and mission. … Janko is calling me every night from London, the Beneš's are coming to Lány every week – I have the warmth and understanding of those closest to me. … But God gives hearts like those of my parents only once."[161]

Alice went into exile a fortnight after Nazi Germany occupied the Czech lands on 15 September 1939. She would return after the war, only to see her country being occupied a second time by the Communist Party in 1948. After Jan's mysterious death on 10 March she left Czechoslovakia for good in December 1948 and moved to Switzerland to join her sister Olga. Both then moved to Great Britain. Alice spent her last years in the USA, her mother's country of origin. She was active in the Czechoslovak exile community, held lectures and broadcasted for Radio Free Europe. She died at the age of eighty-seven on 29 November 1966 in a retirement home of the Czechoslovak community in Chicago.

II. 4 Conclusion

Was Alice Masaryková a feminist? Given the conditions of women at the turn of the 20th century, yes; yet she did not declare herself a feminist, since she grew up in a family that regarded women as equal to men. To her, university education, earning a salary and working

---

[161] ANM, fond Masarykovi – rodina, karton 2, inv. Č. 54, korespondence s Pavlou Horváthovou, roz. Lehotskou, dopis ze dne 30. XI. 1937, quoted from Lovčí, 313.

was normal: her norm, the values she was brought up with. Gender in professional life was not an issue she talked about, but she went to great lengths to support the education of girls and make the lives of families better for the generations to come.

From our perspective of the 21st century, her focus on social care and disinterested attitude to politics might seem a bit odd, considering that she grew up in an intellectual atmosphere that was focussed on politics. But Alice followed her father's political principle of the "small works" in the profession she had chosen. She tirelessly worked also at home, caring for her sick mother during the war and later, acting for a short period as First Lady at her father's side. Whenever the family needed somebody to step in, they relied on Alice. Her parents took her for granted, while her siblings went their own ways. Alice had no visible private life and was fulfilling her duty as a daughter, obeying what Czech and Austrian society expected of a woman.

As a sensitive intellectual and because she had experienced American gender-equality and democracy in practice, Alice was very much aware that women's rights had to be promoted, that Czechoslovak society had to modernize. She knew both worlds: US democracy and Austrian absolutism. She also knew that many Czech women and girls were not as blessed as she was with a critical father and a loving and supportive mother. Yet she was tolerant and did not condemn women who chose the life of a housewife, taking care of children and engaging in unpaid charity. She had an immense understanding for the women of the low social classes who bore the burden of childbearing, slaving for a low salary and, often, had to put up with a drunken husband. That was the reason why she became active in the abstinence movement. To improve the misery of the poor was Alice's mission and the task of her life; thanks to her organizational skills, the Czechoslovak Red Cross came into being.

Alice's life illustrates, to a certain extent, the condition of university-educated women in the early 20th century in a Central European urban environment. We have no documents at our disposal that would allow us to make a sound judgement about how her career decisions affected her private life. Her two sad and unfulfilled love stories remain a mystery, since she was discreet – and the three men who played a major role in her life were equally discreet. Her father, an *Übervater*, relied on her all his life. The short relationships with the Austrian physician Richard Fröhlich and the Slovenian architect Jože Plečnik did not have a happy end. It is not clear, whether Alice wanted to have children of her own; she did not comment about her private life.

Most admirable, but in those times rather the norm, was her care for her family; with her mother, she had an almost symbiotic relationship and was her only support in the dire years of WWI. Her closest sibling Herbert, her younger brother, died of typhus in 1915; her younger sister Olga married twice, had children and moved to Geneva in the 1920s, and with Jan she got closer only after the death of her father. Her friendship with Hana Benešová was a great comfort to her, in particular in her exile during WWII.

Alice was never alone, she had friends and associates, but she might have felt lonely in the sense one feels when one doesn't have a partner and children. I think she was most happy when she built the house in Bystrička. It was a modest reward for her efforts on behalf of Czechoslovak society. Alice was in her early fifties, when she bought her own home, and I can vividly imagine how happy she felt to have a place to retreat to. After the many years during which she had put others first, sacrificing herself to the care of others, she could spend her holidays the way she wanted to, surrounded by her books and piano and going for walks in Slovakia's beautiful countryside. She planned to spend her retirement in Slovakia, reading, writing, taking care of her garden, being in contact with the people from the village – peaceful years to come. Yet, Nazi Germany's aggressive foreign policy would not allow her the quiet seclusion she was looking forward to.

Alice lived through two World Wars, the division of her country, with the following occupation by Nazi Germany and the Communist coup d'état of 1948. As a teenager she witnessed how the Czech Press reviled her father, how students rallied to his lectures; she survived the abysmal conditions of the Vienna prison, rushed back home to take care of her sick mother and managed to make ends meet by teaching English until the end of WWI. At the age of sixty, she had to witness Nazi Germany's occupation of what was left of the Czechoslovak Republic. At the age of sixty-nine, she witnessed how the Communist Party assumed power. After the mysterious death of her brother Jan, she left the country for good. Her father's legacy, democratic Czechoslovakia, was dead. She sought comfort for her last years in the USA, where she had friends.

She dedicated her life to others and the values she believed in: democracy as the political system that embodied liberty, equal rights and the Christian love of others. In 1904, she could have stayed in the USA and embarked on an academic career; in 1918, she could have refused to participate in the building of the Red Cross and focussed on her private life; in 1945, she could have stayed in Great Britain or emigrated to the USA. Yet, Alice always came back to Czechoslovakia and her activities were not a duty to her, but her chosen way of life: to put into practice the values she believed in. Following her father's philosophy of "small works", she embodied them by her daily, unspectacular and unremitting efforts to improve herself and Czechoslovak society. This courageous, sensitive and intelligent woman is warmly remembered in the Czech Republic, Great Britain, Slovakia and the USA.

III. Eva 'Mimi' Jiránková (1921–2015) – a witness of Democracy and Nazism (OHI)

Eva "Mimi" Jiránková[162] was born in Prague in 1921.[163] After the coup d'état by the Communist Party on 25 February 1948, Mimi and her husband Miloš Jiránek (1909–1989) fled to Paris and thence to Great Britain. In the years before her death in April 2015, she lived in Devon close to her daughter; she had three grandchildren and eight great grandchildren. Mimi visited her native Prague regularly.

JB: Dear Mimi, could you please describe how you grew up in the First Republic?

MJ: I had a wonderful childhood. My mother was often ill and my father, a lawyer, spent the days at his office in Prague. He left in the morning, was driven to Prague by his chauffeur and returned in the evenings. That's how my brother and I came to grow up, in complete freedom. Personnel took care of the household. In the summer, we lived in our villa in Řevnice, not far from Prague. I went to the local school in Řevnice and later enrolled at the high school in Prague. With our friends, my brother and I used to do a lot of sports: in the

---

[162] Oral History Interview, Prague, 12 September 2014, 11.00 – 14.15, conducted in Czech.

[163] Minor parts of this chapter have been published in my "Surviving Totalitarian Regimes. An oral history interview with Mimi Jiránková and Nataša Lišková", *New Eastern Europe 4*, no. 1 (2014): 157-170. The Czech cultural journal *Dobrá Adresa* published a longer interview with Mimi: "Vždicky jsem hrála s klukama", *Dobrá Adresa 3*, no. 10 (2002): 50-65. A PDF version of the issue can be found in the journal's archive on http://www.dobraadresa.cz/old.htm; accessed 24 February 2015. In Great Britain, Mimi's story appeared in a much shorter version in *8000 Years of Wisdom* (London: Accent Press Ltd, 2010), 80-82.

summer we played volleyball, tennis, went canoeing, on hiking tours to the Tatra mountains in Slovakia and on bicycle tours. My father was the founder of the Řevnice tennis club and for many years its chairman. Martina Navratilova (*1956), the Czechoslovak Wimbledon champion, started her career as a ball girl at the Řevnice tennis club.

In the winter, we were in Prague. We used to skate and play ice hockey on the frozen Vltava, as our family home was on Masarykovo Nábřeži, just opposite Žofín Island. But what I most loved was skiing: I spent many happy hours in the mountains. Back then, there were no ski lifts; we carried our skis up the mountains and rode down. I remember that our skiing team went to a competition in St. Anton in the winter of 1938. My then boyfriend and future husband Miloš warned me: as Austria was about to become a part of the German Reich with the *Anschluss* of March 1938, it would be dangerous. But I think he had also another motive, since he asked me to make a decision: either go skiing or spend Christmas with him in Prague. I didn't think a minute about it: I told him that I would go skiing and couldn't abandon our team. We did fairly well in the competition in St. Anton; on our way back home, we spent a day in Vienna, and the city's houses were displaying the Nazi flags, the swastika was everywhere. I think I was in my eighties when I last skied downhill with my grandson and his friends in the Swiss Alps.

JB: If it is not too personal a question to ask – how did you and Miloš meet and how did you end up a married couple?

MJ: Miloš Jiránek was the most coveted bachelor in Prague in the mid-1930s. I thought he was too handsome for me; he had many beautiful and perfectly groomed lady friends and the reputation of a kind of a playboy – thus not a man I should marry. Many warned me that such a coveted man would have affairs. He was a doctor of law and the stepson of Jaroslav Stránský (1884–1973) who was the owner of *Lidové Noviny*, the newspaper close to the Castle (*hrad*).[164] Stránský was a close confidant of Masaryk and President Edvard Beneš and would leave with Beneš for Great Britain in October 1938. During the war, he acted as Minister of Justice of the Czechoslovak exile government in London and kept this position in the post-war Czechoslovak government (1945–1948).

Miloš and I frequented the same social circles, so it was only natural that we met. He asked me for a rendezvous. I remember that I arrived late at our first rendezvous at the National Theatre – and with only one glove, since I couldn't find the other one.

Miloš and I soon became a couple; in those years, courtship was very innocent, of course, no sex before marriage. We went to the cinema, to the theatre, met friends for drinks or went to museums. He loved literature and poetry, and the famous journalist Ferdinand Peroutka (1895–1978) was his best friend. I never expected that Miloš would propose marriage to me; I was a kind of tomboy and after I had decided to go skiing with our team to St. Anton instead of celebrating Christmas with Miloš in Prague, I thought that's it. We didn't see each other for six months, but then he got in touch again. Our wedding was beautiful. We couldn't have possibly known what fate had in store for us, what we would have to go through.

JB: How did you live through the occupation and the war?

MJ: The Germans invaded Prague on 15 March 1939.[165] Our lawyer called my father early in the morning, which woke me up. Father and

---

[164] The Castle was an informal group of intellectuals, journalists, scientists, economists and politicians who promoted President Masaryk's values of Czechoslovak democracy, social welfare and market economy.

[165] An excellent volume about how Nazi rule changed the look of all fifteen Prague districts in the years of the Protectorate is Jiří Padevět, *Průvodce*

I stood at the window of our flat on Masarykovo Nábřeži and saw the German tanks. It was snowing heavily and the tanks were heading to Prague Castle. I was seventeen years old. It was the end of our lives, our way of life. In those minutes, my happy youth was over. When the Munich Agreement was signed in 1938, we teenagers had not given it much thought; it was all talk to us. Now, it was reality. What shocked us most was that we had to give up our army, and that concentration camps were established.

After finishing high school in September 1939, I planned to study medicine, but the Germans closed down all universities in the protectorate. Miloš and I were married in dramatic circumstances. After the attempt on Heydrich's life in May 1942, we all prayed that he would die. After his death on 4 June, the terror started: the fate of the village of Lidice[166] is well known. I remember walking past the church of St. Cyril and Methodius where the Czechoslovak officers hid in the crypt.[167] I was on my way to visit my grandfather who lived nearby and witnessed how the Germans were flooding the crypt to flush the officers out. Also, I saw how they picked up people at random and shot them in the streets. The terrible terror lasted until August 1942.

Miloš and I married on 15 September 1942. We had a big reception in my family's apartment; after church and the festivities, we went back to our flat on Národní Třída 9. Among Miloš's friends were some of the most famous Czech poets, for example the future Nobel Prize Laureate Jaroslav Seifert (1901–1986), Eduard Bass

---

protektorátní Prahou. Místa – události – lidé (Praha: Academia, Archiv hlavního města Prahy, 2014).

[166] About the destruction of Lidice see http://www.lidice-memorial.cz/default_en.aspx; accessed 24 February 2015.

[167] A very good movie portraying the assassination of Heydrich by the Czechoslovak officers Jan Kubiš and Jozef Gabčik is *Operation: Daybreak* by Lewis Gilbert from 1975: http://www.imdb.com/title/tt0075019/ accessed 24 February 2015.

(1888–1946) and Vladimír Holan (1905–1980); they congratulated us with poems and short texts. In Masaryk's Republic, everybody was equal, regardless of confessional origins. We were used to a liberal atmosphere; artists, scientists, politicians, every citizen enjoyed the same civil rights.

In the Protectorate, the confession suddenly became important, in particular for our Jewish friends. Add to this the political loyalty to the exile government in London. Miloš was not Jewish, but that didn't matter to the Germans; what mattered to them was that his stepfather Jaroslav was a member of Beneš's exile government in Great Britain.

On our wedding day, we thought that the terror was over, but our Jewish friends Rafael Kubelík (1914–1996),[168] his wife and her brother were arrested. At 4 am, three Gestapo men knocked on our door. Miloš opened and was told to get dressed at once. He was arrested on our wedding night. A Gestapo man told me that I should stay where I was and that they would come back. After they had left, I called my father who arrived in ten minutes and took away all documents that might be dangerous. For three days I did not hear from Miloš. Then I learnt that they had deported him to Svatobořice near Kyjov in Southern Moravia. After one month, I received his first letter; he asked me to send sugar, bacon, salami and cigarettes, as he was a heavy smoker. I was allowed to visit him in Svatobořice. After three months, they deported him to the *Kleine Festung* (*malá pevnost*) in Theresienstadt (*Terezín*).

Around Christmas 1942, the BBC broadcast a speech by Jaroslav Stránský. The German-controlled Czech radio announced a few days later that governor Frank had decided: "Dr Miloš Jiránek and Stránský's sister are going to be transferred from the

---

[168] Kubelík was a world famous conductor; his biography on http://vagne.free.fr/kubelik/timeline.htm; accessed 4 April 2015.

internment camp to a concentration camp because of the Jew Stránský's speech on the BBC."

Stránský's sister was sent straight to the gas chamber at Auschwitz. Miloš was deported to the Gross Rosen camp near Auschwitz; father and I took the train to Breslau (today Wrocław in Poland); we were allowed to visit him. Thanks to my father's intervention, Miloš was able to get a position in the *Schreibstube* (administrative office), which saved his life, since he was originally sentenced to work in the stone quarry.

I stayed in Prague during the war. The Germans confiscated all cars for the war effort and we had only bikes at our disposal. As everybody was required to work, I got a job as an assistant in a dentist's practice. I lived alone in our flat, but did not feel lonely since friends came to visit me.

Somehow, the years went by, but I clearly remember one event. The Czech Quisling Emanuel Moravec (1893–1945), who served as Minister of Culture under the new governor Frank, had Ferdinand Peroutka brought to Prague from Buchenwald, where he had been interned since 1939. He offered him the opportunity to work for the German-controlled *Lidové Noviny* – which Peroutka declined.[169] He was sent straight back to Buchenwald.

---

[169] The Germans' rationale was to co-opt the intellectuals of the occupied countries. Had Peroutka accepted their offer, he would have had to advertise the Nazi ideology directed against the exile government in Great Britain, undermining the Czech resistance. One can only admire Peroutka: to be in Prague after three years in Buchenwald, being fed and pampered and offered the chance to work for the newspaper he used to write for – and then to decline, knowing what awaited him back in Buchenwald. Very recommendable about the Czech print media in the protectorate is Jan Gebhart, Barbara Köpplová, Jitka Kryšpinová a kol., *Řízení legálního českého tisku v Protektorátu Čechy a Morava* (Praha: Univerzita Karlova, Nakladatelství Karolinum, 2010). A very recommendable literary memoir of life in the Protectorate and under Communism is Jozef Škvorecký, *The Cowards* (London: Penguin, 2010).

JB: And then, in May 1945, the war was over.

MJ: Yes, there was fighting in the streets, and we hoped that the Americans would liberate Prague, but the Allies had to stick to the agreement with Stalin, so the Red Army liberated us. From December 1944 on I had no news from Miloš; he was on the death march from Gross Rosen to the Flossenbürg camp in Bavaria. Of all prisoners, only a third survived this ordeal. The Americans liberated Flossenbürg a week before the end of the war; Miloš had to wait two weeks in Domážlice. Then, he travelled with the American army to Plzeň, and American doctors took him to Prague. On 10 June he called me from Vinohrady, a part of Prague, and asked if he could come home. When he arrived at our flat, he was skin and bones, his head was shaven, and he wore these horrible prisoner's rags with a red cross painted on his back. The first thing he asked me to do was to give him a white shirt.

JB: Did Miloš tell you how he survived the camp?

MJ: He didn't talk about the camp, about what he had witnessed there, but every year around the same time, in January, he fell into a deep depression. This lasted up to two, three months. He went to work, but was clearly not in form. Once, he told me that, around Christmas time, the Gestapo had him rounded up with Soviet and Polish army officers. They shot everybody, but, for some reason, they spared him. When Peroutka came to visit us for the first time after he got back to Prague, he greeted Miloš with the joking words: 'Mr Jiránek, you blockhead! You told me when we said goodbye that it wouldn't be for long, but it's been six years.'

His novel about the end of the war dispelled the Communist myth of the heroic Czechs fighting the Germans; *Zbábelci*, published in 1958, marked the beginning of the thaw in Czechoslovak culture.

I often cooked for them. In the first months they didn't eat meat, they just wanted bread and pasta; their stomachs had to get used to food again after the years of starvation. They picked up crumbs from the table.

JB: How would you describe the atmosphere in Prague preceding the Communist Party's putsch of February 1948?

MJ: Miloš and Peroutka immediately went back to work at *Lidové Noviny*. The editor's office was in our house on Národní, and they sat entire nights there, discussing politics and the newspaper with editors and journalists. Often they drove to Brno where the *Lidovky* was printed. Their chauffeur, a certain Mr Biedermann, whom we considered a nice man, reported them to the Communists after the putsch in 1948; he would inform the Security Service about Miloš and Peroutka's discussions in the car. Compared with the war years, we lived a fantastically luxurious life In 1946, our daughter Tina was born, but I never changed a nappy, since we had a nanny. We also had a cook and a housemaid.

In November 1947, Miloš and I were in London. We met Jan Masaryk (1886–1948), then Foreign Minister of Czechoslovakia, who warned us not to go home, to stay in Great Britain. But we went home and spent a beautiful Christmas in Prague.

Right after the Communist putsch of 25 February 1948, we decided to leave. Peroutka and his wife escaped with the help of some students who had found a route through the *Šumava* (the Bohemian Forest). Our daughter Tina was two years old. We left on 1 May because the Communist festivities provided a good cover. We took the train to Klatovy. Our contact person waited for us in a villa in the woods. At midnight, the police arrested us. We never found out who betrayed us. They imprisoned me in the local prison in Klatovy, without my daughter. Miloš told the authorities that it was all a mistake; that we had just been on a holiday trip to the woods.

The worst moment was when that old woman, the prison guard, told me that I would never see my child again, that my daughter would be brought up in a proper Communist family. Two days later, the police from Prague came. Miloš was sent to the Pankrác prison; I to the infamous Bartolomejšska 4 in downtown Prague, the political prison. After a couple of days, they released me and I got my daughter back.

Thanks to the amnesty issued by President Klement Gottwald (1896–1953) in June 1948, Miloš was released. He heard in Pankrác prison that Prime Minister Antonín Zapotocký (1884–1957) had announced on the radio that everybody who did not want to live in Communist Czechoslovakia could apply for an emigration pass! We sold our Prague flat and applied for passports to France. Our friend Hubert Ripka (1895–1958) who was in Paris arranged for visas, and we left around Christmas 1948. My father accompanied us to the train; at the border in Cheb, the train stopped, and the authorities searched us for two hours. It was the last time I saw my father. He died in August 1950.

Politics in Central Europe is absurd, Kafkaesque, since I was really happy when we crossed the border and reached Germany.

In Paris, we lived in terrible poverty and often we were hungry. I sold my gold bangles to buy food because, as refugees, we were not allowed to work. My gold bangles saw us through, since gold could be weighed, it had real value, not like diamonds. We lived in a cheap hotel, with no washing facilities other than a bidet and wore our winter coats since coal was so expensive. Day in day out we ate only crepes and bread and drank wine because that was the cheapest to be had, all we could afford. To this day, I can't stand crepes! Our relatives in Great Britain sent us money to pay for our room. Some of the men, all university-trained intellectuals, got menial jobs like rolling condoms onto tubes for inflation-testing, which Miloš found too demeaning and did not do. But we lived in our

Czechoslovak community, in the company of our friends, and for twenty centimes we could sit in the Café de Flore, nursing a glass of wine. It was the Paris of Jean-Paul Sartre, Simone de Beauvoir and Juliette Greco, the Paris of Existentialism. Paris was like Prague, you live in the streets, a Bohemian culture, you can walk everywhere. Miloš would attend lectures at the Sorbonne, and my friends and I walked along the Seine. I felt very much at home in Paris. And I learnt to cook and how to iron a shirt, things I didn't have to care about in the past.

JB: Then you left for Great Britain, your final destination.

MJ: Yes, after three years in Paris, things could not go on. Luckily, Miloš got a job in the British Foreign Office as a political analyst; it was the Cold War and they needed experts on Communist countries. He asked Mrs Stránská, the wife of his stepfather Jaroslav, to get a tourist visa for our daughter and me, while he was waiting in Paris for his entry visa.

    In the first weeks after my arrival in London, Tina and I lived with the Stránskýs. I decided to find us an apartment. I went on a walk with Tina in the pram and saw this beautiful house in Hammersmith. I rang the bell, and a nice elderly lady answered the door. I asked her if she had an apartment to let. She asked me in, served me tea, and I told her our story. The lady, a devout Catholic and the widow of a wealthy American oil tycoon, told me that once Miloš had arrived, she would give us two rooms and a kitchen. We could pay once we'd found jobs. Later, when we lived in Devon, we learnt that Elizabeth Taylor had once rented a flat in that house.

    In Great Britain, our lives improved: Miloš worked at the British Foreign Office, and I found employment with Liberty's, a fashion house. It was the great 1960s: I travelled first class, stayed in the best hotels and bought fashion. We could afford holidays in the mountains and go skiing.

In 1989, we moved to Devon, where our daughter Tina and her husband Paul had opened an art gallery. Miloš died on 18 October 1989, a month before the Velvet Revolution began in Czechoslovakia. I applied for a Czechoslovak visa at the end of 1989 and met my brother in February 1990 in Prague. I was finally able to go home after forty years in exile.

JB: How did you, personally, cope with these difficult times? What kept you going?

MJ: When you are young, you are just doing what you want to – you are not aware of the consequences, of the dangers your decisions might have. But, the feeling of freedom, the freedom to move and the freedom of the press was what motivated me. Miloš's and my family had been middle class because our hard-working fathers had acquired some wealth. We were brought up in that wealth and that was the reason we didn't like the Communists who extinguished individual effort and oppressed civil rights.

When Miloš and I left in 1948, we lost everything, but we were free and did not have to live in fear any longer. I was raised a Catholic, but I am not religious – I rarely go to church. But I do think that there is something like a divine principle, a God or a moral principle above us – something bigger than man, something beyond man.

JB: Dear Mimi, thank you very much for your time and consenting to this interview.

IV. Milada Horáková (1901–1950) – executed for her belief in Democracy

"In struggle you fall. And what else is life but struggle."[170]

IV. 1 Historical context

The quote above illustrates the tragic fate and strong personality of the courageous woman who worked tirelessly as a lawyer and politician to improve the lives of Czechoslovak women and men. The circumstances of Milada Horáková's trial, the "biggest political trial"[171] in Czechoslovak history, are well researched.[172]

---

[170] The last sentence of Milada Horáková's last letter to her relatives dated 27 June, 2.30 am, three hours before her execution; *Dopisy Dr. Milady Horákové. Z pankrácké cely smrti 24–27.6. 1950* (Praha: Nakladatelství Eva Milan Nevole, 2013 (3)), 43. A few letters are available in English translation on http://chnm.gmu.edu/wwh/p/230.html; accessed 8 April 2015.

[171] Karel Kaplan coined this commonly used term. Kaplan considers the trial of Milada Horáková and co-accused as the biggest political trial because it is a symbol of the regime's violation of basic human rights and the end of the rule-of-law state. The trial, sometimes also referred to as *monstrproces* (monster trial), prompted further trials in the Stalinist 1950s; Pavlína Formánková and Petr Koura, *Žádáme trest smrti! Propagandistická kampaň provázející proces s Miladou Horákovou a spol. (historická studie a edice dokumentů)* (Praha: Ústav pro studium totalitních režimů, 2008), 19.

[172] A selection in alphabetical order: Petr Blažek, "Rekonstrukce. Prameny k proces s Miladou Horákovou a jejími druhy", in *Sborník Archivu ministerstva vnitra, č. 4, Archiv bezpečnostních složek MV* (Praha, 2006); Zora Dvořáková and Jiří Doležal, *O Miladě Horákové a Milada Horáková o sobě* (Praha: Klub Milady Horákové v nakladatelství Eva Milan Nevole, 2001); Miroslav Ivanov, *Justiční vražda aneb smrt Milady Horákové* (Praha: XYZ, 2008); Karel Kaplan, *Největší politický proces. "M.*

In this chapter, I shall focus on two lesser-known aspects recently analysed and presented in Czech scholarly publications: first, Milada Horáková's impressive personality[173] and second, the

---

Horáková a spol." (Praha, Brno: Ústav pro soudobé dějiny Akademie věd České republiky, Doplněk, 1995). See also the website of the Czech Institute for the Study of Totalitarian Regimes http://www.ustrcr.cz/en/milada-horakova-en; accessed 10 April 2015 and Totalita website on http://www.totalita.cz/vysvetlivky/o_horakovam.php; accessed 10 April 2015. Czech television made a documentary about the trial: *Proces H* (10x52 min), written and directed by Martin Vadas: on http://www.ceskatelevize.cz/porady/10153697395-proces-h/ accessed 6 May 2015. The bill of indictment of Milada Horáková and co-accused was published in 1950: *Proces s vedením zaškodnického spiknutí proti republice. Horáková a společníci* (Praha: Ministerstvo spravedlnosti, 1950).

[173] Michaela Košťálová, *Soukromí Milady Horákové* (Praha: Petrklíč, 2014). Košťálová's book focuses on Milada Horáková's private life, her childhood, relations with her husband, family and friends, hobbies, the houses she lived in, her love of poetry and literature, her work in various social institutions and sense of fashion. Save for the chapter about Milada's horoscope (178-186), where the author delves into numerology (!), the book is an interesting contribution, in particular the rumours that were being spread about the famous politician. One rumour was that Milada had participated in the tearing down of the column of Mary Mother of God in Old Town Square in November 1918. This event did indeed take place; it symbolized the citizens' joy about Czechoslovak independence and the end of the rule of the Habsburg Monarchy and the Catholic clergy alike (46-49). Another rumour had it that Milada was the personal secretary of Beneš, which was in fact one of the suspicions of the Germans who had her arrested in 1940 (122-131). Košťálová is an art historian, thus the book's strengths are certainly the chapters on how the arts, especially sculpture (144-156), film and theatre (158-163) portrayed Milada after the *Velvet Revolution* of 1989. Košťálová's book is written in a popular style lacking references, but her sources are serious academic studies from well-respected scholars. The Czech Internet sources she consulted provide interesting and helpful information.

propaganda campaign[174] that the Communist Party organized to discipline the citizens and muster mass support for the government. But first, let me present a brief summary of the events that would not only affect Milada Horáková, but also millions of Czechoslovak citizens. The events are referred to in the academic literature as *unor 1948* (February 1948) or coup d'état.[175] The distinguished Czech historian Karel Kaplan called the Communist Party's assumption of power very aptly "The Short March",[176] comparing it with the Chinese Communists' legendary 'long march' to power.

Post-war Czechoslovakia from 1945 to 1948 was neither a republic nor a parliamentary democracy, but it was no totalitarian regime either – not yet. In constitutional terms, the Czechoslovak political system was a hybrid, a democracy limited by the stipulations of the Košice Agreement that had, under the psychological and political authority of Beneš and Stalin, secured the dominant position of the National Front:

> "This fact was of key significance, and worked to the disadvantage of the non-Communist parties. These parties jointly shared in building up the new system, and they accepted the political conception of a regulated democracy. Beneš was a prominent advocate of the latter as a defensive measure taken to prevent a repetition of Munich. A regulated democracy was a limited democracy and was conditional on the fact that if one or more government parties were to try to take full power, it would limit the forces of democracy to acting in its own self-defence. A regulated democracy can be justified only when there

---

[174] Formánková and Koura, 25-121.
[175] Recommendable for its focus on international relations and the economic consequences the coup d'état prompted is *1948. Únor 1948 v Československu: Nástup komunistické totality a proměny společnosti* (Praha: Ústav pro soudobé dějiny AV ČR, 2011).
[176] Karel Kaplan, *The Short March. The Communist Takeover in Czechoslovakia 1945–1948* (London: C. Hurst & Company, 1987).

is cooperation between democratic parties with equal represent-tation in the coalition."[177]

Limited democracy is justified if all involved parties from all shades of the political spectrum agree on fair play, on keeping to the rules of democratic procedure – which the Communist Party patently did not. Cooperation to achieve a common political goal is important, but equally important is consensus about procedural ethos, agreement on how to behave. Political parties naturally have different goals; but in the particular situation of the National Front, the non-Communist parties just assumed that the Communists would stick to the same rules they adhered to, although there was ample evidence before 1948 that they would not.

After the war, the majority of politicians shared the general attitude that the multi-party system of the First Republic had got out of control; they considered in particular the former integration of the parties of the Sudeten Germans and Hungarians a political mistake they did not want to repeat. These minorities had betrayed the Czechoslovak Republic with their anti-state activities as soon as Hitler supported them. Thus, a slimming-down of the party system was required, which enabled the Communists who had only contempt for democratic rules and fair play to achieve total power within three years.

The party enjoyed wide support and sympathy among the citizens. Many perceived of Munich 1938 as treason of the West and were grateful to the Soviet Union for the liberation. Also, the KSČ announced that its policy would focus on specific national needs, improving Czechoslovak economy and social welfare. This suggested they could forge their own road to Socialism, without the influence of the Soviet Union. The KSČ won the parliamentary elections in May 1946 in the Czech lands with 41%; the National Socialists came

---

[177] Kaplan, *The Short March*, 189.

second with 23.6%; the People's Party got 20.2% and the Social Democrats 15.5%.[178] In Slovakia, however, the Democratic Party won 62% of the vote and the KSS only 30.37%. The lost elections in Slovakia and changes in Soviet foreign policy would lead the KSČ decision-makers to change their strategy.

Pressed for time since parliamentary elections were scheduled for 1948, the Communists stepped up their efforts in 1947; they orchestrated demonstrations of workers' unions and farmers' councils and increased their populist propaganda. The resignation of 12 of 26 non-Communist ministers in February 1948 demonstrated the pressure the Communists put on the government with their maximalist demands for reforms. The centre-right ministers resigned because they had unsuccessfully fought three issues the Communists wanted to push through: first, a reform of the wages of state personnel, and second, a law intended to fix the conditions for the ownership of land. The third and most pressing issue was the conspiracies instigated by the secret service: 13 officers of the secret service were downgraded because of their participation in planning attempts on the lives of the centre-right politicians Prokop Drtina (1900–1980),[179] Peter Zenkl (1884–1975) and Jan Masaryk.

---

[178] Kaplan, *The Short March*, 58.
[179] See Prokop Drtina's memoirs: *Československo, můj osud* (Toronto: Sixty-Eight Publishers, 1982). The Czech intellectuals Jozef Škvorecký and his wife Zdena founded Sixty-Eight Publishers in their Canadian exile in 1971. For the Czechoslovak authors blacklisted by the regime the Canadian publisher acted as *Tamizdat*, publishing them outside Czechoslovakia. It was also a forum for emigrants like Drtina. After the invasion of 1968, the dissidents created their own *Samizdat* and published their works independently, which the regime persecuted as a criminal offence. For a list of forbidden authors under Communism see Jiří Brabec, Jan Lopatka, Jiří Gruša, Petr Kabeš and Igor Hájek, *Slovník zakázaných autorů 1948–1980* (Praha: Státní pedagogické nakladatelství, 1991).

The centre-right government members demanded the establishment of a special commission to investigate the activities of the secret service and the justice department, but Prime Minister Gottwald simply refused to appoint the commission. The StB and the justice department were already in the firm hands of the KSČ. The ministers who had handed in their resignation expected President Beneš to reject it. On 21 February, the Communist Party called for a demonstration on Prague's Old Town Square; Gottwald accused the ministers who had resigned of reactionary subversion, portraying them as traitors for having left the National Front. All over the country, demonstrations and mass protests, instigated by the Party, supported the Communists' demands. The population, exhausted after five years of war and occupation wanted a change and believed the promises and accusations of the KSČ.

On 23 February, President Beneš, already gravely ill, promised the centre-right parties to refuse the resignation of their ministers, but he succumbed to the pressure of the Communists: two days later, he accepted the resignations and appointed a new government according to Gottwald's suggestions. Key ministries such as the Ministry of the Interior, Defence and Justice were now firmly in the Party's hands. The crisis the Communist Party had artificially created seemed to be solved with the support of the president. When the non-Communist politicians understood what had happened on 25 February 1948, it was too late.

> "Jointly with the Communists, they [the non-Communist parties, add. JB] created the National Front, a people's democratic coalition but in no way confirming to the norms of parliamentary democracy. But, in spite of that, the non-Communist parties behaved as if they were a parliamentary democracy, and their opposition to the Communists' efforts towards a power monopoly never deviated from this ideological framework."[180]

---

[180] Kaplan, *The Short March*, 193.

Roughly one month after the Party assumed power, the oppression and elimination of the non-Communists began: General Jozef Bartík (1897–1968) was the first to be arrested in March 1948 and was sentenced to five years' imprisonment in November.[181]

The reasons for the purges and show trials the citizens would have to endure until the mid 1950s were twofold: international and domestic. Moscow dictated Czechoslovakia's foreign policy, as it dictated the foreign policy of every country in the Soviet sphere of influence. No state was allowed to participate in the Marshall plan for the reconstruction of Europe. Yugoslavia insisted on her own independent way to build Socialism, with Tito suggesting to Bulgaria a confederation of the Balkan states – much to the anger of Stalin:

> "The Boss received both delegations [the Bulgarian and Yugoslav, add. JB] in the Kremlin in the cold February of 1948. He yelled at Dimitrov: 'You and the Yugoslavs never report on what you're doing.' ... The Yugoslav Kardelj, trying to smooth over the situation, told him that 'there are no disagreements between us'. This brought a furious outburst from Stalin: 'Nonsense! There are disagreements, and very profound ones at that.' ... They resolved to consult each other regularly in the future. But the Boss had made up his mind to rid himself of Tito. He knew that 'one bad sheep can spoil the flock'. Tito would be now more useful to him as an enemy – as Trotsky had once been. ... By anathematizing Tito, he would tighten the bonds of obedience within the camp."[182]

Expelled from the Socialist camp, Tito created the non-aligned movement (NAM), which Stalin condemned as treason of the Communist cause and an international threat to the Soviet sphere of influence alike. The foundation of Israel in 1948, a stout ally of the

---

[181] Jan Kalous, "KSČ jako iniciátor a vykonavatel politických čistek a procesů", in *Český a slovenský komunismus (1921–2011)* (Praha: Ústav pro studium totalitních režimů, 2012), 87-93; 88.

[182] Edvard Radzinsky, *Stalin* (New York: Anchor Books, 1997), 517, 518.

Capitalist and Imperialist West, was another event that put Stalin on the alert. The fear of renewed international conflict, which would be fought with nuclear weapons, demanded the firm discipline of the states in the Soviet sphere of influence.

In domestic affairs, the Czechoslovak Communists embarked on a brutal course of elimination, a process that all Communist Parties in Eastern Europe went through once they were in power: a more-than-thorough liquidation of the opposition, existing or not. The citizens had to be ideologically disciplined, in particular those who had fought in the first (1914–1918) and the second (1939–1945) *odboji*.[183] Thus, veterans from both wars, members of Masaryk's *legia*, fighting the Bolsheviks in Russia during WWI, intellectuals and politicians who had survived Nazi concentration camps, bishops, priests and vicars, members of Beneš's exile government and everybody representing the values of the First Republic had to be silenced.

> "The terror that was unleashed hit everybody. Even in the tiniest village citizens suspected of political opposition were found. The purges were carried out ruthlessly in all social strata. Privacy, a private life was completely eliminated, which hit the farmers and tradesmen particularly hard. Those who stood up against the terror had to expect that their families' fates were at stake."[184]

To force citizens to toe the line, the Party rationally and cold-bloodedly created an atmosphere of insecurity and anxiety; the propaganda the KSČ unleashed provoked such hatred against the alleged enemies of the people that even school children, instructed by their teachers, rushed to send letters in support of the government. The Czechoslovaks, once the only democratic society in Central Europe, turned into a totalitarian mass of persons, no more citizens, let alone individuals.

---

[183] Kalous, 89.
[184] Kalous, 89.

The concomitant psychological phenomena of fear, denunciation, ruthless ambition, hitherto unknown vulgar words and behaviour and despair ruled in the country. Nobody was safe and anybody could be arrested; from 1948 to 1954, 23,000 citizens were imprisoned in labour camps.[185] In the purges starting in 1948, between 250 000 and 280 000 citizens were imprisoned. In connection with the trial of Horáková et al. 632 persons were arrested; 191 were civil servants and 337 members of Beneš's National Socialist Party,[186] which demonstrates the regime's focus on purging state institutions of adherents of the 'bourgeois' centre-right party, the former political and intellectual elite.

The fate of Dagmar Šimková (1929–1995)[187] from Písek in the South, who emigrated in 1968 and died in Australia, illustrates the frightening atmosphere of the 1950s: the StB arrested the 23-year-old nurse in 1952 for the simple fact that she was from a 'bourgeois' background – she had the wrong parents: her father had been a successful entrepreneur, achieving some wealth, in the First Republic. In 1948, the government confiscated the Šimek family's villa and confined Dagmar, her mother and her younger sister to two rooms in their house. Very much like in the scene in the film version of *Doctor Zhivago*, the former owners of the villa had to share their house with other people. Dagmar Šimková spent fourteen years of her young life in various prisons where she, like Alice Garrigue Masaryková some sixty years previously, experienced the solidarity among the political prisoners and the hatred, physical violence and verbal abuse of the common criminals.

---

[185] Kalous, 91.

[186] Karel Kaplan, *Druhý proces. Milada Horáková a spol. – rehabilitační řízení 1968–1990* (Praha: Univerzita Karlova, Nakladatelství Karolinum, 2012), příloha č. 2, 502.

[187] Dagmar Šimková, *Byly jsme tam taky* (Praha: Monika Vadášová-Elšiková, 2011).

Six (!) male StB agents were sent to arrest the innocent nurse on a Saturday morning in the autumn of 1952. Dagmar had just returned home from a night shift at the local hospital and was looking forward to a quiet week on holiday, meeting friends on Saturday night for drinks and dancing. She was also looking forward to catching up on sleep, to enjoying mornings where she could sleep without the call of duty dragging her out of bed.

Dagmar's memories of her arrest provide us with an example of the elaborate psychological manipulation and vulgar newspeak the Party instructed its agents to use when dealing with the 'class enemy'. The agents told Dagmar's mother that her daughter was required at the local police station for a signature, a mere formality. She would be back in no time. One agent caressed the cat; others wandered about the flat, complimenting Dagmar's mother on the antique furniture and paintings. They all behaved in a very civilized, very polite, manner. The fifth agent, as Dagmar called him in her memoirs, was an elderly gentleman in his fifties and had a distinct air of melancholy about him, looking depressed as if he had just learnt that his family had died. He didn't seem to be interested in anything. I think that his role was to evoke pity, the natural sympathy of women when they meet a sad male. Agent no. 5 was successful in lulling young Dagmar into feeling safe; she fell for his devious trick. She had no clue what awaited her, but I think that her mother knew that something unusual, something bad was happening. Mothers often have an instinctive foreboding, a premonition:

> "I put my raincoat on and did not bother to say good-bye to my mother. I was calm, not afraid, they were so civilized. The blond one opened the door for me, showing all the grace and manners of perfect social upbringing. ... At the gate, I turned around and looked at the terrace. Mother stood there until I stepped out into the street.

'Now have a good look around, you reactionary whore! You'll never come back' said the depressed-looking guy. And he was right."[188]

The show trials followed a brutal but effective rationale and were directed against, first, the clergy and orders of both Christian confessions, accusing them of anti-state conspiracy in collaboration with the Vatican. Second, centre-right politicians were accused of conspiracy with the Imperialist and Capitalist West. Third, the KSČ purged itself or rather, eliminated those Party members who had been in the Capitalist West during the war and had fought the Fascists in the Spanish Civil War. Some were imprisoned in Nazi concentration camps.[189] They were not reliable because they had an independent and strong mind, considerable organizational skills and friends and acquaintances in the West. At the peak of the purges, the Party accused high-ranking members of Zionism, Titoism, sabotage and conspiracy with Western Capitalist states. The accusations mirrored precisely the international development that the Soviet Union perceived as a serious threat to her sphere of influence since these events were strengthening the West: Tito's rejection of surrendering Yugoslavia to Stalin was used as a pretence for the accusation of Titoism and the foundation of Israel as the West's foothold in the Middle East as Zionism. The international events of

---

[188] Šimková, 18.
[189] See the memoirs of Artur London, *On Trial* (London: MacMillan, 1970). In 1970, Simone Signoret and her husband Yves Montand starred as Lise and Artur London in the movie *L'aveu* (*The Confession*), which was based on London's memoirs. The movie shows how the Czechoslovak authorities, instructed by Soviet NKVD officers, prepared the victims for the show trials by depriving them of sleep, subjecting them to beatings and long and exhausting discussions about the principles of Marxism-Leninism and the duties of a party member. For an account of what the wives of the accused had to undergo see the memoirs of Heda Margolius Kovály *Under a Cruel Star. A Life in Prague 1941–1968* (London: Granta, 2012); and Jo Langer, *Convictions. My Life with a Good Communist* (London: Granta, 2011).

the year 1948 had thus direct implications for the KSČ's domestic policy; Czechoslovakia's political future was determined in Moscow and carried out by willing Party members in Prague.

The chronology of political persecution was accompanied by mass hatred and an irrational lust for blood, instigated and instilled by the print and broadcast media and the cinema; it began on 31 March 1950 with the so-called "trial of the orders (*proces s řády*)".[190] In May 1950, the trial of Milada Horáková and co-accused followed. The peak of the purges was the trial of Slánský et al. in October 1952, all high-ranking Party members such as Vladimír Clementis, Foreign Minister after Jan Masaryk's death in March 1948. According to the preconceived script, Husák and the other Slovaks accused should have been prepared to act as witnesses in the trial of Slánsky and co-accused. Yet the authorities did not reckon on Husák's bravery: the doctor of law withstood the torture, refused to sign the protocol and thus saved his own and his colleagues' lives. Pressed for time since Stalin wanted to see results, the authorities decided to go ahead with the trial of Slánský. The Slovaks were condemned to life imprisonment in a separate trial in 1954.[191]

Why did the KSČ, eager to push forward the integration of women into the workforce focus its attention exactly on Milada Horáková as the principal accused?

---

[190] Formánková and Koura, 25.
[191] Excellent analysis of the trial of the 'Slovak bourgeois nationalists' and its connection with the Slánský trial is Jan Pešek, "Nepriateľ so straníckou legitimáciou. Proces s tzv. Slovenskými buržoáznymi nacionalistami", in *Storočie procesov. Súdy, politika a spoločnosť v moderných dejinách Slovenska* (Bratislava: Veda, 2013), 210-226.

IV. 2 Milada Horáková – a democrat and feminist

From the Party's point of view, Milada Horáková was the perfect accused, the no. 1 in the script of the trial that would present her to the public as the ringleader of a band of traitors in the pay of the Capitalist West. She was a symbol of the First Republic, embodying everything the Party wanted to get rid of in its pursuit of constructing the Communist society: university-educated with a doctorate, from a 'bourgeois' background, a delegate for the centre-right National Socialists before and after the war, hence a follower of Beneš, a respected feminist and well connected to politicians from the First Republic. Milada had also the right age: not too young to have no experience in politics and not an elderly lady either whose standing trial might spark the public's pity and sympathy. The Party could take no risks in this matter: nobody wants to see a frail and white-haired *babička* (grandmother) of seventy years or older on the witness stand.[192]

---

[192] The word *babička* is a positive term in the Czech collective memory: it connotes the famous novel *Babička* by Božena Němcová (1820–1862), an admired author and founder of Czech prose in the years of the Czech national renaissance (*národní obrození*) in the second half of the 19th century. This is pure speculation, but I deem it possible that the KSČ had consulted the Party member and famous philosopher Zdeněk Nejedlý (1878–1962) about this particular issue. The Party wanted to avoid a connection of the word *babička* with the trial of Milada, since it had the psychological and political potential to provoke resistance against the regime. Vladimír Handl, a prominent Czech political analyst and specialist for the history of the Communist Party, thinks that my speculative thoughts can explain the mindset of the Czechoslovak and Soviet scriptwriters of the trial. For a biography of Nejedlý see Jiří Křesťan, *Zdeněk Nejedlý. Politik a vědec v osamění* (Praha: Paseka, 2012). Miroslav Michela wrote a review of Křesťan's volume that is forthcoming in *Historický Časopis 63*, no. 2 (2015). I thank Vladimír Handl and Miroslav Michela for discussing these issues with me.

The rationale of the purges was to change the citizens' mindsets, to rid them of 'bourgeois' thought and behaviour. In Socialism, everybody was equal; women enjoyed the same rights as men and they had to fulfil the same duties as the men. Therefore, a woman could be a traitor too and deserved no special treatment, neither leniency nor clemency. That is the principal reason why Milada Horáková had to die.

During the liberal months of the Prague Spring, the Dubček government wanted to find out the truth about the trial of Milada Horáková et al. and established a commission that interviewed those involved in the trial. Yet, the Party had to tread carefully, and some of the functionaries who interviewed the former victims were personally involved in the purges of the 1950s. The full truth and rehabilitation of the victims would be accomplished only after the collapse of the regime in 1990. Karel Kaplan's analysis of the archive material[193] of the interviews conducted in 1968 and 1969 allows us to get a clearer picture of KSČ's policy of choosing women for the trials. Let us have a brief look at the age of the women accused, prepared for the trials and sentenced.

Antonie Kleinerová,[194] born in 1901, and Františka Zemínová, born in 1882, were both accused together with Milada Horáková. Kleinerová had survived Ravensbrück, the women's concentration camp; she and Zemínová received long prison sentences, but were released in President Novotný's amnesty of 1960. In 1950, the prosecutor's office had summoned 27 witnesses, but the court rejected five. Of those interviewed by the commission in 1968 and 1969, only one woman, Leontina Neumannová, born in 1890, was called as a witness. The authorities prepared Milada Šubrtová, born in 1902, as a witness, but the court rejected her; she

---

[193] Kaplan, *Druhý proces,* 171-492.
[194] Kaplan, *Druhý proces,* 183.

was sentenced to 30 years' imprisonment and released in 1960. Eleonora Buchvalová, born in 1923; Hermína Čížková, born in 1908; Jiřina Hauková, born in 1904; Františka Hofmannová, born in 1911; Márie Nedvědová, born in 1912; Milada Rumerskirchová, born in 1904; Jarmila Taubenestová, born in 1918, and Valerie Vrabcová, born in 1898, were accused in the trials following the Horáková trial. Thus, the majority of the accused women were middle-aged. The eldest was Františka Zemínová, who was 68 years old in 1950, and the youngest the 27-year-old Eleonora Buchvalová.

The KSČ, eager to convince the citizens of Horáková's evil character, had designed an entire plot that was based on Milada's physical mobility, political activities and acumen and her intellectual faculties. The doctor of law was a natural leader, a politician who had the rare gift of mobilizing the citizens, of instilling civic enthusiasm for democracy and women's rights – and women who had listened to her radio broadcasts in the First Republic and who trusted and admired her. She was prominent, popular, intelligent and energetic, and her network of political acquaintances and friends a further asset. Accusing her of conspiring with the Capitalist West against the People's Republic would prompt an immediate disciplinary effect, hammering into citizens' minds that not even prominent politicians could be trusted.

Two years later, the mass hysteria the Party organized would peak with the trial of Slánský et al. Now, traitors were everywhere – even at the very core of the Party. Nobody could be trusted; the propaganda created an atmosphere of hatred and bloodlust, which was isolating the citizens already numb with fear. The fear prompted the results the Party wanted to achieve: absolute belief in the Socialist cause and complete loyalty to the Party.

Let us now have a closer look at the woman, who became a symbol of the political crimes committed by the KSČ. In 2004, the Czech government declared 27 June, the date of Milada's execution, an official state holiday in memory of the victims of the Communist regime.

With Ema Destinn, Alice Garrigue Masaryková and Mimi Jiránková, Milada Králová shared one important facet that would dominate her life: all four had emancipated fathers who believed that girls were equal to boys. Like Emanuel Kittl, Tomáš Garrigue Masaryk and Karel Zimmer before him had done, Čeněk Král supported his eldest daughter in her talents, encouraging her to enrol at high school and university. The four fathers were progressive and modern thinkers and convinced democrats in support of the independence of Czechoslovakia. Only Alice's mother Charlotte had studied; Ema, Mimi and Milada's mothers had spent their lives in the traditional ways of wife and mother.

As it was the social norm for girls, young Milada used to help her mother with the housework; as she grew older, her father noticed that she had a talent for analysis and independent thinking. Father and daughter used to read together and discuss various topics and themes, among them the works of the President-Liberator Masaryk. Milada was like a son to her father, and Čeněk was proud of her intellectual faculties.

I think that Milada developed her peculiar sense of responsibility, empathy and interest for the wellbeing of others because of three events she experienced as a teenager: first, in 1914, at the tender age of thirteen, she witnessed the deaths of her fifteen-year old sister Marta and her six-year old brother Jiří. Both died of scarlet fever. Second, their deaths took a grave toll on her mother, who could not deal with her children's death and was physically and psychologically ill, relying on Milada's care. Third, when her little sister Věra was born in 1915, Milada became a kind of surrogate mother to her. They were as close as siblings can grow with the elder sister taking care of the younger and replacing a parent, but besides the intimacy, such a constellation also affects the siblings' professional and private lives. Věra would concentrate on a family of her own and did not pursue a professional life in public; until her death, Milada would remain the dominant one in the relationship.

The first time Milada drew the attention of the authorities to herself was with a symbolic act of affirmation of Czech national identity and political protest. The eighteen-year old high school student participated in a demonstration on 1 May 1918 in Prague:

> "When the Czech troops marched past the barracks at Újezd, a young girl stepped out from the crowd and threw the soldiers a rose. Milada Horáková's act had unfortunate consequences. The school authorities explained to her father that Milada had committed a provocation and they had to expel her."[195]

To us in the 21st century, throwing a rose to soldiers is rarely considered an act of political protest – it is a modest gesture, an offering of hope and peace. Yet, in the last months of WWI, Milada's act was a clear sign of an anti-Habsburg attitude, and the rose a symbol of peace. The states at war in 1918 considered pacifism treason and defeatism, a criminal offence.

After the *maturita*, which she accomplished at a different high school for girls in 1921, Milada planned to study medicine. Yet her father disliked doctors; he had not forgotten that the doctors could not save Marta and Jiří and suggested Milada study history and languages.[196] She eventually decided to study law, because she did not want to become "a dusty academic" who worked only for herself.[197]

---

[195] Košťálová, 47. Košťálová often quotes from Zora Dvořáková and Jiří Doležal, *O Miladě Horákové a Milada Horáková o sobě* (Praha: Klub Milady Horákové v nakladatelství Eva Milan Nevole, 2001); from Zora Dvořáková, *Kdo je ... Milada Horáková* (Praha: Středočeské nakladatelství a knihkupectví, 1991); and from *Dopisy Dr. Milady Horákové*.
[196] Košťálová, 52.
[197] Košťálová, 52.

In 1927, when the young doctor of law married her boyfriend Bohuslav Horák (1899–1976), a doctor of agrarian engineering and scientific presenter with the Czech radio, she was already politically active in the Czechoslovak Women's Council (*Ženská Národní Ráda, ŽNR*). She had met the chairwoman and founder of the Council Františka F. Plamínková (1875–1942) in 1924; Plamínková was personally acquainted with President Masaryk whose support for the women's movement was well known. Both women shared a passion for social work and politics. Plamínková was a senator for the National Socialists and worked also as a journalist. She never married and had no children.[198]

Milada chose a different way of life: she married, joined the National Socialists in 1929, and in 1933, her daughter Jana was born. Milada's life reflected the changes in society and women's lives: she was a modern woman with a family and a professional life. She and Františka would remain close friends until the war separated them. The Germans arrested Milada and Bohuslav in 1940. Františka once told her never to cry over spilt milk,[199] a lesson that taught Milada to look ahead, think positive and not get distracted by things she could not change. The Gestapo arrested Plamínková, the energetic intellectual and political activist, in 1939 and again in 1942 in the *Heydrichiáda*, the wave of arrests following Heydrich's execution by the Czechoslovak officers Jozef Gabčik and Jan Kubiš. Františka was interned at the Kleine Festung in Theresienstadt (*Terezín*) and shot in July 1942.

In the First Republic, Milada held various functions: she was deputy chairwoman of the organization *Demokracie dětem* (Democracy for Children), chairwoman of the Czechoslovak Society for the Friends of the United Nations (*Společnost prátel Spojených*

---

[198] Košťálová, 64.
[199] Košťálová, 79.

národu v ČSR), chairwoman of the Womens' Council and delegate for the National Socialists in parliament.[200] She also represented Czechoslovak women to an international public; because of her contacts with women's organizations she held lectures and attended meetings in various European countries such as Switzerland, Sweden, Great Britain, and France. She was personally acquainted with Eleanor Roosevelt (1884–1962), the wife of US President Franklin D. Roosevelt (1905–1945), who was an internationally respected feminist and diplomat.

A look at public life in the First Republic is fascinating in terms of relationships and networks: the political and intellectual elite was a prestigious, an almost intimate circle that met on many social occasions, bound by their loyalty to Masaryk's democracy and rule-of-law state. Milada was a close friend of Beneš and his wife Hana and other members of the political elite; they used to meet at the Community Club at the Dientzenhof Palace on Přikopě in Prague's city centre.[201] Milada's admiration for Masaryk had begun in her teenage years, when she and her father had read his works and discussed his thoughts and ideas. Thanks to her acquaintance with Alice Garrigue Masaryková, she finally got an invitation to the Castle in 1933.[202]

Milada's meeting with the President lasted an entire evening; Masaryk sat quietly at the table, had his modest milky coffee with a biscuit for dinner and listened to Milada who talked about the Women's Council and her ideas about education and social welfare. When the hour of taking leave had come, when the President was tired, Milada was still so agitated and nervous that she forgot the twig of azalea the President had presented her with when she had arrived. Masaryk picked it up from the table and gave it to

---

[200] Košťálová, 69.
[201] Košťálová, 130.
[202] Košťálová, 111.

her when she was at the door. Milada was deeply impressed by Masaryk's pragmatism, straightforwardness and grace.[203] She shared with her husband Bohuslav a deep admiration for the president's achievements and political principles. When they learnt about Masaryk's death in the broadcast on 14 September 1937, they rushed back to Prague from their holidays in the *Šumava* (Bohemian Forest) and queued to pay their last respects to the president.

Did Milada have a foreboding, a premonition of what awaited her? Mrs Lewis was an American friend of her's and Františka Plamínková's; she remembered her last meeting with Milada in 1947. They were walking through Prague's city centre:

> "I told her: 'Milada, you have to get out.' And she started to explain, much the same way as Plamínková did, that the people needed her ... that she was convinced that they could resist the pressure, hold out until the elections and then win them. 'Milada', I said, 'you and your colleagues from the party are not seeing this tragic situation in its fullness. Understand the gravity of the situation: you, as delegate to the parliament, are receiving me, your American friend, yet you have no place where you can safely and openly talk to me, we have to keep moving about town. Get out now, you are making the same mistake Plamínková did.' Milada replied: 'Perhaps I am really making a mistake and perhaps I'll end up like her.' It was very clear to me then that her life was in danger – while she was trying to convince me that the situation was going to change for the better. I could have got her out, that would have been no problem at all, but it was impossible to convince her of the real danger she was in."[204]

Milada would not leave and she would not see her American friend again. I think that she could not imagine giving up her life-long beliefs in the principles of Masaryk and Beneš's politics. In her way of thinking, leaving was treason, an act of cowardice and selfishness. Mrs Lewis might have had more information at her disposal about

---

[203] Košťálová, 111.
[204] Košťálová, 81.

how the international political situation would develop; if not, then she must have become acutely aware of the danger while in Prague, feeling the tense atmosphere, the fear, the whispers, the rumours. As a pragmatic American who had witnessed the war, Mrs Lewis wanted to save Milada from the Communists as she had tried to save Františka from the Germans.

Milada, on the other hand, may have thought that Mrs Lewis was overreacting; she did not feel threatened. The National Front bound the Communists into co-operation with the centre-right parties; the Communists had won the 1946 elections, hence were participating in the system of limited democracy. They were not a foreign enemy occupying the country like the Germans; they were Czechoslovak citizens. The current situation was but a minor crisis. After all, or so she must have thought, she had survived the war in Nazi prisons and Terezín – what could be worse? Beneš was President and would see to it that the system of limited democracy would survive until the elections in 1948. Milada was convinced that her party would come out victorious; Beneš would then steer the country towards a truly democratic course. The patriot Milada did not see that danger can also emerge from within the nation, not just from the outside; she underestimated the Communists' lust for power and their dedication to achieve it, at all costs. She did not see that the Communists had a very different view of Czechoslovak patriotism.

After the mysterious death of Jan Masaryk in March 1948, Milada laid down her mandate in protest. She was arrested on 27 September 1949 and imprisoned at Pankrác. In her cell, she remembered the good times of the First Republic. One woman she was particularly fond of was Alice Garrigue Masaryk. Since both women had shared an interest in social care and the women's movement, it had only been natural that Milada and Alice, the chairwoman of the Czechoslovak Red Cross, had met. They had come to know each other well. In her first letter from prison, dated on 24 June 1950 and addressed to her father and sister, Milada remembered an impressive event with Alice:

> "If I had to reproach people at all it would be to say that many of those great and loving hearts overvalued me. I am not saying this as a simplistic confession. I know that I worked hard and did much good and I am also telling you that I fervently and deeply loved you, but I might have needed you to criticize me, from time to time, the way Alice Masaryková once did around Christmas 1947: 'Lady, don't put on airs'. She meant it as a joke, but it hit home. She should have told me this more often."[205]

This quote illustrates not only Milada's calm and poise while waiting for her execution, but also the deep feelings she had for her family and her ability to look at herself with a critical eye. Was the successful lawyer arrogant and obsessed with her achievements? Alice certainly thought so, but then the President's daughter was unusually modest and from a generation that considered the efforts of women for society a natural duty. In terms of her father's "small works", one could be a bit proud of one's achievements and activities in the seclusion of one's study, but one should not boast it about in public.

Her last days in the Pankrác prison cell on death row made Milada remember good and bad times. Obviously, Alice's alleged joke had hurt her but she also understood what the President's daughter wanted to tell her: be more modest, it's not about you, but about what you can do to help others, to make life better for all of us. Milada was certainly self-assured, determined and used to people working with her listening to her suggestions and following her advice, but I

---

[205] *Dopisy Dr. Milady Horákové*, 9. Alice's dressing down of Milada in Czech is "Paní, nedělejte se wichtig", which is quite rude in tone. As we have seen above, Milada was not the only one hurt by Alice's lack of diplomacy and directness.

don't deem it likely that she was bossy, arrogant or narcissistic. An arrogant person is usually disliked by many and provokes the criticism of family members and the resistance of people having to deal with her at work. This did not seem to be the case with Milada. Růžena Pelantová who worked with her in the Main Social Services Department of Prague described her with admiration and affection:

> "For fifteen years, we had been sitting at each other's side in the office. Not once did she have a cooked meal at lunchtime. She used to drink coffee from a modest mug while attending to her tasks."[206]

Knowing that she soon would die, I think that Milada wanted to achieve two last things in her life: first, to say good-bye to her loved ones, and second, to find inner peace. Her letters are full of memories conveying how grateful she was for friendship, love, loyalty, and also criticism. She was not at all sentimental; she didn't complain, she didn't accuse, she was not bitter. She accepted the death sentence and used her few remaining days to comfort her family. She apologized to her husband for not being a role model as a wife, for working too much and neglecting him. Particularly painful to Milada was the lack of news; in her letter to Bohuslav dated on 26 June 1950, she expressed her anxiety and affection, but particularly visible is also Milada's taciturnity, her strong will to preserve her independence. She was calm and had herself under control:

> "I am writing to you, as I am writing to everybody [close to me, add. JB] and I don't even know if you are still among the living, whether you will be able to read these words at all. This is the biggest pain in my heart, that I know nothing about your whereabouts, that I don't even have that sad certainty [of your death, add. JB] ... I was more a lover than a wife ... I had wide wings and you, at the price of your own happiness, never hindered me from flying. – You were the perfect husband and companion and you never forced yourself indiscreetly into the depths of my soul. ... I kiss you, my husband I

---

[206] Košťálová, 86.

press your hand, my comrade! If you are alive, live a long and healthy and happy life. ... That's my wish."[207]

In her letter, Milada mentioned also that Bohuslav "had left their daughter",[208] which she couldn't understand. She wrote that she did not mean this as a reproach, but it was one. She had no information about Bohuslav; he could be dead, had fled the country or was arrested too. According to Věra Hložková, who claims that she and Milada had shared a cell at Ruzyně prison, Milada returned from the interrogation on 25 April 1950; she was despondent and in tears and did not want to talk about what had happened.[209] Allegedly, the authorities had given her a letter from her daughter Jana; Milada was used from her years in Nazi prisons to read between the lines, to gather hidden information. She thought that Jana had told her that Bohuslav and her father Čeněk were dead. Did the authorities give her a faked letter? Or was Milada mistaken in her interpretation of the letter's contents? Either way, without further information Milada's reproach makes no sense; perhaps she hinted at something that had happened in their relationship before her arrest. If this was the case, let us not speculate any further and respect the privacy of Milada and Bohuslav.

---

[207] *Dopisy Dr. Milady Horákové*, 35, 36, 38.
[208] *Dopisy Dr. Milady Horákové*, 36.
[209] Košťálová, 71-72. I have some doubts about the accuracy of Věra Hložková's account: she mentioned that they shared a cell at Ruzyně prison, but Milada was incarcerated and executed at Pankrác prison. Perhaps Věra confused prisons and dates. Ruzyně prison was not yet operative at the time of Milada's arrest. In April 1949, the Party began the reconstruction of a building in the vicinity of Ruzyně airport in the North-West of Prague; the prison complex was declared ready in October 1949, and soon the first victims of the Slánský trial were imprisoned there; Igor Lukes, *Rudolf Slansky. His Trial and Trials. Cold War International History Project Working Paper no. 50* (Washington, D.C.: Woodrow Wilson Center, 2008), 16-17; http://www.wilsoncenter.org/sites/default/files/WP50IL.pdf; accessed and downloaded 25 April 2015.

Dr Trudák, the chairman of the court, knew that Bohuslav had fled in September 1949, but he deliberately told her nothing. Intent on breaking her, the regime wanted her to suffer as much as possible, but it did not succeed. On 8 June, the court gave her the opportunity for a last speech after the announcement of the verdict. Milada told the court that she accepted the death sentence and would remain faithful to Masaryk and Beneš's politics.[210]

In her letter to Marie Švehlová, who had been taking care of the Horáks' household since 1945, Milada thanked her for her service and asked her to be there for her daughter Jana in the future. She fondly remembered how Marie had accompanied Jana to dancing lessons when she was at work. Milada's wording was friendly; she addressed Marie with the tender name Maruška and praised her as "faithful and honest associate and a pillar she could always rely on".[211] She did not treat Marie as a servant, but as a member of the family.

Not every relative could deal with Milada's strong character; often, wives have a complicated relationship with their mothers-in-law, and Milada was no exception in this regard. She asked her mother-in-law for forgiveness and apologized for not showing the respect the elderly lady deserved:

> "You gave me ... your only son Bohuslav. And you wanted nothing but a bit of appreciation and my permission to spend some time with your jewel. And, young as I was, in my self-assured pride, I was engaging in an incomprehensible competition, a competition that is easily won by a young woman. I was so selfish. ... That's why, for the 23 years that Bohuslav and I were living together, I always kept my distance from you."[212]

---

[210] Milada's last speech at court on https://www.youtube.com/watch?v=Spii_fjdgXs; accessed 25 April 2015.
[211] *Dopisy Dr. Milady Horákové*, 26.
[212] *Dopisy Dr. Milady Horákové*, 17-18.

She comforted her mother-in-law and tried to give her strength, focussing on their common pain caused by the lack of information about Bohuslav. Had she never been a respectful or loving daughter-in-law, her letter was a touching attempt at reconciliation. Milada's bad conscience was torturing her and she wanted her mother-in-law at least to know that she was sorry for her past behaviour.

In all her letters, Milada's anxiety about her daughter Jana is very tangible. She asked everybody to take care of Jana, although she knew that her sister Věra and her husband Jozef would be the principal persons in Jana's young life, replacing her parents. I think that Milada wanted to make sure that Jana, who was sixteen years old in 1950, would grow up as normally as it was possible in a hostile environment that had accused her mother of high treason and killed her. Milada was realistic enough to anticipate the social stigma Jana would grow up with as the daughter of a traitor; that is why she implored all her relatives to take care of Jana. As a mother, she wanted to create a nest, a comforting zone for her daughter. Milada wanted to keep the family together after her death and time and again asked her family not to waste their lives mourning, but to live. If her death made any sense, or so she must have thought, the family should remember her, but not too long. Life was too precious; they should focus on the future, on their lives together as a family.

I think that in her last days, with ample time to remember the persons she had known, Milada often thought of Františka's homily that one should never cry over spilt milk. That advice had been with her for her entire life; but now, facing death, Milada allowed herself to put matters to rights, things she now thought she had neglected in the past. She had always wanted only to improve citizens' and especially women's lives, but she had neglected those closest to her. She did not regret the way she had led her life, but she wanted to prepare them for a life without her.

On the morning of the 26 June Milada wrote to her daughter Jana; she did not know yet that she would see Jana in a few hours.

She still had no news of Bohuslav. The authorities allowed Věra, Jozef and Jana a first and last visit on the evening of 26 June; she learnt from them that Bohuslav had fled to the West.[213] In her letter to Jana, Milada told her how much she and her father loved her, but the principal message in her letter was to prepare Jana for the life that lay ahead of her. She apologized for having worked too much and being away too often, but she had to live her life as she did. She had to follow her conscience. Jana should focus on her future:

> "You must not mourn and be sad thinking that I won't come back. Learn, my child, right now in your young years to look at life as an important thing. Life is hard, it won't pamper you, and for one caress it will inflict ten injuries. Better get used to it now, but don't give in – decide to fight. Have courage and clear goals and you shall defeat even life. You are still young … And at one point in time, as you are growing up, you will ask yourself why your mother, even though she loved you and to whom you were the greatest gift, led her life in such an unusual manner. … My girl, you have to find your way. Find it independently …"[214]

Milada wanted to instil strength and a distinct sense of independent thinking into Jana and left her a particular legacy: a list of books her daughter should read. Most of the books were Czech novels, but two recommendations are particularly interesting. Milada recommended Jana to read Stalin's historical treatises about the Great Patriotic War and the concise history of the Soviet Communist Party; she also recommended Gottwald's book *With the Soviet Union forever*.[215]

I think that Milada wanted to achieve three things with her reading list: first, to make sure that her letter would pass the censor. Had she listed the books of Masaryk, Beneš or other authors of the First Republic, the censor would have most probably had to

---

[213] "Závěřečné poznámky", in *Dopisy Dr. Milady Horákové*, 45-47; 47.
[214] *Dopisy Dr. Milady Horákové*, 27, 29.
[215] *Dopisy Dr. Milady Horákové*, 34.

confiscate the letter. Second, I deem it very likely that Milada recommended the books of Stalin and Gottwald driven by a desire to make Jana see the nature of the regime she was living under. The careful study of these texts would teach Jana a lesson for life, make her understand how the regime treated those who did not share its creed. Jana should understand on what ideological basis Comrade Gottwald was running the state. Gottwald, after all, had the power to save Milada's life, which he refused to do.[216]

Third, Milada was bright enough to anticipate the immediate political future: in 1950, as Stalin and Gottwald were alive, one could not realistically expect a change in the political conditions anytime soon. I don't think that Milada wanted her daughter to become like her, engaging in politics and sacrificing herself in a struggle against the regime, a struggle she could not possibly win. In these conditions, any activity that was not in strict compliance with the Party line was simply too dangerous. I deem it likely that Milada hinted at emigration between the lines; if the political course would ever change for the better, Jana would have to decide if she stayed in the country or leave. Jana would leave for the USA in 1968.

Milada was executed at 5.35 a.m on 27 June 1950. She died last; Záviš Kalandra (1902–1950), Jan Buchal (1913–1950) and Oldřich Pecl (1903–1950) were hanged before her. According to Martin Vadas, the author of the documentary series *Proces H*, it took each of them, hanged by asphyxiation, approximately seven to eight minutes to die, not 15 minutes as was recently published in the Czech press.[217]

---

[216] Milada had the opportunity to ask Gottwald for mercy, which she refused. Her sister Věra did, but, from the KSČ's point of view, mercy would have undermined the political sense and goal of the trial: to create the public's shock, fear and hatred of the accused.

[217] Email conversation with Martin Vadas, 6 May 2016. According to Vadas, the alleged 15 minutes it took Milada and co-accused to die is most probably an exaggeration by the press, less so a mistake by the historian

The regime's absolute lack of humanity cast two last cruel blows at Milada's family. First, they did not receive her mortal remains. Milada's ashes were disposed of at an unknown place to prevent citizens visiting her grave. She should not become a martyr. Second, the authorities did not respect her last wish: the family did not receive her letters, about whose existence they had learnt from their visit on the evening of 26 June. In 1968, Milada's sister Věra filed a claim with the Ministry of Justice, asking for the release of the letters, to no avail. Thanks to a few courageous persons at the Ministry, the letters were kept safe and hidden.[218] Milada's family finally received them in 1990, after the Velvet Revolution had swept away the KSČ's monopoly of power.

In terms of retribution, justice and coming to terms with the past, the trial of Milada Horáková and co-accused found a last end in January 2015 with the death of Ludmila Brožová-Polednová (1921–2015). In 2007, the Ministry of Justice of the Czech Republic indicted Brožová-Polednová for her active participation in the politically motivated murder of Milada and co-accused.[219] She had been a people's prosecutor, slavishly followed the instructions of the trial's script and fervently demanded the death sentence; no mercy should

---

Aleš Kýr: "Horáková umírala čtvrt hodiny" on http://zpravy.idnes.cz/horakova-umirala-ctvrt-hodiny-zjistili-historici-fs3-/domaci.aspx?c=A050629_090843_domaci_lkr; accessed 8 April 2015. See also a Kýr's short history of the executions at Pankrac prison from 1926 to 1989: "Pankrácká popraviště z let 1926–1989" on http://www.historickykaleidoskop.cz/1-2006/pankracka-popraviste-z-let-1926-1989.html; accessed 8 April 2015.

[218] "Závěřečné poznámky", in *Dopisy Dr. Milady Horákové*, 47.

[219] Brožová-Polednová excelled in her function as prosecutor especially when women were on the stand: "Zemřela Ludmila Brožová-Polednová, prokuratorka z procesu s Horákovou" on http://www.lidovky.cz/ve-veku-93-let-zemrela-ludmila-brozova-polednova-f5k-/lide.aspx?c=A150124_124718_lide_mct; accessed 25 April 2015.

be shown to the traitors.[220] The court found Brožová-Polednová guilty of judicial murder in 2008 and sentenced her to six years' imprisonment. Because of her advanced age she was imprisoned in a special geriatric ward and released in March 2010 in an amnesty issued by President Václav Klaus. She spent a year and nine months in prison.

Brožová-Polednová never admitted her guilt; she had not the slightest qualms about her past deeds and never showed any remorse. She kept claiming that she was the only former prosecutor prosecuted now for an alleged judicial murder she did not commit;

---

[220] Allegedly, Brožová-Polednová had played a particularly nasty role in Milada's execution, shouting at the executor not to break their necks, which would have caused a quick and painless death, but, with a special focus on Milada, to "slowly suffocate the bitch; "I leave this world without hatred" on http://coldwarradios.blogspot.ch/2010/11/i-leave-this-world-without-hatred.html; accessed 25 April 2015. There is no documentary proof. Markéta Doležalová, a specialist on the 1950 trials at the Czech Institute for the Study of Totalitarian Regimes in Prague: "On the internet one can find many appalling and unlikely claims with regard to the trial of Milada Horáková. I can tell you though that the events you referred to, would, had they really happened, have never appeared in the protocol of the execution. The protocols of the death of other prisoners who had died in mysterious circumstances did not reveal the real cause of death; in those days, the protocols were faked; no written traces of the regime's violence should be left behind." Email conversation with Markéta Doležalová, 29 April–5 May 2015. Martin Vadas, also familiar with the archive material, considers the alleged cruelty of Brožová-Polednová unsubstantiated gossip. Brožová-Polednová said in a short interview in 2008 that at the execution she had been sick, did not watch and people had to give her some cognac when it was over: "Pri popravě Horákové mi bylo špatně" on http://www.novinky.cz/domaci/149236-ludmila-brozova-polednova-pri-poprave-horakove-mi-bylo-spatne.html; accessed 6 May 2015. I thank Martin Vadas for recommending this link to me. Attendance at executions was the duty of the prosecutors, not a matter of personal choice.

back then in the 1950s, she had been but a student, had no knowledge about how the trial had been planned and what political purpose it served. She had believed her instructors blindly. The other prosecutors at the trial of Milada et al. could not be indicted as they had all died.

Yet, the prosecution had ample evidence at its disposal that Brožová-Polednová, known in 1949 under her maiden name Biedermannová, was guilty; prior to Milada's trial, she had fervently demanded the death sentence for a pregnant 26-year-old woman in a trial in Hodonín at the end of 1949.[221]

The daughter of a middle-class civil servant, she had grown up in Prague and trained at the workers' law school in a crash course in law for a few months before she got her first assignment as assistant prosecutor in the trial of the Catholic priest Josef Toufar in Cihosť in 1949 and the Hodonín trial.[222]

---

[221] "Brožová-Polednová návrhla i smert těhotné žene" on http://www.lidovky.cz/brozova-polednova-navrhla-i-smrt-tehotne-zene-ted-bude-volna-prb-/zpravy-domov.aspx?c=A100301_205502_ln_domov_ani; accessed 25 April 2015. The Eastern Moravian village Hodonín was Masaryk's place of birth; the Party had 'found' anti-state activities in the region and deliberately chose this location for the trial. Biedermannová was assistant prosecutor with the task of holding the closing argument, a moral speech. Condemning 'class enemies' in Hodonín in a show trial was a clear sign to everybody that the times had definitely changed. The judge spared the young woman's life; she was sentenced to life imprisonment and released in the amnesty of 1960.

[222] "The story of a Czech priest who saw a miracle and was killed for it" on http://www.catholicnewsagency.com/news/the-story-of-a-czech-priest-who-saw-a-miracle-and-was-killed-for-it-66326/; accessed 30 April 2015. According to Markéta Doležalová, Ludmila Biedermannová played a shameful and ignominious role in the trial about the 'miracle' of the moving statue of Christ in the Catholic church in the village Cihost; in her interrogations of small children in Cihosť, she suggested to them that Toufar had abused them; email conversation with Markéta Doležalová, 29 April–5 May 2015.

An interesting psychological aspect can be found in her past; according to the documentary *The Story of an Actress*, written by the historian Petr Zídek and produced by Czech television in 2011,[223] she had been a member of the Prague *Divadlo mladých pionýrů* (Theatre of the Young Pioneers), performing under the name of Lída Biedrmannová.

To the Party that was in the process of creating a new judicial elite to have politically loyal prosecutors, judges and lawyers at its disposal, she was a promising people's prosecutor: young, female, pretty, extraordinarily talented in performing in public, with excellent rhetorical skills, eager to please and follow, with a sharp mind and the rare ability of exercising an absolute lack of clemency and forgiveness. These characteristic qualities made her the perfect people's prosecutor for the persecution of 'class enemies'. At the Party's request, Biedermannová changed her German name to the Czech maiden name of her mother Brožová. She was sent to the capital to assist in the trial of Milada and co-accused. Until her retirement in the 1970s, Brožová-Polednová would perform in more than a hundred trials; after the trial of Milada, she was posted to the court in Plzen and worked there as a state prosecutor. One of her former colleagues in Plzen said in the documentary that many people were afraid of her, since Brožová-Polednová "was a bit of a fanatic".[224] The retired People's prosecutor enjoyed her last months in freedom,[225] thanks to the generous gesture of President Klaus, an act of humanity she was never capable of or interested in exercising.

---

[223] The documentary "Příbeh herečky (The Story of an Actress)" on http://www.ceskatelevize.cz/porady/10366883725-pribeh-herecky/21156226416; accessed 29 April 2015.

[224] "Příbeh herečky": http://www.ceskatelevize.cz/porady/10366883725-pribeh-herecky/21156226416; accessed 29 April 2015; position 37'48".

[225] "Zemřela Ludmila Brožová-Polednová, prokuratorka z procesu s Horákovou" on http://www.ceskatelevize.cz/ct24/domaci/299321-zemrela-lud

President Havel awarded Milada Horáková *in memoriam* the Order of Tomáš Garrigue Masaryk First Class for her courage and loyalty to the democratic principles of Masaryk and Beneš in 1991.

IV. 3 The propaganda campaign creating the Socialist Citizen

Since the end of the war, the KSČ was continuously disseminating its propaganda, fighting the centre-right parties until the day it would launch its coup d'état. Lies and misinformation should convince the citizens that a Socialist government with specific Czechoslovak features would not only be in their best economic interests but also prevent a second Munich and another war. Back in Moscow in March 1945, all negotiating parties had agreed that a crucially important stipulation of the Košice Agreement had to be the expulsion (*odsun*) of the Germans and Hungarians.

In the election campaign in 1946, the KSČ did not present itself to the electorate as a "momentum of the European revolutionary wave",[226] which might have raised fears of the Bolshevik aim for world power that had been virulent in the 1930s. On the contrary, the comrades shared in the widespread anti-German and anti-Hungarian sentiment, adamant in dispelling suspicions that the Party was at Moscow's beck and call. This clever strategy suggested to the citizens that Czechoslovakia could forge its own road to Socialism, focussing on the country's specific needs was a realistic alternative to the old-fashioned and weak democracy of the First Republic. The First Republic had been a Capitalist stronghold and a stout ally of the West; but Czechoslovakia's democracy and liberty had not been important enough to the West.

---

mila-brozova-polednova-prokuratorka-z-procesu-s-horakovou/; accessed 25 April 2015.

[226] Kaplan, *The Short March*, 55.

Munich 1938, the Nazi occupation and the clerical fascist regime in Slovakia were still traumatic events in the Czechoslovak collective memory; many citizens felt that the West could not be trusted, and the KSČ made use of that attitude, turning citizens' minds to its advantage. The German-born political theorist Hannah Arendt (1906–1975) superbly described the totalitarian mindset and the atmosphere it yielded:

> "More specific in totalitarian propaganda, however, than direct threats and crimes against individuals is the use of indirect, veiled, and menacing hints against all who will not heed its teachings ... The important factor for the movements [Nazi and Bolshevik, add. JB] is that, *even before they seize power,* they give the impression that *all elements of society are embodied in their ranks.* ... The claim inherent in totalitarian organization is that *everything outside the movement is 'dying'.*"[227]

The Party was systematically undermining farmers' associations, professional councils, youth organizations, the civil service, administrative institutions, schools, universities, the army and the secret service – from 25 February 1948 on, the totalitarian state was being perfected by the rule of terror and fear.

Until the collapse of KSČ's monopoly of power in December 1989, the regime would not only micromanage citizens' lives by determining housing, education, the choice of profession and individual mobility, but also control citizens' minds with technological means and the finely tuned application of psychological pressure, punishment and reward. The goal was to construct the Socialist Citizen, who, thanks to the Party's perennial wisdom, would build the best of all worlds. Justice, equality, humanism and freedom would reign in the utopian future paradise – but to embark on this revolution in the first place, citizens' minds had to be changed.

---

[227] Arendt, 303-507; 345, 371, 381, italics by me.

Intellectuals and writers were particularly important to the movement, since they had at their disposal the faculties to teach the people, to impress them with rhetoric, to explain the Party's goals with simple words. Socialist Realism was declared the politically correct form of art in literature, film and poetry. Stalin was spot on when he described the writers as "engineers of the human soul",[228] expressing the materialist principle that the strict application of science was a life-guiding rational agenda. What he meant with 'soul' was a rational appeal to those who still believed in the concept of the human soul, an area of human life he 'knew' did not exist. Materialism does not accept a life after death; there is no metaphysical space, no sphere beyond the physical, no immortal soul. Man is flesh, matter, and when he dies that is the end. Man is machine determined by the laws of biology, physiology and chemistry, and writers, doctors, and psychiatrists take care of that machine.

The proper materialistic-scientific *Weltanschauung*, its limits naturally defined by the Party, had, by the sheer power of its inherent rationalism, a solution to every problem. According to this way of thinking, the human mind was a machine that could be repaired, reset, altered, and fine-tuned. If the mind of a citizen, however, was resistant, if he did not see or refuse to see the shining truth, then he had to undergo repair. In this way of thinking, he who dared cast the slightest doubt on the scientifically established truth of Marxism-Leninism was simply ill, literally out of his or her mind –

---

[228] Andrei A. Ždanov's (1896–1948) speech at the Soviet Writers' Congress in August 1934; he referred to Stalin's wisdom: https://www.marxists.org/subject/art/lit_crit/sovietwritercongress/zdhanov.htm; accessed 27 April 2015. See the famous novel of Josef Škvorecký, *The Engineer of Human Souls* (London: Vintage, 1994). Škvorecký's title is irony *par excellence*; the chapter titles of his autobiography are dedicated to great 'engineers of the human soul' such as Edgar Allan Poe, Mark Twain, Joseph Conrad and F. Scott Fitzgerald.

in need of psychiatric treatment. It was therefore but a logical consequence that citizens openly critical of the regime were treated and medicated in psychiatric wards, a practise the Soviet Union under Brežnev excelled in.[229]

In his famous novel *Darkness at Noon,* first published in 1940, Arthur Köstler (1905–1983), the Hungarian-born British novelist, brilliantly described the European intellectuals' fascination with Marxism-Leninism and the elitist mindset of his generation born at the turn of the 20th century:

> "It is said that No. 1 [the fictitious Chairman of the Party, in reality, Stalin, add. JB] has Machiavelli's *Prince* lying permanently by his bedside. So he should: since then, nothing really important has been said about the rules of political ethics. We were the first to replace the nineteenth century's liberal ethics of 'fair play' by the revolutionary ethics of the twentieth century. In that also we were right, *a revolution conducted according to the rules of cricket* [a synonym and metaphor for fair play in the English-speaking world, add. JB] *is an absurdity.* … Politics can be relatively fair in the breathing spaces of history; *at its critical turning points there is no other rule possible than the old one, that the end justifies the means.*"[230]

The intellectuals were besotted with Socialism; they considered the ideology the best answer to the problems of the 20th century and were convinced that Socialism was the only creed that could establish real justice and true liberty. A particular psychological facet of the believers was their arrogance, the belief that only they,

---

[229] A comprehensive account of the (ab)use of psychiatry in Communist Europe is Mat Savelli and Sarah Marks (eds.), *Psychiatry in Communist Europe* (London: Palgrave, 2015).

[230] Arthur Köstler, *Darkness at Noon* (London: Vintage, 2005), 81, italics by me. Köstler's novel is a fictitious account of the Moscow show trials of the 1930s, which he observed as a young Party member from Europe. The Moscow trials served as a blueprint for the show trials of the 1950s in the Eastern bloc.

the initiated, were entitled to teach people how to live and think. He, who did not see the light, had to be forced to his own good, his happiness, whether he liked it or not. If he was resistant, stubborn, he had to be sacrificed, for the greater good of mankind. Sir Isaiah Berlin described this particular arrogance with unprecedented clarity and insightfulness:

> "If I know that I am right, if I know that what I seek is the true good, then people who oppose me must be in error about what it is that they themselves seek. No doubt they too think that they are seeking the good, they assert their own liberty to secure it, but they are seeking it in the wrong place. Therefore I have a right to prevent them. In virtue of what have I this right to prevent them? ... It is because if they knew what they truly wanted, they would seek what I seek. The fact that they do not seek this means that they do not *really* know – ."[231]

If one wants to establish a power monopoly as a platform to embark on a global revolution, one has to have not only reliable comrades at one's side carrying out directives and commands. More important for the revolutionary and totalitarian movement are individuals with particular capabilities, persons who have no scruples and stop at nothing. One of the most loyal Party members, a true revolutionary Lenin would have fondly approved of because of his ideological enthusiasm and discipline, was Rudolf Slánský (1901–1952), who had spent the war at Gottwald's side in Moscow. They had known each other since the 1920s. The Gottwalds and Slánskýs had experienced together the horrors at the Hotel Lux in Moscow, very aware of how many comrades vanished into the depths of the Soviet Union in the years of the war.

In many accounts of the history of the Cold War and Czechoslovakia alike, Slánský, elected General Secretary of the KSČ

---

[231] Isaiah Berlin, *Freedom and its Betrayal. Six Enemies of Human Liberty* (London: Pimlico, 2003), 45-46.

in 1948, is usually presented as the most prominent victim of the 1952 show trial, in which 13 high-ranking Party members were accused of Titoism, Zionism and conspiracy with the West. The Slánský trial was the peak of the purges that had been ongoing since 1948 and it had a particularly nasty antisemitic character, since 11 of the 14 accused were Jewish. Yet, Slánský was not only a victim. From 1949 on, the ruthless Party functionary played a crucial role in the organization of the purges:

> "A major impetus for this wave of arrests came from the CPC General Secretary Rudolf Slansky, who said in September, at Edvard Benes's funeral in Prague, that the country needed labour camps to deal with the class enemy and it made no difference that the West was going to complain about communist concentration camps in Czechoslovakia. Attempts at ideological education would be insufficient for dealing with enemies of communism."[232]

When comrades Klema (Gottwald) and Ruda (Slánský) could no longer ignore the pressure from Stalin to find Czechoslovak traitors connected to the Hungarian Rajk group, they began to organize the trial; the first Soviet advisors arrived in Prague in early October 1949. With two other members of the politburo, Slánský supervised the renovation of a large building in Ruzyně, where a prison complex was built for the interrogation of the suspects written into the script of the trial. He declared the prison ready on 29 October 1949.[233] Little did he know that just two years later he would be arrested, subsequently interrogated and tortured at the very prison complex, whose building and installation he had overseen.

It was not so much a cruel irony of history that Slánský fell victim to the very agenda he had helped to set up for rooting out 'class enemies', but a logical consequence consistent with the

---

[232] Lukes, 13-14.
[233] Lukes, 13-14.

rationale of the purges: the building of Socialism required a clean body of personnel, also within the Party.

A crucially important aspect of Slánský's arrest was the operation *Great Sweeper*, planned and carried out by OKAPI, a group of high-ranking members of the Czechoslovak army and intelligence officers, who had fled in 1948.[234] They planned the operation *Great Sweeper* together with the OSS immediately after Slánský's 50th birthday on 31 July 1951. An OKAPI officer noticed that there was no mention of Stalin's traditional birthday telegram in the Czechoslovak press. He drew the right conclusion: Slánský had fallen from Stalin's grace, and something was going on against him at the top of the Party.

OKAPI's plan was simple, but ingenious: OKAPI would warn the deputy Prime Minister of his forthcoming arrest and offer him a chance to defect to the West. If he defected, the OSS would have a top member of the Czechoslovak Communists in their hands; if he did not, the letter could always be played into the hands of the Party where it would foster suspicion and cast doubts among the comrades about Slánský's loyalty, and thus accelerate his fall.[235] In either case, OKAPI and the OSS would only gain.

Because of a double agent who was caught, the letter never reached Slánský, but the StB and Moscow learnt about the planned escape. The letter with the instructions how to get in touch with OKAPI was shown to Gottwald, who had for 13 days withstood Stalin's command to have Slánský arrested.[236] The letter and the

---

[234] Lukes, 39. The name *Great Sweeper* was OKAPI's code name for Slánský, referring to his organization of the purges. Lukes's brilliant paper conveys the merciless atmosphere of the Cold War, with secret services fighting each other in the shadows. OKAPI members wanted to take revenge on the KSČ for the many citizens who had been killed or were suffering in the prisons and labor camps.

[235] Lukes, 39-40.

[236] Lukes, 46.

codes how to contact OKAPI were broadcast on Radio Free Europe from Munich, Bavaria; they eventually ended Gottwald's resistance. He issued instructions to the StB, and his closest confidant and friend was arrested on 24 November 1951 shortly after midnight.

Slánský had not been in the West during the war like Vladimír Clementis or Artur London but that did not matter to Stalin. He had mistrusted him since the war; the arrest of his closest confidant and friend was proof of Gottwald's obedience and loyalty. The *Great Sweeper* operation was a full success: a wave of arrests followed with the Party sweeping itself thoroughly clean. The particular combination of Stalin's mistrust of Slánský, the OKAPI letter and the KSČ's need to organize a show trial brought down many prominent Party members, to the delight of the OKAPI and OSS officers.

Before he became a victim himself, Slánský was merciless; he had not the slightest compassion with the 'class enemies'. An excellent interpretation of his character with regard to the trial of Milada can be found in a TV play.

Often, artists, poets and writers have a psychological insight, a special gift for portraying persons, showing with the help of fictitious dialogues what a particular historical situation could have looked like, how events and decisions we have no record of could have occurred.

Czech Television produced the series *České Století* (*The Czech Century*), written by Pavel Kosatík and directed by Robert Sedláček, based on the latest historical research. The series shows the major events of Czech and Czechoslovak history from 1918 to 1992 in nine TV plays.[237] Part 5 is entitled *Zabíjení soudruha* (*The Murder of a Comrade*), telling the story of Slánský and Gottwald's friendship and

---

[237] Košťálová, 104; "Zabíjení soudruha" on http://www.ceskatelevize.cz/porady/10362011008-ceske-stoleti/21251212043-zabijeni-soudruha-1951/; accessed 30 April 2015.

how the General Secretary ended up at the gallows. Slánský, played by David Novotný, had no mercy with Milada. A fictitious dialogue with Gottwald, played by Jiří Vyorálek, illustrates Slánský's arrogant mindset. In the afternoon of 27 June 1950, Slánský and Gottwald, sitting in the President's office at the Castle, receive written confirmation of the execution of Milada and co-accused. The sober, disciplined and energetic Slánský to the slightly depressed Gottwald who is in dire need of another drink:

> "You know what her problem was? As a young girl, she fell in love with Masaryk from afar. Once she had grown up, she could not stop and continued with Beneš."[238]

This fictitious quote reveals the sexist thinking of the Party's male members: save for the female comrades, of course, every woman who engaged in politics, putting her beliefs into practice, did so following a low motive: love, not the platonic feeling of deep friendship and respect, but erotic love that binds women to men. After Masaryk's death, Milada had allegedly converted her feelings to Beneš. This is another vulgar thought conveying the assumption that women have only one interest: following their heart. If the object of their desire cannot or does not want to reciprocate their feelings, they simply shift their affection to somebody else. They have no sense of faith and are incapable of loyalty. Certainly, this dialogue is fiction, and Slánský did not say these things, but the quote illustrates his arrogance, lack of respect for the beliefs of others and the vulgar view that non-Communist women were brainless creatures who went into politics only to pursue calls of the heart.

One might be tempted into thinking that Slánský eventually got what he deserved, much like the sorcerer's apprentice in

---

[238] "Zabíjení soudruha" on http://www.ceskatelevize.cz/porady/1036201 108-ceske-stoleti/21251212043-zabijeni-soudruha-1951/; accessed 30 April 2015; position 15'26".

Goethe's famous poem: *Spirits that I've cited My commands ignore.*[239] The Party he had been so eager to serve not only stripped him of his power and destroyed his reputation, but also sentenced him to death – and the very fact that he was utterly innocent of the charges brought against him could be interpreted as poetic justice.

Yet, poetic justice or even *Schadenfreude* is neither helpful nor appropriate in the context of historical study. What one should look at more closely are the reasons why so many citizens truly believed that Milada and co-accused deserved to die.

The purpose of the trial of Milada et al. was to reveal to the people "the ugly face of the forces of reaction".[240] The authorities began with the preparation of the trial in the autumn months of 1949; on 26 November 1949, the deputy Minister of Justice Karel Klos invited members of the Czechoslovak association of journalists (*Svaz československých novinářů*) to attend, with instructions how to report on the trial.[241] Each newspaper would appoint one journalist, whose only task was to make himself familiar with the trial and publish a daily summary of the court proceedings after briefings from the Ministry of Justice.

The meeting of 24 March 1950 took place at the KSČ's headquarters. Gottwald's son-in-law Alexej Čepička (1910–1990) demanded that film should play a major role in covering the trial: news footage should report live and in colour to arouse the people. They should see what means the forces of reaction used against the *národ*.[242] KSČ specialists for propaganda held that this might work against them; only parts of the trials should be shown. Some of the

---

[239] "Die ich rief, die Geister, werd ich nun nicht los"; the English translation by Edwin Zeydel from 1955: germanstories.vcu.edu/goethe/zauber_dual.html; accessed 29 April 2015.
[240] Formánková and Koura, 28.
[241] Formánková and Koura, 34.
[242] Formánková and Koura, 34-35.

accused were physically weak and to show them on film might provoke only pity and compassion – which had to be prevented at all costs.

At a further meeting, the Party and ministries involved agreed on procedural details: templates should be prepared for the newspaper articles and the film coverage in such a way that the human side of the accused would not appear. The last meeting took place four days before the start of the trial; members of the CC, representatives of the court, the prosecution, Ministry of Domestic Affairs and Ministry of Justice gathered to discuss the last pressing details, for example, how to choose the public for the courtroom: only reliable Party members should sit in the front row.[243] The script determined precisely how the prosecution should act and react and what it should focus on:

> "... then we'll come to the question of the war. The moment Horáková starts talking about the war, specify immediately this issue. ... Show Horáková that if she wants to go on a political level what she did was not politics, but espionage."[244]

The past of the accused, in particular their resistance activities during the war and the occupation had to be strictly ignored, and the prosecutor to prove that they had been enemies of the people ever since, regardless of the political regime that was in power. Particularly demagogical was the display of swastika flags, weapons and ammunition in the courtroom, which had allegedly been found at the hiding places of the accused; the public had to be convinced that the defendants held deep and hidden sympathies with Fascism and were preparing terrorist activities against the state in the pay of the Capitalist West.

---

[243] Formánková and Koura, 38-39.
[244] Formánková and Koura, 39.

The trial's script was written, but the Party wanted to make sure that it would reach its goal; it organized the peoples' reaction. The day after the beginning of the trial, on 1 June 1950, the KSČ issued secret instructions to the regional and district Party hierarchies. All over the country, *stengazety* (wall newspapers) were posted to allow as many people as possible immediate access to the latest news.[245] In factories, offices, railway stations, pubs, restaurants, clubs and all public places broadcast news was reporting on the trial, naturally following the prepared information bulletin. Public discussions with persons that had attended the trial were held and citizens asked to write resolutions in favor of the prosecution. This organizational 'overkill' came along with an artificially created mass hysteria spreading the fear of a political overthrow organized by the forces of reaction. Leading Party functionaries all over the country had to implement special security measures:

> "On the days the court is convening, make sure that the security of the public buildings, offices, factories and so on are checked and if needed, improved. Do not allow for the slightest provocation to happen in the factories."[246]

Furthermore, the Party made sure that the citizens attending the trial were carefully chosen: Party functionaries from every region and district compiled lists with the names of politically reliable citizens. The attendees were from all areas of society: workers, army personnel, teachers, intellectuals, factory managers and farmers. The citizens were driven to the capital and allowed into the courthouse only after thorough verification of their identity cards and their personally issued pass for the trial (*vstupenka na proces*).[247]

---

[245] Formánková and Koura, 41.
[246] Formánková and Koura, 41.
[247] Formánková and Koura, 45.

Every little detail was thought of: the citizens attending the trial were also chosen according to where they lived and worked. The guiding principle was that they had to originate from the area or region where the accused came from;[248] when Milada was on the stand, the public in the courtroom was from her constituency of České Budějovice. This subtle and cruel measure made sure that the citizens, once back home, would talk about their impressions of the trial to friends, families and colleagues at work, thereby destroying any doubts about the guilt of the accused among those who might still have some sympathy because they knew the accused.

This was a devilishly clever means of psychological manipulation and torture alike, since it worked twofold: citizens familiar with Milada, her former voters sharing with her the local customs and identity and political values were made to believe that she was guilty – which, in turn, put immense psychological pressure on Milada. It was one thing to have citizens from a distant town or village who did not know her against her, but quite another to experience that citizens of her own constituency attending the trial lost their faith in her. To a person so dedicated to society and the welfare of the citizens as Milada was, the loss of trust was a cruel psychological punishment. She must have felt cornered, as nobody believed in her innocence, not even the citizens who had once trusted her with their vote.

The public in the courtroom was changed on a daily basis; nobody, save for the prosecutors and judges, had a full picture and overview of the trial. The public saw only a part, which made it difficult for them to form an opinion of their own, since they lacked the larger picture, the context. For the eight days of the trial, some 4000 citizens from all over the country were driven to Prague and

---

[248] Formánková and Koura, 53.

attended the trial in the courtroom, which was a major organizational task.

In view of the massive propaganda machine manipulating the citizens' minds and broadcasting lies and defamations, it was no wonder that the majority of the citizens became agitated and anxious; stirred up on a daily basis with accusations that portrayed the defendants as terrorists and enemies of the people, they wanted revenge. The vulgar 'newspeak' the Party was promoting had no limits and it was an effective means to unite the citizens in hatred, suffocating independent reasoning, decency and tolerance, the old values of the bourgeoisie. After the verdict was spoken on 8 June 1950, some lower Party secretary wrote:

> "Hang them all, bullets are wasted on these lumps. Here in Lanškroun, the workers are looking with disgust at the brazenness of Dr Horáková, whom our enemies consider a heroine. Only a strict sentence can prevent the forces of reaction from raising their heads."[249]

Comrade Božena Svobodová thanked the government for exposing the low lives of reactiontionaries by exceeding her work quota. From thousands of letters and resolutions citizens sent to the court and the Party offices it transpires that the propaganda was effective and fulfilling all expectations. An atmosphere of hatred and bloodlust was uniting the country. In the North, some comrades were so shocked and angry at Horáková's cynical behaviour in court that they smashed the wireless – which they then had to quickly send in to repair to be able to continue following the trial.[250] Thousands of resolutions were carried in baskets into the courtroom every day; they were used as proof of the people's will, which caused the

---

[249] Formánková and Koura, 48.
[250] Formánková and Koura, 49.

defendants and witnesses further distress. At the end of the trial, an estimated 6300 resolutions had arrived.[251]

Some citizens were not satisfied with just signing the resolutions composed at the workplaces and the Party's offices: they sent personal letters to the prosecution, demanding the death sentence. The fanaticism that made these citizens act independently was a further proof of the propaganda's success. Nobody had forced them to sit down in their homes, write a letter and post it. An interesting detail that Formánková and Koura, the historians analysing the propaganda campaign, found was that the majority of these 'overachievers' were women.[252] An example: eager to demonstrate their political loyalty and commitment to Socialism, Alžběta Jandová and Marta Egerová wrote to assistant prosecutor Ludmila Brožová, most probably motivated by the young woman's emotional closing argument:

> "On 8 June 1950, we were at the National House in Smíchov, where the trial took place. We have followed the whole trial on the radio and in Rudé Právo and heard with terror, what they had prepared for us all. After the verdict was out, a wave of indignation and outrage arose about the lenient sentences passed on these murderers and traitors. Everybody protested and demanded the death sentence for all of them."[253]

Not only workers and farmers, but also intellectuals and members of the other political parties, which the KSČ had 'kept alive' after February 1948, rushed to express their support for the prosecution. The parties of the National Front and their newspapers such as the former prestigious centre-right *Lidové Noviny* were but Potemkin villages; they had been brought into strict line with the KSČ and were used to suggest to the citizens that the pluralist system of the

---

[251] Formánková and Koura, 57.
[252] Formánková and Koura, 61.
[253] Viz document č. 141, quoted from Formánková and Koura, 61.

National Front still existed. The most demagogical article was published in *Svobodné Slovo* (*The Free Word*), the newspaper of the Czechoslovak Socialist Party ČSS. Josef Šafařík, delegate for the ČSS, excelled in his rhetoric:

> "What is the difference between the well-known beast of Buchenwald – Elsa Koch – who used to put to death political prisoners wearing tattoos and then had toiletries and book-bindings made from their skins and the former delegate of the National Socialists Dr Horáková, who, at the price of a new world catastrophe, wants to reverse the achievements [of 25 February 1948, add. JB]?"[254]

The Party had written the script, including the defendants' alleged plans to risk a nuclear war and plunge mankind into the abyss. The more citizens from different areas and political pseudo-spectres joined in the campaign, the more effective it was, suggesting that the people were standing firmly behind the Party.

Milada was the special target of the trial, which showed features similar to the witch trials of the 17th century in Europe: the accused had no chance to prove their innocence. By admitting their guilt in court they 'proved' that the prosecution had been right all along. Some compared Milada to Hitler, others thought that her behaviour in court was similar to that of a guard at a Nazi concentration camp, and others again considered her activities as being motivated by a hunger for fame, dominated by a lust for power and, of course, financial greed, the despicable wish to enrich herself at the people's costs.[255]

Citizens acquainted with her in the past, like former party colleagues, were also calling for her blood. Some were motivated by

---

[254] Formánková and Koura, 91. The correct spelling of the name is "Ilse Koch"; see "Ilse Koch" on https://www.jewishvirtuallibrary.org/jsource/biography/ikoch.html; accessed 5 May 2015.

[255] Formánková and Koura, 92.

true belief in Socialism and the Party's protection of the nation, others joined in using the trial as an opportunity to present themselves to the regime as trustworthy, since they had had, in the Party's eyes, a suspicious past. Now, by identifying themselves with the aggressor, they were demonstrating that they were on the right side and might evade a similar fate.[256]

According to its totalitarian goal of uniting society and getting it to toe the ideological line, it was only consistent to get children involved. Teachers and head-teachers had to make the trial a significant part of instruction at all levels. The trial and the media campaign were promoted on a daily basis and an important part and theme of the children's school experience:

> "One recommendation was '… to organize exercises in stylistic writing with the task to write about the theme 'Traitors of their own nation'. … Teachers should draw the children's attention in particular to 'the degenerate character of the accused'. In the classes, so-called five-minute sessions (*pětiminutovky*) were held that were informing the children about the trial. It was their duty to listen to the school radio that broadcast the latest news from the courtroom, and the trial was a major theme in the class instructions of Czech and the class teachings about state and society (*vlastivěda*)."[257]

Children's journals, like *Pionýr*, were full of the propaganda that taught the young ones with simple words and colourful cartoon-like pictures what the accused were guilty of. Naturally, the children, the youngest ones six years old, were incapable of defending themselves against the powerful propaganda and believed the tale of the traitors' intentions of drawing the country, and the world, into a nuclear war, which would lead to millions of deaths. The hatred shown to everybody who did not heed the Party's course, the concomitant arrogance of 'knowing' that one was on the right side

---

[256] Formánková and Koura, 89.
[257] Formánková and Koura, 67.

was poured into the young minds; the loyalty of the next generation was safe – or so the responsible functionaries and ministers must have thought.

The children also received instructions from their teachers to report about their parents and relatives,[258] early lessons of denunciation that had proven effective in the 1930s in the Soviet Union with Pavlik Morozov (1918–1932), a sad symbol of the Party's ideological child abuse.[259] The teachers kept asking the children what was said at home; the little ones had to write letters at school describing their views of the trial and then present them to their parents, asking or rather, instructing them to support and join them in their views.[260] This was a particular clever means of manipulation: controlling citizens' minds via their offspring. What loving parent would not feel it a sheer human impossibility to tell its child that he or she did not share its views about the traitors? Indoctrinated at school on a daily basis, the child found it equally difficult to understand why the parents considered Milada and co-accused decent people in view of the horrendous crimes the court had presented to the public, with ample evidence. Confused children are prone to talk and, given that the trial was an ever-present topic at school, it was very likely that they mentioned their parents' opinions to their teachers and classmates. The campaign turned children into informants without their being aware of it, while the parents were given a warning through their offspring: better join in the mass condemnation of the accused or else …

Most of the letters, written by children and adults alike, ended with a promise to the government, a pledge and commitment thanking the Party for watching over the nation and saving the

---

[258] Formánková and Koura, 69.
[259] "Pavlik Morozov: Soviet Boy Hero" on http://www.mod-langs.ox.ac.uk/russian/childhood/pavlikmorozov.htm; accessed 5 May 2015.
[260] Formánková and Koura, 69.

citizens from the traitors' evil plans: the adults usually promised to raise the target at their workplace, to accelerate the accomplishment of the five-year plan, while children pledged to clean the school floors, collect garbage or, most importantly, join the Party's pioneer movement.[261]

A further aspect of the mass campaign was the mustering of loyal international journalists and reporters from the Soviet Union and the countries of the Eastern European bloc. Journalists of the leftist British *Daily Worker*, the Italian *Unità* and the French *Drapeau Rouge* and *L'Humanité*, but also non-leftist Western newspapers were present at the trial.[262] The authorities tried to influence the Western press with carefully selected translators, which was not always to the liking of the Western comrades. Sam Russel, the editor of the *Daily Worker*, complained that the best interpreter was assigned to the "reactionary" press, which prompted the Ministry of Information to reply that interpreting to the reactionary press was a demanding and complicated task that could be assigned only to politically reliable and experienced persons.[263] The government held daily press conferences with members of the Ministry of Justice, the prosecution and the senate.

The trial provided the main headlines in the press; the most influential newspaper was the KSČ's Party organ *Rudé Právo* with the highest number of copies sold and the largest distribution network. *Mladá Fronta Dnes* addressed the young citizens, and *Vlasta* was the women's journal. Only *Mateřídouška*, the journal for

---

[261] Formánková and Koura, 71.
[262] Formánková and Koura, 79.
[263] Formánková and Koura, 79. For an insightful account of Western Communists who lived in Czechoslovakia see Kathleen Geaney, "At home among Strangers: The Extraordinary Year 1950 in the Life of an Ordinary American Family in Communist Czechoslovakia", *COMENIUS. Journal of Euro-American Civilization II*, no. 1 (2015): 25-42.

the smallest children at kindergarten age did not report the trial. A brief list of headlines demonstrates how the press manipulated the citizens who could not escape the propaganda:

> "The Traitors at the People's Court; The Spy Horáková Confesses Activities against Republic and Peace; Agents in the Pay of the West in Front of the State's Court; Traitors of the People; To the Wreckers Our Women React With Work; Traitors without Masks; The American Agents Unmasked; In Thousands of Resolutions our People demand: Have the Spies, Criminals and Traitors Strictly and Justly Sentenced!"[264]

The contents of the articles published in the newspapers and journals were equally repetitive and followed the agenda that the government had precisely determined: "agents in the pay of the traitor-emigrants", "hyenas seeking nuclear war" and "selling out their own nation".[265]

Renowned academics with an international reputation joined the campaign, often with elaborate words: the famous linguist and rector of Charles University Jan Mukařovský, the equally well-known literary scholar and dean of the Faculty of Philosophy Bohuslav Havránek, and Josef Tureček, the dean of the Faculty of Law and a specialist in Ecclesiastical Law, issued statements in support of the death sentence. The author of the *Česká mluvnice* (*Czech Grammar*), a textbook still in use today, expressed his opinion with elegant wording, stating that the defendants were no human beings, since consumed by their hatred of the people and intent on warmongering in support of and in conjunction with the enemy.[266]

Yet, there is also evidence that the authorities forced citizens to issue statements against their will. It was very difficult to find a way out of or around the political pressure without losing one's self-

---

[264] Formánková and Koura, 80.
[265] Formánková and Koura, 80.
[266] Formánková and Koura, 90.

respect, and, in the harsh economic reality of the post-war years, some modest material privileges. The Olympic champion Emil Zátopek (1922–2000) wrote and signed the statement *Rozsudek vynesl všechen československý lid* (*The whole of the Czechoslovak people passed the judgement*), but his text was different from the usual wording. The long-distance runner who would win three gold medals at the Olympic games in Helsinki in 1952 condemned the traitors and spies, but did so in a general and superficial manner; not once did he mention the name of a defendant, which is a clear sign that he did not identify with what he was forced to do – he did the minimum and simply refused to elaborate.[267] The authorities pressed Zátopek into the statement, using the world-famous athlete as a 'weapon' against his relative abroad: Emil's wife was the niece of general Sergei Ingr (1894–1956), a former member of the London exile government and active in Czechoslovak exile, who was fighting the Communist regime from abroad.[268]

A minority of citizens could not be cajoled into toeing the Party line; with respect to the overbearing propaganda, their independent thinking and courage is admirable. Elderly women from the Olomouc area in Moravia, where the population traditionally occupied itself with farming, met on an evening and declared that they considered "Horáková and Zemínková heroines because they spoke up, from their hearts."[269] The Party's local office in Jihlava reported to the capital that the most conservative citizens from town and countryside did not trust the defendant's statements; they believed that the accused were innocent and forced into confessing, like the Catholic priest Jozef Toufar in the trial of the 'miracle' in the Eastern Bohemian Cihošť seven months ago.[270]

---

[267] Formánková and Koura, 91.
[268] Formánková and Koura, 91.
[269] Viz document č. 17, quoted from Formánková and Koura, 49.
[270] Formánková and Koura, 50.

Others were shocked about the death sentence passed on a woman; they thought that the accused were rightly condemned but they expected the state to be merciful since the execution of a woman had never happened before:

> "In the village Janov, women were discussing the sentence while occupied with the processing of beetroot. They said that the condemned should be imprisoned, but it was not necessary to have them executed. In a pub in Litomyšl, three citizens left after they heard the sentence in the broadcast."[271]

Many citizens who wrote letters of protest against the death sentence argued with mercy, asking the President to spare Milada's life as a symbolic gesture. They did so knowing that the regime would punish them, risking their freedom and safety. Vlasta Kálalová, who, as a young doctor had built up a hospital in Bagdad and enjoyed the financial support of President Masaryk in the years of the First Republic, wrote to Gottwald:

> "For her death we all would be responsible with our conscience – You, Mr President as much as I, the last citizen of the People's state. And I am convinced that a person, who is trying to always act in a humane way, cannot act, not even when thinking about issues of the state, the way an old, enslaving, animal and inhumane society would. The Germans shot my husband and my children – they shot my 19-year old son and my 14-year old daughter. I have thoroughly reflected about and experienced violent death in my life."[272]

The following event illustrates not only how the regime punished 17 innocent teenagers, but also how exile organisations used the trial to promote their own beliefs, not always sticking to the truth they so fervently defended in their admiration of President Masaryk. But then, it was the Cold War, a merciless and brutal struggle about beliefs, words, concepts and creed.

---

[271] Formánková and Koura, 51.
[272] Formánková and Koura, 113.

The exile journal *Zpráva o Československu* (*News about Czechoslovakia*) published in its issue 15 the article *Dozvuky procesu s dr. Milady Horákové* (*Echos of the trial of Dr Milada Horáková*): at the end of the school year in the early summer of 1950, a class of the high school in Český Brod in Central Bohemia went on a trip to the countryside.[273] The teenagers carried a pieta with them and, resting in some forest, talked about Horáková and co-accused; eventually, they adopted the names of the 13 accused as a symbolic gesture of their solemn reverence to the defendants,[274] viz, to the West and the exile Czechoslovaks. Back from the trip, a student told her father about what they did; he immediately contacted the local StB. The StB came to the high school and started the investigation, which led to the expulsion of all students involved. The young ringleader was quickly identified and walked through town having to wear a plate marked with 'This is the boss of the degenerate Czech youth'.

The rector of the high school of Český Brod Jaromír Klenka, however, remembered in his testimonial what had really happened at the end of the school year 1949/1950:

> "The class, among them some good singers, went off with their guitars. They had a large repertoire; one of the songs was from Voskovec and Werich and they chanted the words 'These Nazi pigs, where are they hiding ... probably in Argentine ... Sieg Heil!' Just the usual provocative behaviour of teenagers! Nothing would have happened, had not somebody described the situation in a completely different light. A student of this class was the daughter of the chairman of the MNV Josef Brt, and she told her father what had happened on the trip. He immediately saw the opportunity to rise in the Party's rank and file and reported the incident to the KSČ's local office. And the affair was in the making. ... back then, some of the students were from Kostelec, busy with performing in a theatre play; the slogan was a part of the script, and the swastika was stitched

---

[273] Formánková and Koura, 71.
[274] Formánková and Koura, 77.

onto the costumes the youngsters took with them on their trip. Finally, the connection with the traitorous group of Dr Ripka, who was in London, and the refugee Corn from Kostelec, who was in Canada, was found! That's how the silly joke became a state affair. 'The Nazi Group at the high school in Český Brod', 'Subversive group of Ripka revealed' – these were the headlines in the newspapers."[275]

Apparently, Josef Brt who reported the youngsters to the authorities had had a somewhat dubious past as a teacher in the last year of the Protectorate. He was eager to ingratiate himself with the Party and prove his loyalty to Socialism.

The investigation at the high school and the town lasted a few days; the authorities used the opportunity to have a thorough look around. Some students' parents were large-farmers, so-called 'kulaks', others were shop-owners, others members of the educated upper middle-class, the intelligentsia – which chimed in well with the Party's long-term policy of nationalizing farms and shops and getting rid of independent minds, the entrepreneurial middle class. The investigating authorities composed lists of unreliable students; some of the teenagers with a 'bourgeois' background were expelled from the high school and could not accomplish the *maturita*, others did not receive the recommendation to enrol at university.[276] Every little joke about Gottwald's wife Marta and petty ironic comments about the current political situation were put on record and filed.[277] At the end, 17 teenagers were expelled from the high school for a silly joke, like Milada in 1918, who had been expelled from her *gymnasium* for throwing a rose at Czech soldiers.

Letters and telegrams from Czechoslovaks in exile and prominent citizens asking President Gottwald for mercy poured into

---

[275] Formánková and Koura, 77. Kostelec is a little town in Central Bohemia, known to the readers of Josef Škvorecký's *Zbábelci* (*The Cowards*).
[276] Formánková and Koura, 78
[277] Formánková and Koura, 78.

his office. The Nobel laureate and professor of physics Albert Einstein (1879–1955), for example, sent Gottwald a telegram from Princeton, imploring him to spare the defendants' lives, since they had suffered in Nazi concentration camps.[278] Naturally, the regime did not publish these protests; the citizens learnt about them only if they had access to Western broadcast.

After Milada's execution, the Party continued with its plan to build the Socialist Citizen: the last show trial was in the making. This time, prominent functionaries and loyal Party members would be on the witness stand. Persons, who had participated in the planning of Milada's trial, lost their influential positions.[279] They were used as witnesses in the trial of Slánský and arrested in the first months of 1951; the trial would begin in the autumn of 1952. They had to undergo the same treatment as Milada and the victims of the 1950 show trial. The Party's rationale was to *leave no witnesses behind*; they were prepared for the stand as witnesses of Slánský's crimes, having to learn by heart their 'confessions'.

The former Minister of Education Jaroslav Stránský (1884–1973), Mimi Jiránková's father-in-law and Miloš Jiránek's stepfather, commented from his London exile:

> "First and foremost, Milada Horáková was a woman, a mother of a teenager, a distinguished fighter in the *odboj* against the German oppressors and a victim of their persecution. She was an educated and noble person. As a delegate to parliament, she was a colleague of Gottwald and Slánský, who determined her fate. She was strangled one morning because these two wanted her to die."[280]

---

[278] Formánková and Koura, 99.
[279] Formánková and Koura, 115-117.
[280] Formánková and Koura, 107.

IV. 4 Conclusion

Milada was a democrat and feminist, a woman who wanted to improve women's lives. She had the opportunity to emigrate in 1947 – but she did not. Even warned by Mrs Lewis, her close friend, Milada was still optimistic, she believed in Beneš and his authority. The current crisis would peter out. She believed that Masaryk's rule-of-law state could be resurrected.

Arrested and put on trial, portrayed by the government as a spy, terrorist and warmonger, she was courageous. The authorities could not break her; she declared her loyalty to the politics of Masaryk and Beneš in her last speech. Milada's courage is a shining example to everybody whose civil rights are taken away. As a lawyer, she believed in the rule of law; she did not understand that the rule of law was of no importance to her political adversaries. She died a heroic death and is remembered with admiration and affection.

Emmy Destinn as Aida, date unknown
Source: Wikimedia Commons

Ema Destinn in private, date unknown
Source: Wikimedia Commons

Alice Masaryková, the chairwoman of the Czechoslovak Red Cross, daughter of T. G. Masaryk, atelier F. Drtikol
Photo: Drtikol František. © ČTK – Photo 2015.

Alice Masaryková, the chairwoman of the Czechoslovak Red Cross, daughter of T. G. Masaryk, atelier F. Drtikol
Photo: Drtikol František. © ČTK – Photo 2015.

Eva 'Mimi' Jiránková in 1938
© Ladislav Sitenský

Eva 'Mimi' Jiránková in Prague in 2012
© Josette Baer, 2012

Czechoslovak President Edvard Beneš and the chairwoman of the Czechoslovak Women's Council Dr. Milada Horáková, Prague, 1947.
Photo: Neznámý. © ČTK – Photo 2015.

Milada Horáková on trial in 1950
Source: Wikimedia Commons, © Cassius Chaerea.
Licensed under CC BY-SA 3.0
(s. https://creativecommons.org/licenses/by-sa/3.0/deed.de)

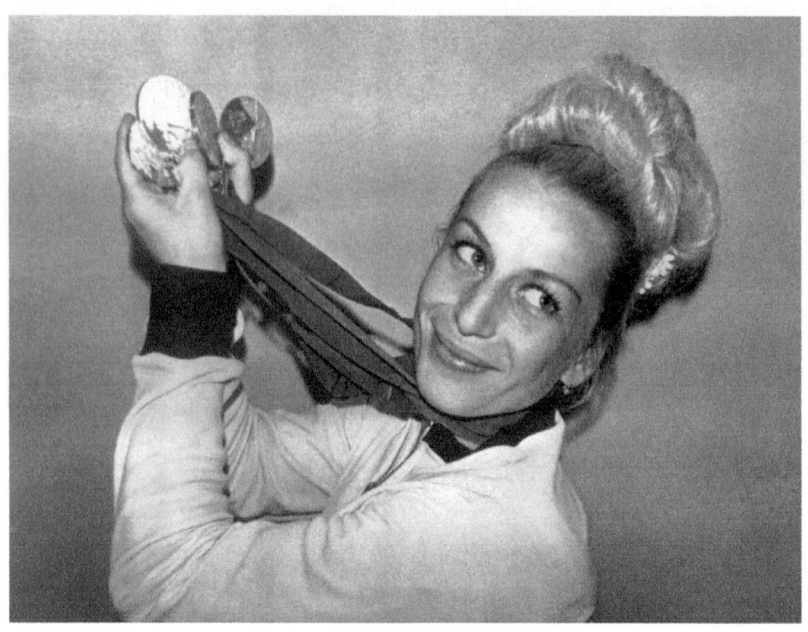

Věra Čáslavská-Odložilová, member of the Czechoslovak Olympic team with her four gold medals.
Photo: ČTK. © ČTK – Photo 2015.

Věra Čáslavská's famous lotus flower
Source: Wikimedia Commons, © Kroon, Ron / Anefo.
Licensed under CC BY-SA 3.0 NL
(s. https://creativecommons.org/licenses/by-sa/3.0/nl/deed.de)

Nataša Lišková in Prague in 2014
© Josette Baer, 2014

Tereza Maxová in 2012, surrounded by 'her' children
© Tereza Maxová Foundation for Children

Tereza Maxová in 2009
© Tereza Maxová Foundation for Children

**Terezie Sverdlinová,
the director of the Tereza Maxová Foundation for Children**
© Tereza Maxová Foundation for Children

V. Věra Čáslavská (*1942) – an Olympic champion punished with silence

> *"If I wanted to live in another country or thought badly about our society, I would have thousands of possibilities at my disposal to change my life. I would not have to live as miserably as I am living now. … With a quiet conscience I assure you, dear Comrade Husák, that I have nothing against Socialism. I hold, however, strong reservations about persons, who, in implementing your party's Russian policies, are doing its dirty work, violating even the most basic principles of the constitution."*[281]

V. 1 The historical context

When Věra Čáslavská was born on 3 May 1942 in Prague, Alice Masaryková was in exile in the USA, and Milada Horáková imprisoned in Pankrác. Mimi Zimmerová and Miloš Jiránek were enjoying their last months of freedom, a beautiful summer in Prague, occupied with preparations for their wedding that was scheduled for September. 24 days after Věra's birth, Josef Gabčik and Jan Kubiš would shoot Heydrich.

Věra's father had a little grocery shop, and her mother took care of the three girls. The family survived the Protectorate, and Věra and her sisters grew up in relative comfort. When the Communist Party assumed power in February 1948, their father's shop was nationalized, and he was assigned a manual job. The parents supported the girls' talents for dancing since their children were their only future. They could not imagine that Věra would one day

---

[281] Pavel Kosatík, *Věra Čáslavská. Život na Olympu. Autorizovaný životopis* (Praha: Mladá Fronta, 2012), 115.

become an Olympic champion. Neither did Věra imagine that she would become a target of the Party, a political person.

She was only ever interested in sports; she was no *homo politicus*, but she would prove with her resilience that she was a *zoon politikon*, a *citoyenne* who cared about her rights, a responsible member of the community, in the very sense that the great Aristotle saw human life as an element of that which matters to all: politics.

In this chapter, I will focus on how the Party treated the Olympic champion in the years of the normalization. Věra Čáslavská's life illustrates the pressure the Husák government was putting on citizens who refused to toe the line. Before I present the most important events of Věra's career and life after the Olympic games in Mexico City in 1968, a brief summary of the normalization shall introduce the reader to the political situation after the invasion of the Warsaw Pact troops in the night of 21 August 1968. Tanks ended the eight months of the Spring of Prague; Socialism with a Human Face was over.[282]

After the invasion, the Soviet Politburo was seeking to replace Dubček, which was no easy task, since there were no sensible options. Oldřich Černík (1921–1994) and Vasiľ Biľak (1917–2014) were candidates, and Brežnev offered the position to

---

[282] A selection: Gordon H. Skilling, *Czechoslovakia's Interrupted Revolution* (Princeton, NJ: Princeton University Press, 1976); Kieran Williams, *The Prague Spring and its Aftermath. Czechoslovak Politics 1968–1970* (Cambridge: Cambridge University Press, 1997); Dubček's memoirs *Leben für die Freiheit* (München: Bertelsmann, 1993); *Hope Dies Last. The Autobiography of Alexander Dubcek* (London: HarperCollins, 1993). For a chronology of 1968 see *Rok Šedesáty Osmý. V usneseních a dokumentech UV KSČ* (Praha: Svoboda, 1969); with a focus on Slovakia Valerián Bystrický a kol., *Rok 1968 na Slovensku a v Československu* (Bratislava: HÚ SAV, 2008); *Sedm pražských dnů. 21–27. srpen 1968. Dokumentace* (Praha: Academia, 1990); and Jan Pauer, *Prag 1968. Der Einmarsch des Warschauer Paktes. Hintergründe – Planung – Durchführung* (Bremen: Edition Temmen, 1995).

Černík, but Černík refused once he learnt what he was supposed to do. His conscience forbade him to implement the harsh neo-Stalinist measures the Soviets insisted on.[283] Biľak was no option: as one of the conservative Party members who had signed the letter of invitation to the Soviet Union for brotherly assistance, the people considered him a traitor. To appoint him General Secretary would lead to more unrest and bloodshed – the Soviet analysts were spot on.

This was Husák's hour: without a mandate from the KSČ, which could not make up its mind, he took matters into his own hands. He clandestinely met Brežnev on 13 April 1969 at the airport of Mukačevo (formerly the Soviet Republic of Ukraine, today Ukraine).[284] The Soviet Politburo subsequently suggested Comrade Husák. The Central Committee elected him General Secretary on 17 April 1969 after Dubček was forced to step down. The Soviets could now concentrate their forces on a most difficult task that was of global importance for the future of Socialism; they started to prepare the CSCE negotiations scheduled to begin in 1973. Most pressing to the Soviet Union was the recognition of the GDR's western border.

The normalization began: everybody in a higher position, writers, poets, doctors, academics, factory managers and teachers had to sign the official declaration that condemned the reforms of the Prague Spring as counter-revolutionary, publicly declaring the invasion and occupation as the rightful political course. The normalizers (*normalizátoři*) were responsible for putting the measures into practice, that is, placing loyal Party members in key positions and purging the institutions, factories, schools and academia. The goal was the *status quo ante* January 1968. The KSČ purged itself: in the first large wave of 1969/70, some 70,000

---

[283] Stanislav Sikora, *Po jari krutá zima. Politický vývoj na Slovensku v rokoch 1968–1971* (Bratislava: HÚ SAV, 2013), 118.
[284] Sikora, 126.

members were expelled (*vyloučený*), and some 400,000 suspended (*vyškrtnut*); those suspended got a second chance to prove their loyalty in a special hearing for which they had to apply.[285]

Apart from the normalizers, Czechoslovak society consisted of three groups or socio-political strata: the dissidents (*disidenti*) were a small group of approximately 200 to 300 citizens who obeyed the law, but refused to accept the social norms of the normalization, which resulted in their political persecution. They founded the *samizdat* in the mid-1970s and *Charter 77* in 1977.

The grey zone (*šedá zona*) consisted of citizens who refused Party membership but trod carefully in order not to lose their positions in the administration and academia.[286] The citizens (*obyvatelé a občané*), approximately ten million persons, were the largest group; they found a *modus vivendi* with the regime, trying to lead a normal life and securing their offspring's chances for higher education. They were careful not to draw the attention of the authorities to them.[287]

The only explanation and description of the normalization could be found in the document issued by the CC in December 1970, the *Lessons Learned from the Critical Developments in Party and State Following the XIII Congress of KSČ* (*Poučení z krizového vývoje ve straně a společnosti po XIII. sjezdu KSČ*).[288] The people conceived of the document as "the normalizers' simplistic catechism" and a

---

[285] Jan Měchýř, "O lidech v čase normalizace", in *Česká a slovenská společnost v období normalizace. Slovenská a česká spoločnosť v čase normalizácie. Liberecký seminar 2001* (Bratislava: Veda a Ústav politických vied SAV, 2003), 93-108; 96.

[286] Měchýř, 100. A prominent member of the grey zone was Václav Klaus, who worked at the Institute of Prognostics as an economist, was a principal figure of the OF in November 1989 and later founded the ODS.

[287] Měchýř, 99-100.

[288] "Poučení z krizového vývoje ve straně a společnosti po XIII. sjezdu KSČ" on http://www.totalita.cz/txt/txt_pouceni.php; accessed 15 May 2015.

"manifesto of neo-Stalinism" alike[289] that advocated the return to the old methods of governing: oppression of civil rights, censorship, closed borders, Prague's dominance in Slovak matters and a centrally planned economy according to the Soviet model.

A brief look at some figures illustrates the despair of the Czechoslovaks who withdrew from public life. The consumption of hard liquor, that is, drinks with an alcohol content of 40% and higher, increased dramatically during the years of the occupation: in the Czech part, in 1965 a citizen consumed an average of 2 litres of liquor per annum, in 1970 it was already 4.2 litres and in 1978 6.8 litres; the equivalent statistics for Slovak citizens' intake were: 4.3 litres in 1965, 9.5 litres in 1970 and 14.1 litres in 1978.[290]

The opposition against the normalization was stronger in the Czech lands than in Slovakia; the Czechs had specific historical experiences of political self-organization that united them in protest. The Slovaks, on the other hand, had had a different past: they were used to that politics were made from above, that the ordinary citizen had no say in politics. Until 1918, higher education had been available to the Slovaks only in a foreign language (Hungarian, German or Czech), and the economic structure was agrarian until the Communist government started to industrialize the country in the 1950s. Many Slovaks were grateful to the KSČ and KSS for building up industry and social institutions after WWII. Yet, the normalization affected everybody; those who spoke out against the Husák regime had to expect repression, regardless of their national identity.[291]

---

[289] Kováč, *Dejiny Slovenska*, 300.

[290] Juraj Marušiak, "Slovenská spoločnosť a normalizácia", in *Česká a slovenská společnost v období normalizace. Slovenská a česká spoločnosť v čase normalizácie. Liberecký seminar 2001* (Bratislava: Veda a Ústav politických vied SAV, 2003), 136.

[291] An excellent account of the opposition to the normalization and the persecution by the government is Jaroslav Pažout, "Trestněprávní

To illustrate the mechanisms of the normalization, I shall focus on two particularly interesting areas: first, the purges at the Faculty of Philosophy at Charles University in Prague,[292] and, second, the legal restrictions regulating foreign currency and travel.[293]

František Černý (1926–2010) was Professor of Drama Studies (*teatrologie*) and a renowned specialist in Czech theatre; after the Velvet Revolution of 1989 he was appointed dean of the Faculty of Philosophy. Černý witnessed the normalization at the faculty, and his memoirs provide us with a rare and personal insight.

The invasion happened in the summer holidays; many students did not bother to return to the university at the beginning of the winter term of 1968/69.[294] Those who did show up were united in protest: the last free meeting at the faculty took place from 21 to 23 April 1969, a few days after Dubček's abdication.[295] The students' academic council secretly convened and announced a strike. The result of the meeting was the manifesto of the Prague students that called for the re-establishment of civil rights, the re-establishment of the state's sovereignty and the academic freedom of research and teaching. The inviolability of the premises of the university should be guaranteed, and the academic functionaries democratically elected; the academic community should be granted self-organization and self-government without interference from

---

perzekuce odpůrců režimu v období tzv. Normalizace (1969–1989) – faktor stability a indikátor rozkladu kommunistického režimu", in *Český a slovenský komunismus (1921–2011)* (Praha: Ústav pro studium totalitních režimů 2012), 174-192.

[292] František Černý, *Normalizace na Pražské Filosofické fakultě (1968–1989). Vzpomínky* (Praha: Mnemosyne, Filosofická Fakulta Univerzity Karlova, 2009).

[293] Jan Rychlík, *Devisové přisliby a cestování do zahraničí v období normalizace* (Praha: Ústav pro soudobé dějiny AV ČR, 2012).

[294] Černý, 8.

[295] Černý, 10-11.

Party and state.[296] The StB called Deputy Dean Černý for interrogation at the infamous Bartolomejšská 4; yet, the StB had him just sit there for a couple of hours. They did not interrogate him, which was most probably just a first measure of humiliation and intimidation.

The authorities began to pressure the Faculty's governing body into obedience: academics who accepted the new course, among them persons without an international reputation who had not even published one book were 'elected' into the faculty's key positions. Persons who did not even have the *maturita* but excelled in their Marxist beliefs were catapulted into the highest academic positions.[297] Although the elections were conducted in secret, the political pressure beforehand pre-selected the candidates, and the plenum's members, already intimidated and fearing for their jobs, voted for the candidate they knew the authorities wanted. Some of the younger faculty members and hitherto unsuccessful academics saw their window of opportunity to achieve power, position and the concomitant rise in salary, social prestige and political reputation. Academics without political scruples occupied the positions of dean, deputy dean, prorector and rector. Naturally, the quality of research and teaching immediately plummeted. Revenge, envy, jealousy and ruthless ambition replaced academic excellence and scholarly talent.

Some of the best teachers and researchers were expelled, among them the famous literary scientist Václav Černý (1905–1987) and the philosopher Jan Patočka (1907–1977), the intellectual father of *Charter 77*. The philologist and expert in Russian linguistics Vladimír Barnet (1924–1983) committed suicide.[298] Others were offered a special arrangement: if they agreed to publicly declare that they had taken early retirement, they would receive a better

---

[296] Černý, 10.
[297] Černý, 28.
[298] Černý, 25.

reference,[299] keeping their pension. This way, their leave from the faculty looked like their personal decision, and nobody would see what was actually going on.

A small number of distinguished academics stayed on, and astonishingly few emigrated. Černý thinks that the main reason for their staying in the country was the academics' distinct sense of responsibility; they were committed to their students and did not want to leave in these difficult years.[300] As scholars and citizens, they were cast into oblivion; they were no threat to the regime anymore – or so the authorities must have thought. But they were still there, and the phenomenon of the 'black university' emerged: students and citizens, everybody interested in studying themes and topics that had been deleted from the universities' curricula used to gather in a flat to listen to a 'normalized' professor's lectures. The 'black university' was an element of the *parallel polis*,[301] an independent space, an area of civil society the authorities had no control over, a vanishing point. Eda Kriseová (*1940), a writer and close friend of the Havels, remembered how Professor Patočka's lectures impressed the listeners:

> "He was my professor, I attended his lectures about phenomenology. ... To him, Plato and Aristotle were not theoreticians in the modern sense, ... but individuals occupied with the basic human need to enquire about the meaning of life, ... nobody can relieve us from that responsibility. ... Not only students, but also teachers of the faculty came. These lectures were events, happenings. He never sat down, he used to walk through the room, gesticulating. ... When they expelled him from the Faculty of Philosophy, it was as if they had expelled Kant from Philosophy; some courageous citizens let him

---

[299] Černý, 25-26.
[300] Černý, 23.
[301] The philosopher Václav Bělohradský (*1944) coined the concept of 'parallel polis' to describe the dissidents' solidarity in his *Krize eschatology neosobnosti* (London: Rozmluvy, 1983).

use their flats for the so-called black university. ... Ten to fifteen persons attended his lectures, sitting on the floor, side by side. ... After his lecture, Professor Patočka went to collect signatures [for *Charter 77*, add. JB] with his old friend Zdeněk Urbánek who drove them. Allegedly, when he came back down breathless from a flat on the fifth floor, he always said: 'He did not sign, he will end up in hell too.' Many friends disappointed him."[302]

The guiding principle of the purges was 'divide et impera'. The normalizers separated those who still stubbornly supported Dubček's reform politics from the realists, who understood the terms of the trade and the fickle tides of political power in Central Europe. The authorities concentrated on forming a new academic body, pressuring the undecided into obedience with promises and threats. Naturally, the government could not sack the entire Faculty, since the students needed teachers to educate the next generation of scientists and researchers.

After the first large sweep, the normalizers in Party and faculty came to a decision about the already decimated personnel; the *ad hoc* decisions were largely influenced by personal animosities and affinities. This was more an arbitrary regime than a system with clear-cut rules, but it was quite effective: arbitrary decisions were spreading fear and insecurity among those who still had a job. One was advised to behave, to have good relations with the offices of the dean and the rector. But arbitrary rule, as is its nature, also led to unexpected results:

> "I have no explanation for the fact that I survived the purges at the Faculty of Philosophy. To this day, I do not understand it, since I was vice-dean from 1966 to 1969 and acting dean during the eventful days of Jan Palach's death, replacing the dean who was on sick leave.

---

[302] Eda Kriseová, *Václav Havel. Životopis* (Praha: Atlantis, 1991), 72, 74. Zdeněk Urbánek (1917–2008) was a writer and translator and a member of *Charter 77*. In Poland, the phenomenon of the 'black university' was called 'the flying university'.

> The sad days after Palach's suicide brought me into the public eye; I spoke on TV and the broadcast the night before his funeral. Also, I had published quite extensively in the 1960s ... From the archives of the StB that were opened in the 1990s it transpires that the StB considered me a person hostile to the regime for my activities as deputy dean."[303]

If we believe Černý's account, and I think that he was truthful in his memoirs, there is one reason that can explain why he was spared: the long-term policy of the StB Václav Havel so aptly described in 1979:

> "You know much better than anybody else that the decision whether to arrest Gruša or Vaculík has absolutely nothing to do with the risk each of them took, but everything to do with the regime's cold and cynical calculations. In terms of tactics, it is sometimes more advisable to arrest Gruša to intimidate Vaculík; sometimes it is better to arrest Vaculík to intimidate Gruša."[304]

With the goal of positioning normalizers in key faculty positions achieved, the strategy of the StB was to gain full control over the smooth functioning of the personnel at the Faculty of Philosophy. Certainly, Havel's quote refers to dissident colleagues who had made their decision to speak out. Yet, I think that specific tactical calculations of the StB can explain why Professor Černý could keep his position.

We cannot know the exact reasons why the authorities spared Černý, but I deem it possible that they had considered the following, which is, of course, speculation. I think that a clever Party

---

[303] Černý, 45-46.
[304] Václav Havel, "Milý pane Ludvíku (25 leden 1979)", in *O lidskou identitu. Úvahy, fejetony, protesty, polemiky, prohlášení a rozhovory z let 1969–1979* (Praha: Rozmluvy, 1990), 204-206; 204. In his letter, Havel criticised Vaculík's suggestion to publish the dissidents' texts anonymously, which would have broken the principle of legality the dissidents adhered to.

functionary familiar with the situation at the faculty would reason as follows: 'Leave that František Černý alone now, for the time being. We have the faculty under control; we have sacked the most notorious members of the reaction. Theatre and drama studies are not politically sensitive areas such as historiography or political science. We need to keep some of our experts as an alibi to demonstrate to the citizens and the West that we are not persecuting intellectuals for political reasons. If Černý behaves, fine. If he does not, we can always offer him early retirement, and if he won't accept that, we can still sack him for his counter-revolutionary activities back in 1968.'

To us in the 21st century, going on a trip with family or friends, booking a flight and a hotel and hiring a car is very easy; thanks to the Internet and the credit card system, holidays and trips can be arranged within minutes.

To the Czechoslovak citizen in the 1970s and 1980s, who wanted to visit relatives in the West or make a trip to the countries of the Socialist bloc, travelling abroad was a lengthy and nerve-racking endeavour that required time, patience, personal relations with the authorities and, above all, money. The normalization regime did not conceive of travelling and tourism as a human right; it did not acknowledge freedom of movement. Mobility was a political issue, a privilege bestowed on those who deserved it because they were reliable in political terms.[305]

On 21 December 1970 (č. 142/1970 Sb), the government issued a new bill of law about foreign currency: citizens wanting to travel to the West and Yugoslavia as tourists, hence not on a business trip, had to apply for a foreign currency exchange permit (*devisový příslib*).[306] With the permit granted by the authorities, they then had

---

[305] Rychlík, *Devisové přisliby...*, 30.
[306] Rychlík, *Devisové přisliby...*, 19.

to apply for a special exit permit (*výjezdní doložka*) that was attached to the passport. Anyone who did not have a valid passport had to apply for one. The maximum permitted length of stay abroad was 20 days. The citizen had to exchange Czechoslovak crowns for foreign currency at a branch of the ČSNB and could leave the country only with a valid exit permit. This system was based on political and economic considerations: the government held the monopoly of foreign currency and was intent on imposing restrictions on citizens travelling to the West and Yugoslavia – from where they could easily get to the countries of Western Europe. To the Czechoslovaks, Yugoslavia as a member of the NAM was the way to the West, to freedom, since it allowed its citizens free movement. Once on Yugoslav territory one did not require an exit permit.

The Czechoslovak State Bank issued a limited number of foreign currency exchange permits every year in January. To apply for one, a citizen needed the stamp of his employer. Every citizen had the opportunity, not the constitutional right (!), to apply[307] for a foreign currency exchange permit once a year in January, but this did not yet mean that he or she would automatically receive the permit. The system was prone to corruption and nepotism; some citizens received permits for several trips to the West in one year, while others, who had no personal contacts at the offices issuing the permits, never received one.

A special commission investigating the activities of the Brno branch of the ČSNB found the following:

> "The branch issued foreign currency exchange permits to 340 applicants who went on private trips to the West in the years from 1977 to 1979. 243 of these applicants neither lived in Brno nor worked there. ... 38 functionaries of the local CC of the KSČ went to Vienna on 12 April 1980, where they met members of the Austrian

---

[307] Rychlík, *Devisové přisliby*..., 23.

Communist Party. ... The director of the bank's local branch got off with a disciplinary warning."[308]

The Czechoslovak crown was not freely convertible, which also made trips to the brotherly countries of the Socialist bloc very difficult. Citizens wanting to visit Bulgaria, the GDR, Hungary, Mongolia, Poland, Romania or the Soviet Union did not have to apply for an exit permit, but needed an invitation from a citizen of the state they wanted to visit as well as the foreign currency exchange permit.

Given these barriers, it is no wonder that an ordinary Czechoslovak citizen did not even try to travel – it was just too much of a hassle. On Friday afternoons, citizens left Prague and Bratislava, drove to their *chalupas* and *chaťas* in the countryside, met up with friends for a barbecue, listened to music, read books, drank some wine or home-made *šlivovica* and just relaxed. Věra would never relax.

V. 2 From Olympic stardom to social isolation

Věra Čáslavská inherited her talent for sports from her father.[309] To be successful in artistic gymnastics, one needs not only a special talent, but also the right physique to perform the difficult movements. Like Olga Korbut (*1955), the Soviet Olympic champion of Munich 1972, and Nadia Comaneci (*1961), the Romanian Olympic champion of 1976, Věra had an athletic, almost male physique with long and strong legs, narrow hips and wide shoulders. From childhood onwards, she was always moving; she was full of energy and used to play football with boys. She not only had talent, but was also physically fit; her endurance seemed to have no limits. From a very young age, she was conditioning her body, albeit not yet consciously. She just loved to move and could not sit still. One of the

---

[308] Rychlík, *Devisové přisliby*..., 32.
[309] Kosatík, 13.

sisters' tasks was to get coal from the cellar to heat the flat. Hana and Eva soon tired of walking down four floors and carrying up the heavy bucket and struck a deal with their youngest sister: each time Věra would fetch coal, they would give her a little picture with a saint, thus contributing to her collection.[310]

All three sisters had ballet lessons, as the parents' wish was that the girls should have a better life with a solid education. That education was not necessarily an academic one. I think that the parents, both from modest origins, could rather imagine their girls as celebrities, as artists who would perform in public, than as doctors, teachers or lawyers. Hana became a ballet dancer and Věra an Olympic champion, only Eva chose a different profession: she studied economics. In 1948, the three started to perform at the Lucerna in Prague city centre and the cute little Čáslavské girls were soon very popular.[311] They performed for Hana Benešová at the Castle and later for Marta Gottwaldová.

In the 21st century, gymnasts are very young, a new phenomenon of artistic gymnastics that began with the Soviet gymnast Olga Korbut who was 15 years old when she won gold in Munich in 1972. At the age of 15, thus quite old already, Věra decided to focus on artistic gymnastics after a few stints with figure skating and ballet.

An Olympic champion needs not only talent and the right physique, but most important is, I think, an iron will. Top-class sport at an international level requires daily training, discipline and the mental strength to deal with failure and perform under pressure. Věra had all these characteristics. She decided to take up serious training in gymnastics after meeting Eva Bosáková (1931–1991), whom she saw first in a TV show in 1957.[312] Věra's mother invited

---

[310] Kosatík, 15.
[311] Kosatík, 20.
[312] Kosatík, 27.

Eva and asked her to coach her daughter. Eva agreed, and Věra started to go to the sports hall where Eva was training. Often, however, Eva was not there, so Věra was on her own, familiarizing herself with the four disciplines of artistic gymnastics: vault, balance beam, uneven bars and floor exercise. On 13 April 1957 she wrote in her diary that she had tried the uneven bars for the first time.[313]

After a few months, coach Vladimír Prorok supervised Věra's training. Women's gymnastics in the late 1950s was just beginning to develop; in schools, physical education was limited to athletics.[314] Věra's discipline and iron will were extraordinary; she had no fear and was always trying to improve her training regime. Her ease during training sessions was quite remarkable:

> "In the first two years, I was practising the vault … I told myself: today, I'll do ten forward loops and five backwards. Then I was done. … Often, I was thinking of something else or talking to somebody and, without any preparation or concentration, I started to run and did the vault. Coach Prorok often reproached me that I was not focussed, but I could not understand exactly what I was supposed to focus on."[315]

Her favourite discipline was the floor exercise.[316] To move in the rhythm of the music reminded her of her early ballet lessons and figure skating. To her, gymnastics was a kind of communication with the public, a particular way of expressing herself. She taught herself the backward somersault without any instruction or supervision; she started with quick backward loops until her hands stopped touching the floor.

---

[313] Kosatík, 28.
[314] Kosatík, 33.
[315] V. Čáslavská: Vavříny rostou z dřiny, *Sportovní-umělecká gymnastika* č. 3, r. 13, březen 1963, s. 8, quoted from Kosatík, 34-35.
[316] Kosatík, 35.

The balance beam was her least favourite discipline: she was afraid of the beam that is 10 cm wide, 1.25m high and 5 meters long. To us spectators following international competitions in artistic gymnastics, the balance beam is a highly aesthetic discipline, but it is also nerve-racking. To watch gymnasts doing somersaults backwards or a handstand on one hand, and all this on a 10-cm-wide beam, is stomach-churning. A microsecond of wrong movement – and the gymnast falls. In her most feared discipline, Věra would win the gold medal at the Olympic games in Tokyo in 1964 and the silver medal in Mexico in 1968.[317] In Tokyo, she would perform, as the first gymnast ever, a 360º pirouette on her right knee. Another famous element of her routine was the 'lotus flower'.

Sport was the most important part of the young gymnast's life, yet Věra did not neglect her education. After she had accomplished compulsory education at the age of 14, she started to take evening classes at the workers' evening school of economics and learnt stenography and typewriting. Thanks to Eva Bosáková, who always treated her younger competitor in a friendly and supportive fashion, Věra got a job as a typist at the Central Committee of the Czechoslovak Association of Physical Education and Sport (ČSTV). From early morning until lunchtime she worked, in the afternoon she was in the hall and in the evenings she attended the courses at the workers' school.

After her great success at the Olympic games in Tokyo, Věra decided to make significant changes in her private life and training: she moved out of her parents' flat into a little *garsonka* that the Association gave her and also changed her coach: Jaroslava Matlochová was the coach of the national team and her approach to

---

[317] "Věra Čáslavská at the Olympic Games" on http://www.olympic.org/vera-caslavska; accessed 17 May 2015.

gymnastics was different from Prorok's, whose focus was on the discipline's aesthetic and artistic aspects.[318]

In the years of the Cold War, sport became an ideological weapon of the Eastern European bloc; the governments invested millions in training and also doping to demonstrate to the Capitalist West that Socialism was a system that supported a healthy lifestyle and was, in every respect, superior. Under the influence of Soviet instructors and coaches, Matlochová, who a few years earlier had refused to coach Věra, because she had thought that the teenager was too weak, concentrated on getting her ready for the next Olympic games. Her training days always started with reading press releases that were designed to strengthen the girls' ideological awareness and unity in training and competition. The goal was to eliminate individualism and make the girls a team: at the beginning of each training session, one gymnast had to read a brief newspaper article that taught the girls that they were living under a superior system. In this regard, gymnastics was to Matlochová like war.[319] Věra's concentration improved; she now looked at her discipline as a kind of struggle, also against herself, her own weaknesses and fears.

When the public overwhelmingly supported the Soviet gymnast Natalia Kučinskaia at the World Championships in Dortmund in 1966, Věra was disappointed. She was used to being the public's darling, especially in Tokyo. She lost weight, changed her hairstyle and developed a completely new routine in all four disciplines. She wanted to perform what nobody else before her had done. She wrote in her training diary what she planned to achieve in her training that lasted five hours:

---

[318] Kosatík, 69.
[319] Kosatík, 69.

"25 Yamashita vaults, 5 backward somersaults ... 10 rondats and saltos from the beam. At the uneven bars 5 times the compulsory elements ... In one year, from autumn to autumn, I did 4320 Yamashitas."[320]

Věra was not a political person, but she noticed the political change in January 1968, when Alexander Dubček was elected First Secretary of the Party. The liberalization led to a wave of independent articles, the foundation of civic groups, and for the first time since 1948 citizens were allowed to travel to the Capitalist West. Tourists from the West poured into the country, and the new liberty created an almost euphoric atmosphere. There seemed to be no limits; the Dubček government was working on a draft of a new economic programme that should improve the hitherto low economic performance.

However, when the writer Ludvík Vaculík (*1926), in his manifesto *2000 Words*, called for an end to the KSČ's monopoly of power, the Soviet Union's patience with the Czechoslovak comrades was at an end. Věra was among the first 70 citizens to sign the manifesto after its publication on 27 June 1968.[321] Little did she know that she would have to pay a high price for this modest expression of civic freedom.

On 21 August, she was in a training camp in Šumperk for the last intensive preparations before the Olympic games. She woke up at four o'clock in the morning and saw the Polish tanks. She was so shocked that she forgot her training; her coach had to fetch her from the street. After they returned from the Moscow negotiations, Dubček, Černík, Smrkovský and President Svoboda received the Olympic team at the Castle. The citizens did not yet know what awaited them: the return to the old style of governance. But the

---

[320] V. Čáslavská-Odložilová: *Cesta na Olymp*, Praha 1972, s.14-15, quoted from Kosatík, 75.
[321] Kosatík, 77.

government knew that its reform politics were finished; they had high hopes for the Olympic team, and the sportsmen and sportswomen were eager to win to teach the Soviets a lesson. The Czechoslovaks could do nothing against the Warsaw Pact tanks, but they could beat the Soviets in sports. The Czechoslovak ice hockey team would beat the Soviets in the 1969 world championship, a match of historic proportions that showed the whole world how the Czechoslovaks fought against the occupier.

Mexico was the highlight of Věra's career as a gymnast and also her private life. She won four gold medals: individual all-round, vault, floor and uneven bars. She won silver on the balance beam, and her team came second to the Soviet Union in the team competition. The international public understood very well what her gesture on the podium meant: when the Soviet hymn was playing for Larissa Petryk, with whom she had to share the gold medal for the floor exercise, Věra turned her head to the right, away from the flag and looked down to the floor.[322] Her gesture of silent protest wrote Olympic history.

After the games were over, she married her boyfriend Josef Odložil (1938–1993), a middle-distance runner (1500 m) and Olympic champion in 1964 and 1968. The civil wedding took place at the Czechoslovak embassy on 26 October; thousands of fans attended the wedding in the cathedral. The Archbishop of Prague, František Tomášek, later thanked her in a personal letter for her courage in choosing to marry in church.[323]

When Věra and Josef returned to Prague, the good times were soon over, her triumph quickly forgotten. The Dubček government received the Olympic team to thank the members for their successes. Věra, who had decided to end her career in sports after

---

[322] Kosatík, 87; "Olympic Games Mexico 68 Vera Caslavska" on https://www.youtube.com/watch?v=lksI8O8_u7M; accessed 17 May 2015.
[323] Kosatík, 90.

the Mexico games, was looking forward to her future. She wanted to have children and a normal family life; she planned to study at the Faculty of Physical Education and then work as a coach, like her older colleagues did.[324] Yet for the next five years she could not find employment.

The authorities implementing the politics of normalization did not forget what she had signed in 1968. Emil Zátopek and his wife, who had also signed Vaculík's manifesto, were forced to condemn their act in public, and Zátopek vanished from public life for years. Jiří Raška, a famous ski jumper, refused to confess his 'error' until functionaries of the ČSTV threatened him with dissolving the entire ski association.[325] The normalizers concentrating their efforts on the nation's sports associations had but one more to break: the 27-year-old Věra.

The first problem that arose was the contract she had signed with the publisher Mladá Fronta for her autobiography; at the end of 1969, she had her manuscript ready, since she was on maternity leave and had time to write. Ota Pavel (1930–1973), a well-known writer and sports journalist, liked it and forwarded it to the printers. In 1970, however, censorship was re-established, and a well-meaning editor instructed Věra how to change her manuscript with ironic advice:

> "Due to well-known reasons, delete any criticism of politics or remarks that can be seen as hostile to the current ideology. That means: delete the introduction and significantly shorten the chapter about the Castle. Do not quote anybody or refer to those who were there ... it is advisable to mention the Russians so that nobody can reproach you that you don't like them or that you are allergic to them. This is first and foremost a question of wording, certain clever

---

[324] Kosatík, 97.
[325] Kosatík, 107.

tricks – but you can keep your natural and rightful aloofness regarding their generosity and sovereignty."[326]

After many corrections, Věra's memoirs were finally published in 1972 with an edition of 94,000 copies; a second edition or reprint was not allowed.[327] The authorities rejected a very lucrative offer from Hollywood to perform in a movie about her life; Japanese companies that wanted her to advertise their products in Japan, where she had been an admired celebrity since the 1964 Olympic games, were no more successful. The authorities' standard answer was that Mrs Čáslavská was no longer representing the nation abroad, since she had not altered her behaviour. Her immense success in Mexico was forgotten.

Věra was now a *persona non grata*, in the truest sense of the word: she vanished from TV, newspapers and magazines. Her name did not even appear in the memoirs of the famous Soviet gymnast Larisa Latynina (*1943), her former competitor: she was referred to as "the Czech".[328] An admirer who had followed the European championship in women's gymnastics in Minsk on TV in 1971, wrote her a letter:

> "I was very sad about the fact that, in the breaks, our television reporters talked about all the women who had achieved something in this discipline. But you did not get the slightest mention. This was like talking about physics and forgetting Einstein."[329]

I think that Věra gathered her strength from her children; her daughter Radka was born in 1969 and her son Martin in 1974. All her attempts at finding a position failed. She must have felt as though

---

[326] V. Novák V. Čáslavské, b.d. strojopis, archiv V. Č., quoted from Kosatík, 109.
[327] Kosatík, 110.
[328] Kosatík, 112.
[329] Došlá korespondence 19. 10. 1971, archiv V. Č., quoted from Kosatík, 112.

she were in an endless nightmare, a kind of evil bubble she was thrown into for her refusal to cave into the pressure. President Svoboda who had been so kind to her at the Castle's reception in 1968, and to whom she turned in despair, did not receive her. He had his personal assistant tell her in a single sentence: "It is human to commit errors, but to insist on a lie is devilish."[330]

General Secretary Husák was more forthcoming. He received her, and they talked for an hour. Husák tried to convince her to rescind her signature of the manifesto, arguing that everybody had to make compromises in these difficult times. Věra's position was clear: she just could not see the occupation as 'brotherly help' and insisted that, according to the constitution, she had the right to work, to be employed. She had the impression that the General Secretary did somehow understand her and was proud of her courage to speak her mind.[331] When she left, Husák asked her what she was occupying herself with at the moment. The Olympic champion replied that she was painting, spending her time with oil paintings. In those difficult days, with a little baby at home and relying on the salary of her husband Josef, Věra concentrated on art. Painting was to her an inner need, not the beginning of a new career. Painting was relaxing to her; it distracted her from the pressure the Party, the ČSTV, the Ministry of the Interior and the Association of Gymnastics were putting on her:

> "Be reasonable, nothing will happen to you. Your stubbornness will gain you nothing. I am not being stubborn, I am normal – was her answer."[332]

Věra was of course disappointed – who would not be? The authorities were not subtle in their threats: a faked arrest was staged

---

[330] Kosatík, 115.
[331] Kosatík, 116.
[332] Kosatík, 116.

in an attempt to intimidate her and make her fear for her and little Radka's life. Some agents came to her apartment, had her and Radka seated in a car and then drove them away. Yet, the petty action did not prompt any change; an officer sitting to her left and one to her right tried to press her into issuing a public statement.[333] Věra cried, not because she was afraid, but because she could not bear the humiliation and the injustice. When the agents saw that she would not cave in, they released her and Radka, left them standing in the street and did not escort them back home.

In view of the abominable way the government was treating her, Věra could no longer enjoy the memories of her triumph at the Olympic Games. Her great success was no longer important to her. She used her medals from Mexico to distract her daughter Radka, who loved to play with them. She started to study at the Faculty of Physical Education and Sport and thoroughly enjoyed her courses, since they ended her social isolation. Finally, she was among people again and showed a distinct talent for the psychology course. Three weeks before she gave birth to her son Martin, she graduated from the Faculty in August 1974.[334]

After the CSCE treaty had been signed in 1975, the Soviet Union lessened the ideological pressure a bit. Věra, who had been applying for the position of official coach since her graduation in 1974, received an offer from Mexico in 1979: she was asked to train some hundreds of young girls and build up Mexico's future generation of gymnasts.[335] The Mexican authorities also made an offer to Josef, which was her condition for signing the contract. In April 1979, they moved with their two young children to Mexico and would work there for two years.

---

[333] Kosatík, 117.
[334] Kosatík, 125.
[335] Kosatík, 130.

Josef, who, like Věra, had always refused to join the Party, became estranged from her; it was a long process of disintegration, since they had different views about the childrens' education and an altogether different attitude to life. Josef seemed to be jealous of his wife's popularity in Mexico, where thousands of citizens gave the "Queen of Mexico" an overwhelming welcome.[336] His contract terminated earlier, and he returned to Prague.

Věra loved her life in Mexico; she worked in three jobs, and when her contract was terminated in the summer of 1981, she went back home with her children. The Olympic champion had difficult years ahead: she would eventually file for divorce in 1987. Věra had not signed *Charter 77* and had not been active in politics, but that did not matter to President Havel, who knew from his own experience what it meant to be under the surveillance of the normalization authorities. Havel invited her to join his team at the beginning of 1990 and gave her a job she loved. She was appointed Director of Social Affairs, taking care of citizens' complaints and claims.

In 1997, she broke down and had to be hospitalized for almost a decade. She was not only physically exhausted after years of working tirelessly at the Castle, but the circumstances of the death of her ex-husband Josef were the last straw. She fell into a deep depression that could not be healed, since she refused to take the medication the country's best psychiatrists prescribed.

Her son Martin was wrongly accused of having murdered Josef in a row in a pub. Martin used to address his estranged father with Mr Odložil; Josef had never cared about the children, he did not spend time with them and had always gone his own way. The circumstances of his death were reminiscent of fate in a Greek tragedy, involving love, hatred, envy, jealousy, and death – human

---

[336] Kosatík, 133.

passions that, singly, can be managed or controlled. Yet, a fateful combination of these passions can result in violent death.

On an August night in 1993, Josef, visibly drunk, went to a discotheque in the Moravian village of Jeseniky, where he had built his weekend *chalupa*. They had bought some land in the years of their marriage and a plot was assigned to Věra in the divorce proceedings; she spent her weekends in her own cottage just a couple of metres away from her ex-husband's place. That night, Martin was celebrating with friends at the discotheque; he did not know that his father was there, until he saw him on the dance floor.[337] Josef, drunk as he was, hit some of Martin's female friends. A fight started, and Martin, defending his girl friend, hit Josef. He fell down and was hospitalized. On 10 September, one month after the accident, the doctors at the hospital in Olomouc stated that he had died of a brain haemorrhage.

The Czech popular press, supported by Josef's family, was merciless; instructed by its Western teachers, it had quickly learnt that bloodlust sells. It portrayed Martin as a murderer and Věra as a bad mother, who allegedly had seduced her son into getting rid of her ex-husband in order not to have to share the property they had acquired during their marriage. This was too much for her. Věra spent a decade in hospitals and hospices, but she eventually pulled through and was able to live on her own again in 2007.

President Havel granted Martin, who had been convicted of murder in an unfair trial in 1996, amnesty in 1997. In 2009, Věra made a modest comeback thanks to a sports gala broadcast by Czech Television and she gave a few interviews to the press. The Olympic champion lives quietly in Prague.

---

[337] Kosatík, 182.

V. 3 Conclusion

Was Věra a feminist? In terms of her activities, she certainly was. But did she see herself as a champion of women's liberation? I doubt it.

She worked hard and her extraordinary talent and iron discipline made her an Olympic champion. The mindset, the mental strength, is of crucial importance for an athlete. The beautiful blond gymnast was the darling of Czechoslovakia, not only because she had the courage to protest with a silent gesture while standing on the podium in Mexico City. Věra was the perfect embodiment of a young female citizen of a Socialist country, a female role model of Socialism: beautiful, successful, disciplined, and, literally, a good sport, a girl, a comrade. An approachable young women, a friend, who is not arrogant, a girl women and men can go to the pub with for a beer after work. She seemed to be the dream girl of Socialism, but weeks after her return from Mexico, the authorities purged her from public life because of her courage and determination. The dream girl did not behave as expected; she had to be punished with silence. Yet, the dream girl would persevere and prove her mental strength more than once: Věra overcame her serious illness, caused by a combination of physical exhaustion and psychological duress.

Feminism was no issue to her. She just did what she was good at and took the chances life offered her. She once said:

> "I was very hard on myself. The confrontation with the stronger sex never interested me, on the contrary."[338]

Thanks to YouTube, where one can find broadcasts of her performances at the Olympic Games, Věra will always be remembered for her elegance and beauty. Her mental strength can teach us a lot: when she was preparing, as the youngest member of the national team, for the Olympics in Tokyo, she was driven by what

---

[338] Kosatík, 182.

she referred to as "fiendish ambition" (*pekelná touha*).[339] We can learn a lot from her fiendish ambition with respect to daily discipline, strength of will and dedication, in good times as well as bad – whatever it is we occupy ourselves with.

---

[339] Kosatík, 46.

VI. Nataša Lišková (*1949) – a Czechoslovak citizen (OHI)

Nataša Lišková[340] was born in 1949 in Prague; she witnessed the Prague Spring, the normalization period and the Velvet Revolution. She lives in Prague and spends her time in the countryside, taking care of her three grandchildren. Mimi Jiránková and Nataša got to know each other in 1968 when Nataša studied for a couple of months in London, where she became friends with Mimi's daughter Tina.

JB: Dear Nataša, can you describe to our readers the atmosphere during the Prague Spring? You were allowed to travel and censorship had ceased.

NL: In 1967, I finished my secondary schooling and, as the state authorities were generous, I was allowed to travel to England. Later, as a student at the London Polytechnic, I even got permission to stay till the end of my course in June 1968. I had the great advantage of having well-situated relatives in London: Natasha Fisherová was my aunt. She and my mother were born in Russia and fled the Soviet Union on false passports in 1929. After attempts to settle in Constantinople, Athens and Paris, they at last found some comfort in Prague. John Fisher, my aunt's husband, was born in the Moravian town of Ostrava; it is difficult to say what nationality he considered himself to be, since he was the eldest son of a Jewish family, born in 1917 in the Austro-Hungarian Empire. He managed to escape from Prague before 1939. After the war he returned to Prague and left the country legally in 1948.

---

[340] Oral History Interview, Prague, 12 September 2014, 18.00-19.15, conducted in Czech.

This background may explain some of my later decisions. I first met Mimi and Tina in 1967. My aunt had a lot of friends among the Czechoslovak émigré community in London and introduced me to some of the young people who were my age. Mimi and her husband could not imagine ever returning to Czechoslovakia but they managed to teach Tina Czech and, in the 1960s, English society defined their social class as "Bohemian". What a relief and chance for me to meet a Czech-speaking girl who was my age.

The Beatles, Jimmy Hendrix or love at first sight were nothing compared with the Prague Spring. I left London after my studies, passed my entrance exams at the Faculty of Journalism at Charles University in Prague and joined, in spite of my family's protests, a group of students who enrolled in a students' exchange programme to build cowsheds in Siberia.

JB: Was the invasion of the Warsaw Pact troops on 21 August 1968 a complete surprise or did Czechoslovak citizens suspect that the Soviets would intervene?

NL: Who could believe that in peacetime, five civilized European countries could invade their neighbour with tanks and troops? I heard the news of the invasion, the so-called "friendly assistance in difficult times", on the radio while I was on a four-day trip with friends, travelling by train from Novosibirsk to Leningrad. By paying a huge amount of money, we managed to get air tickets and landed in Prague on 30 August. None of us could have imagined then that the troops would stay in our country for more than twenty years!

JB: How did a normal day in your life look after the invasion?

NL: In my "history" of surviving under the totalitarian regime, the question was not one of "life or death", but of "better or worse". So the most difficult decision was whether I should emigrate or stay.

Should I leave for England whilst pregnant and stay with a man who could not understand why my relatives wanted to stay in Czechoslovakia? Or should I stay in Prague and try to make our lives better? Do I want to be a refugee? No, I thought, and made a decision: let's fight together, with my family in Prague.

I studied journalism at Charles University. In 1969, the government introduced the so-called *Marxák*, a compulsory course instructing students in the basic principles of the international workers' movement, naturally to instil loyalty to the regime. Marxist-Leninist ideology was also a compulsory part of the state exam at my faculty. Those students who did not pass the state exam lost their place at the university. I remember my graduation in 1973: the local committee of KČS praised me for my excellent grades in the political course, upon which somebody in the public shouted 'That must be a real b…!'

JB: How did you live through the normalization?

NL: With regard to the "normalization", the loss of illusion would be a suitable explanation for persons of my age, but the loss of reliability or even credibility was such a disillusion; it taught us to be cautious.

The worst thing was the schizophrenic lifestyle: to get by on a daily basis in a system you detest but can't openly criticize; to pretend and lie on a daily basis to protect oneself and one's family from political oppression. But somehow we survived with the support of our families and friends. Good relationships proved to be stronger than politics. I spent time in the mountains with my friends. Surrounded by people we could trust, with a shared sense of humour and absurdity, we were able to fight idiocy, evil, violence and humiliation. Our greatest wish was that oneday the Communists would disappear.

I started to write for a children's magazine and worked as a production assistant in Czechoslovak television; by gradually climbing up the ladder I became a freelance journalist and presenter. I was asked to join the Communist Party, which I refused. I was invited to become an informer of the StB, which I refused. In 1984, I was blacklisted, but I found a job as a promoter of jogging. Be fit whilst queuing for meat, mandarins and toilet paper! Work was a duty; according to our constitution, he who did not work was persecuted as a criminal. I used to work from 7.30 am to 4.30 pm, but there was not much to be done. The regime pretended to pay us, and we citizens pretended to work.

JB: What did you think of Gustáv Husák, who is considered the bogeyman, the principal politician who introduced the regime of normalization?

NL: Husák is a symbol for lost hopes and chances, which the political climate opened up in the late 1960s. Normalization was a tough regime, suppressing any individuality. Specialists lost their jobs and worked as window cleaners. Children were not allowed to study at university because of their parents' political views. There were writers with no chance to publish. There was a lack of goods though all firms claimed 100% fulfilment of the planned production. There was also the restriction on travelling to the West. Special shops offered rare goods for those who had hard currency (US dollars, British pounds, etc). There was that fear that your neighbour might inform StB that you were listening to Radio Free Europe. The envy. Forget your character and cooperate so that you can be better off, in a material and political sense.

All people are equal, but the chosen ones were really more than equal. Those who did not accept that way of life started to build their own micro world, repairing huts and farms in the countryside and having fun to survive.

JB: The Czechoslovak federation was the only reform of the Prague Spring that survived the normalization. What did Czech citizens think about the federation?

NL: The federation came into being on the initiative of the Slovaks, but nothing really changed: we still shared a currency and had our Czechoslovak identity cards. In Slovakia though, they had great books, thrillers, crime novels – just interesting literature. The political atmosphere in Slovakia was more liberal than in the Czech part, in spite of the fact that the boss of Slovak Television was probably an even bigger idiot than the boss of Czech Television. On Mondays, we used to watch the show *Bratislava Mondays* on TV; they showed great theatre plays. In terms of identity, I was a *Pražačka,* a citizen of Prague.

We had our national Czechoslovak sports teams, such as our famous ice hockey team that beat the Soviets in the world championship in 1969. Ondrej Nepela and Karol Divín were famous figure skaters, and we considered them Czechoslovaks. We Czechs all understood Slovak and the Slovaks understood us. I understand why the young today no longer understand Slovak. To my generation, it was natural, since we had a daily course of Slovak on radio and TV, but of course, if you are not challenged, if you don't learn and study, if your little grey cells, to quote Hercule Poirot, are not working … The Slovak language has always been a fact, and the Czechs and Slovaks were two nations, each with its own language. That's why I think that the Slovak language law, issued by the Mečiar government after the separation of 1993, was a sign of an inferiority complex. The Slovak TV presenter Adela Banášová, who fronted the Czechoslovak superstar, is the best example: she understands Czech, speaks Slovak and presented a show that brought young Slovaks and Czechs together.

JB: When Mikhail S. Gorbačev came to power in March 1985, what did you think? Did his election to General Secretary of the Soviet Communist Party raise hopes that something would change?

NL: At first glance, Gorbačev was different from all Soviet leaders we had known. He was younger, seemed more intelligent and less dogmatic than the former leaders Andropov and Černenko. He was just a different type of leader. But it would last some time – 1989 was still a long way to go. We admired what was happening in Poland – Solidarnośc was successfully contesting Soviet might. But the Poles didn't have the Soviet Army in their country; we Czechoslovaks had Soviet soldiers everywhere.

In 1989, hundreds of East Germans climbed over the fence of the West Germany Embassy in Prague and we saw it on TV! This was a great encouragement for the Czechoslovak nation!

After the Velvet Revolution, we experienced times like in the Wild West: our constitution was like an Emmental cheese – full of holes, which was an advantage to those who benefitted from the economic transformation, the privatization of state factories. Old networks of StB personnel and Communist politicians were most successful, enriching themselves. They had no sense of responsibility towards the people.

We are the last generation that grew up in peaceful times. If you look at the world today – Islamic State's ravages, civil war in Ukraine. My biggest wish is peace; my grandchildren should grow up in a peaceful world.

JB: Nataša, do you have a personal motto, a fundamental principle?

NL: Yes, don't do to others what you don't want them to do to you.

JB: Dear Nataša, I thank you very much for your time and consenting to this interview.

VII. Tereza Maxová (*1971) – Beauty and the care of children (OHI)

JB: Dear Mrs Maxová, you were the first internationally known Czechoslovak model in the early 1990s. You have made an international career in fashion and modelling, and your face is globally known for its exquisite and classical beauty. How did you start modelling? How did modelling and the fashion industry in Czechoslovakia in the late 1980s look when you started your career?

TM: In Communist Czechoslovakia, there was no such thing as modelling, no real fashion industry to speak of, only small fashion shows, and the models had regular jobs or were students earning money on the side. In 1989 I had no idea that you could make money with your looks. One day in the summer of 1989, I was asked on the street by Milada Karasová, a scouting agent working for a French agency, if I was interested in modelling. She asked me to come to the French agency's contest in Prague.

I was curious; I was seventeen years old, interested only in sports, didn't wear make up at all, did not colour my hair and never wore high heels. I had just graduated with honours from high school and was getting ready to study law at Charles University. I went to the contest at the Hotel Intercontinental in Prague; everything was very confusing since I spoke only Czech and Russian. They asked us a lot of questions and had our answers translated. We had no idea what modelling was, but eventually, some of us got an invitation to go to Paris.

I had been abroad only once before, with my family; we had spent holidays in Yugoslavia in 1985. This invitation meant that I could go abroad, see Paris, which was a huge opportunity. So, despite the reservations of my family; I accepted. In September 1989, after turning 18, I left by train for Paris for a trial month, my travelling companion and fellow model was Eva Herzigová. I had no idea that a planned one-month stay would turn into a career spanning 25 years. They put us up in an apartment in Paris. I felt like a fish out of water at the many castings I was sent to. I did this on a daily basis; I didn't speak the language and missed my family at home. I had never before been judged by my looks, I was not used to it. Some clients thought that my nose was too big, others said that my breasts were too small, some thought I was too thin, to others I was too fat. I was not judged for who I am as a person, but only for my looks, and this made me feel miserable. I was lonely, got only small jobs that didn't earn me the money to go home, and for a long period, I didn't work at all. One job was particularly humiliating: a company that produced knitted sweaters for pregnant women hired me!

All in all, it was a strange system: the agency paid me 250 French francs per week, from which I had to pay the rent and the tickets for the metro. Very little remained for food, and I often lived on bread and water. Nevertheless when I wrote to my family, I didn't want them to worry and praised my amazing time in Paris and my view of the Tour d'Eiffel.

Things took a turn for the better when I got more confidence, my French improved. I changed my agency and signed with VIVA; they knew how to get the interest of clients, although my looks were quite different from the standard back then. My first cover was the French Glamour. It was a black and white cover with a tattoo painted across my chest. The picture was awarded the best photo of the year. This was in 1991. With Mikael Janssen, the photographer who took this picture, I later worked for British VOGUE. With that picture, my career took a different direction. The early days of my modelling career were challenging, this made my accomplishments later on all the more meaningful.

JB: Can you explain to our readers what it meant to grow up in Communist Czechoslovakia in the 1980s?

TM: I had a great childhood. As a child you don't care about political systems, nothing else is important than your Mum and Dad, your family and friends. We didn't have much information from abroad, and I believed the state's propaganda: We were told that we lived "in a dream country, we enjoyed free education, free medical care. We were not as desperate as people in the Imperialist West who had no jobs and were poor". It was the time of the Cold War and we lived in fear of a nuclear attack from the West. I remember vividly the drills at school when we had to evacuate with our gas masks.

We did not have much money, but my family valued education and knowledge above material possessions. When I was older, I heard stories about 1968 and criticism of the regime. My mother was a teacher, my father a chemical engineer, and they were very family-oriented. We would sit down to dinner together and talk. There was not much to watch on our two TV channels anyway. As a child, I experienced a strong sense of solidarity in my family – and I was ambitious, a pioneer who always volunteered, for example, standing guard at a house or a statue of a Communist hero on national holidays. I suppose I was somewhat brainwashed by propaganda as a child. It is amazing how quickly brainwash evaporates when you see reality with your own eyes as I did when I took that train to Paris in 1989.

When I came to Paris, it was a cultural shock. There were foreign movies, the cult of Hollywood stars, and the supermarkets offered things I had not seen before. I remember the particular smell of pancakes and bananas in Paris train stations; bananas were sold all year round. Back home, we could buy bananas only under the counter.

JB: What was the 'West' to you when you got your first contract? And how did the Czechoslovak government deal with your contracts?

TM: There was the state agency *Pragokoncert*; they had special contracts with the Czechoslovak Symphony Orchestra and sportsmen and sportswomen who travelled abroad. I had a special contract too: the state agency claimed 70% of my salary, the French agency got 20%, which effectively left me with 10% of the sum I earned. After one month abroad I came home and took part in the Velvet Revolution that was initiated by the students of the Law faculty. I didn't want to go back to Paris, but the agency got me that job with the knitted pullovers, so I had to return.

JB: 'Normal' people believe that a top model living in Monaco is drinking champagne all the time, partying, having expensive facials, wearing diamonds and is a regular guest at the Monaco yacht club and the casino. How does a normal day in the life of Tereza Maxová look?

TM: My partner and I live a very normal life with our three children. I don't know where the glamour you speak about is in our lives, perhaps somewhere between our son's basketball game or our daughter's homework, or while we change the baby's nappy. When I am not working I try to spend time on my charity and family. I do what all mothers do: I take the children to school and care about the household chores.

JB: One of the most beautiful pictures I saw of you was the cover of *Reflex*, I think, in the spring of 1996; you and a small child in your arms. You were just about to launch the 'Foundation Tereza

Maxová'.[341] What were the principal motives of the foundation and how did you start? What difficulties did your foundation face in the early years?

TM: Terezie Sverdlinová who is sitting here with us is the director of our foundation and she was with me from the very beginning. We didn't really have a plan. I just thought that here in Prague, where people were occupied with their own daily problems, I could make a difference. That was an idea familiar to me from my years living and working in the USA. There, it is almost a civic duty, a moral duty to engage in charity work when you have the means.

I wanted to help, but not just donate some money to a charity organization; I wanted to provide goal-oriented, effective and sustainable help. So we started the foundation, and a long journey began. Back then, in 1997, there was no law in the Czech Republic that regulated foundations; the government did not support foundations. Children who didn't live with their families were being taken care of by social institutions, but I thought that they were in these institutions not of their own free will but because of the difficult social and financial situations of their parents. These children literally had no future, no sense of that particular security I had experienced in my family. Their entire life was marked by their sad childhood.

We were just five girls when we started and what drove us was female intuition. We took it step by step. We didn't have any experience, did not study the subject, but we were learning by doing. People used to tell me: 'You must be crazy. Why care?'

Terezie Sverdlinová: We went to the UK to learn how they organized the children's homes and orphanages. In 1997, the government

---

[341] The Tereza Maxová Foundation on http://www.nadaceterezymaxove.cz/en/; accessed 19 September 2014.

finally issued a law. Before, there was only chaos. To this day, the Czech Republic has the highest rate in Europe for children not living with their families.

JB: Your Tereza Maxova Foundation is very successful. Can you reveal to our readers the next projects your foundation plans to embark on?

TM: We have plans to continue to fill the gap between what the state provides and what the abandoned children need. We work with partner companies, trying to connect the orphanages to future employers, to make sure that the young adults who leave the children's homes can get jobs and stand on their own feet. At the age of eighteen, they have to leave the children's homes or orphanages, but they don't know where to go or what to do. We help them with education, teaching them how to get jobs, enter professional life, navigate through that difficult moment of their lives.

Terezie Sverdlinová: We also engage in preventing abandonment: children should not have to grow up in institutions. We do field work with pregnant women who feel that they are unable to care for the child that they are about to give birth to. We work with mothers in shelters. Our goal is to prevent the disintegration of the family first, and if this is not possible to make sure that the children who are abandoned get the best care possible through adoption, foster care or education at the children's homes.

JB: Dear Mrs Maxová, dear Mrs Sverdlinová, thank you very much for your time and for consenting to this interview.

Conclusion

This study is the first account in English of the life stories and personal experiences of seven Czech women who rendered or are still rendering outstanding service to their nation. I tried to convey to the reader the complicated and often cruel history Czech women had to deal with, situations of economic and political hardship 'Western' women cannot even begin to imagine.

From the second half of the 19th century to the present day, Czech women have lived through seven political regimes: the Austro-Hungarian empire, the First Republic, the Protectorate, the three short years of postwar democracy, the Communist regime, the brief years of the democratic Czechoslovak Federation and, after the dissolution of the Federation in 1992, the Czech Republic. The Czech Republic became a member of NATO in 1999 and joined the EU in 2004. The young state was now firmly in the West and the traumatic experience of the Soviet occupation a thing of the past.

Ema Destinn was born in the times of the monarchy. Thanks to her spectacular soprano voice, she forged an international career and performed at the world's most prestigious opera houses. Her great successes on stage earned her a small fortune. Ema was a Czech patriot, no great feminist, and her activities for the *maffie* did not earn her any reward from the Czechoslovak government.

The diva married a man who was interested only in her money. From 1916 on, she was confined to her home, Stráž Castle; the house arrest would prompt the end of her international career. Ema ignored the marriage proposal of the British pianist Harold Samuel, which could have changed her sad fate for the better. But she was an artist, acting according to her heart: she was impulsive and did not think ahead. Her slow decline led to her depression, and the once famous singer, who had enchanted the world's opera fans, died young, alone and forgotten.

After her death, the government praised her as a national heroine; she became an icon of Czechoslovakia's music and was buried in the National Cemetery on Vyšehrad. Her early death could have been avoided by paying her the respect she had earned, but the institution of state pension plans did not yet exist. She had no source of income anymore, and her husband, Joe, was spending her money, contributing to her debts. The government could have given her a professorship to honour and thank her for all she had done for the independence movement and the promotion of Czech music abroad.

But times had changed; there was no position for the elderly diva who had made a bad marriage and was incapable of keeping her finances under control. Ema had helped many friends, but could count on the help of only a few remaining friends. With Joe spending her money in Prague, Ema withdrew from public life. She spent her time at her castle, Stráž, fishing and hunting for mushrooms, the Czech national sport. Whenever she was in need of cash, her sister Jitta helped her out. Ema ignored her physician's advice: she indulged in rich food and sat for hours in the sun beside a lake on her domain, patiently waiting for a catch. She suffered from high blood pressure and arteriosclerosis.

The young Republic had to build up the institutions of a modern state, but when Czechoslovak democracy was consolidated in the mid-1920s, the government could have supported her. A symbolic gesture of gratefulness, a modest pension would have meant a lot to her. I don't think that Ema was a feminist; she did not think in political concepts, but she was a Czech patriot and loved her nation dearly.

When Ema died in 1930, Alice Garrigue Masaryková had been building up the Czechoslovak Red Cross for more than a decade. Alice, the President's first-born child, was working tirelessly

Conclusion

to improve Czechoslovak citizens' lives. She had grown up in a loving environment; her parents were supportive, with a modern way of thinking, and brought up boys and girls in a spirit of equality. After receiving her doctorate in history and philosophy, the young, progressive woman worked as a teacher at a high school for girls. When her father left for exile in 1914, Alice became the principal carer of her mother Charlotte, who was mentally and physically ill.

When incarcerated in Vienna by the Austrian authorities, Alice wrote to her mother on a regular basis; both women had a symbiotic relationship. When Charlotte felt that Alice needed her to be strong, she wrote that she was doing fine. She did not want to worsen Alice's delicate mental health that was caused by the abominable hygienic regime in the prison. Once Charlotte learnt of Alice's release, she told her the truth: she was not doing fine, she had heart problems and was very weak. The Austrian authorities decided to release Alice because of the campaign that some of Alice's American friends had started. American feminists and pacifists alike sent letters of protest to Vienna, accusing the government of tarring her with the same brush as her father: the only reason for Alice's arrest and imprisonment was the fact that she was her father's daughter.

Like Ema, who had married the wrong man, Alice's private life was an unhappy one. She had two love affairs that ended badly. In the misogynist terms of those years, Alice was an old spinster, unmarried and with no children. Her younger sister Olga married twice and had children; unlike Alice, Olga lived her own life. Alice was always taken for granted by her family: whenever the Masaryks needed her, she was there, soldiering on, supporting her mother and later, replacing Charlotte as First Lady at her father's side.

As the eldest child, Alice had a particularly strong sense of responsibility. The only luxury she allowed herself after having worked for the Republic for almost twenty years was her house in

Slovakia. She was looking forward to retirement, but the cruel history of Europe would force her twice into exile. Alice left Czechoslovakia after the Germans occupied Prague in March 1939. She would come back after the war in 1945 and witness her brother Jan's mysterious death in March 1948. She left Czechoslovakia for good after the Communist coup d'état and died in US exile in 1966.

In the 1960s, Eva 'Mimi' Jiránková and her husband Miloš Jiránek's lives took a turn for the better: they lived in London, where their daughter Tina was attending school. Mimi worked as a fashion consultant for Liberty's and Miloš at the Czech desk of the British Foreign Ministry. They had met during Masaryk's First Republic and married in difficult circumstances in 1942, just months after Heydrich's assassination and the subsequent wave of cruel repressive measures.

Mimi and Miloš were upper-middle class; their fathers had been entrepreneurs and both grew up in an affluent environment. Miloš's stepfather Jaroslav Stránský was the owner of the *Lidové Noviny*, a centre-right newspaper close to the Castle. The *Lidovky* were comparable with the Swiss *Neue Zürcher Zeitung*, the German *Die Zeit*, and *The Times* of London. Since Stránský had left Czechoslovakia with President Beneš in 1938 and regularly broadcasted on the BBC on behalf of the Allies, the Nazis arrested Miloš on his wedding night.

Mimi survived the war in Prague and often had no news from Miloš. Thanks to Mimi's father Karel Zimmer, Miloš was able to work in the administration of the Gross Rosen camp. He survived one of the death marches of the Holocaust in 1945 and returned to Prague in June of that year. He immediately went back to work, spending his evenings with his best friend Ferdinand Peroutka. When the Communist Party assumed power in 1948, Mimi and Miloš decided to leave. Their daughter Tina was two years old. After an attempt to flee through the Bohemian Forest, they were arrested. Yet, thanks to an *ukaz* (decree) from the government, they were allowed to sell their property and leave Czechoslovakia for good in December 1948. Had they stayed, they might have become victims of the purges the Communist Party instigated in the 1950s.

They spent three years in Paris as refugees before they were able to move to Great Britain. Miloš died of a heart attack one month before the Velvet Revolution would sweep away the Communist Party's monopoly of power. I spent unforgettable days with Mimi in Prague. We used to go for long walks through the city centre, had lunches and dinners with friends and talked about Masaryk's Czechoslovakia and politics. We had set a date in March of this year, where we would meet up, a tradition that had begun after I had met her in Devon in 2009. We used to meet in Prague in the spring and the autumn. But it was too late for Mimi to make one last trip to her beloved Prague. She died in April 2015 in her Devon home, peacefully and without pain.

Milada Horáková's death was not as peaceful as Mimi's. Milada was hanged on the morning of 27 June 1950 for the simple reason that she was a perfect symbolic culprit in the show trials orchestrated by the Communist government. Milada was a feminist and a doctor of law; as the chairwoman of the Czechoslovak Women's Council, she had been an ardent adherent of Masaryk's democracy and rule-of-law state. Milada's life mirrors the cruel history of Czechoslovakia: arrested by the Nazis in 1940, she survived the war and was liberated by the Americans in 1945.

She was a member of Beneš's National Socialist Party and highly respected by women because of her broadcasts on Czech radio about women's issues. She was doomed to die because the government was intent on changing citizens' minds: the creation of the Socialist citizen required victims, and Milada was a symbol of the First Republic. She was acquainted with Alice, and had met the President. Loyal to Beneš, she did not understand the dangerous situation that threatened her life in 1947. She could have left Czechoslovakia with her daughter and her husband, but her particular sense of responsibility made her stay. Milada thought that her party would win the elections of 1948. She was wrong, underestimating the Communists' lust for power and the methods they were prepared to deploy in achieving it.

Weeks before Heydrich was assassinated, Věra Čáslavská was born in Prague in 1942. The talented girl who loved sport would become Czechoslovakia's greatest Olympic champion. Věra was no feminist; she was only interested in sports and spent her young life in the gym and at work. Her discipline was extraordinary; at the age of 15, she started serious training in women's gymnastics. She was determined to win and had the physique and mental strength that would make her an Olympic champion.

When the Warsaw Pact troops invaded her country, Věra was in a training camp, preparing for the Olympic Games in Mexico City due to be held in September 1968. She had signed the *2000 words* manifesto published by the writer Ludvík Vaculík. She would pay for this act of moral courage: after her return from Mexico, where she had won Gold, the government condemned her because of her signature. For five years, Věra could find no employment; she was *persona non grata* in the harsh years of the normalization. She could have applied for political asylum in Mexico, since her two children and her husband were there too, but Věra wanted to go home. She could not imagine living anywhere other than Czechoslovakia.

Nataša Lišková was twenty years old and on a trip with friends in the Soviet Union, when the invasion ended the Prague Spring. She experienced the normalization, the Velvet Revolution and the early post-Communist years that were determined by the Klaus government's privatization plans. She witnessed the dissolution of the Federation. In the 1970s and 1980s, Nataša worked as a freelance journalist.

She could have emigrated in 1969; her aunt lived in London, where she had met Mimi and her daughter Tina in 1967 while studying at the London Polytechnic. Yet Nataša wanted to return home to Czechoslovakia and brought up two children in the harsh years of the normalization. She is an example of strength, courage and humanism, with an admirable sense of humour. She spends her retirement happily with her grandchildren in the countryside.

Tereza Maxová is one of the most beautiful women in the world – and she has a big heart. The 18-year-old, blonde beauty left Czechoslovakia in 1988 for the West, with a contract from a French model agency. After difficult early years in Paris, her good looks catapulted her onto the covers of international fashion magazines. The beautiful Czech, whose delicate features and perfect body earned her celebrity status and highly paid jobs in Europe and the USA, now lives in Monaco with her family.

Tereza was shocked by the dire situation of children who had lost their parents. Orphans lived in state-founded homes in dire conditions. Private organizations, foundations and NGOs were unknown in the young Republic. In 1996, the top model who had made a lot of money decided to do her best to help: with her friend Terezie Sverdlinová, she set up the Foundation Tereza Maxová for Children. Thanks to her initiative, thousands of children now have a future; they are able to grow up in a loving environment and receive an education that allows them to find jobs, earn a salary and live a happy and normal life.

Tereza could have enjoyed her wealth, living a quiet family life abroad, but thanks to her compassion and sense of responsibility thousands of children have been saved from the cruel cycle of poverty, lack of education, alcoholism, drug abuse and criminality. She and her co-workers at the foundation have made a crucially important contribution to Czech civil society and humanism. Civil society is a pillar of democracy and the rule-of-law state; it depends on individual initiative, on the citizens' engagement. Without the Foundation Tereza Maxová for Children, Czech civil society would not have developed the way it has in the years after the Velvet Revolution.

I hope that my study of seven Czech women, their courage and commitment to humanism and enlightenment will lead to a better understanding of the often cruel history and the political circumstances of Czechoslovakia and the Czech Republic. We can learn a lot from these seven women: discipline, intelligence, compassion, and the care of those less fortunate than ourselves.

Chronology

1867	The Austro-Hungarian Compromise (*Ausgleich*) divides the empire into two parts; Austria has no more say in the domestic affairs of the Hungarian kingdom. Although split by the emerging mass parties in the 1880s and 1890s, the Czech national movement is gaining in strength, owing to the relative liberty prevailing in Austria. Unlike Buda, Vienna does not infringe on the language and cultural rights of the Czechs.
1878, 26 February	Emilie Věnceslava Pavlina Kittlová (stage name Emmy Destinn, Ema Destinnová in Czech) born in Prague to Emanuel Kittl and Jindřiška Kittlová, née Šrutová. The Kittls have four other children: Jindřiška (1879), Emanuel (1881), Viktor (1882) and Antonín (1884).
1879, 3 May	Alice Garrigue Masaryková born in Prague. She is the first child of Tomáš Garrigue Masaryk (7 March 1850–14 September 1937) and his American wife Charlotte Garrigue Masaryk (20 November 1850–13 May 1923). Her siblings are Herbert (1 May 1880–15 March 1915), Jan (14 September 1886–10 March 1948), Eleanor (2 March 1890–18 July 1890) and Olga (25 May 1891–12 September 1978). From 1887 to 1891, the Masaryks spend their summer holidays in Bystrička, Slovakia.

1882	Charles-Ferdinand University in Prague opens a Czech section providing higher education in Czech, a significant achievement of the Czech national movement. Not only Czech, but also Slovak students enrol to study in Prague. Masaryk appointed Professor of Philosophy in the Czech section.
1886	Ema Kittlová's first public performance in Kamýk nad Vltavou; she plays the violin.
1891	Ema Kittlová takes up studies in violin, piano and foreign languages with Ferdinand Lachner in Prague. From 1892 on, she studies voice with Thomas and Marie Loewe. Marie's stage name is Destinn.
1892	Alice Masaryková enrols at Minerva, the first high school for girls in Prague.
1893	Ema Kittlová enrols at the Drama School of the Prague National Theatre. First attempts at writing poetry and literature.
1896	Ema Kittlová signs a contract with the Court Opera House in Dresden, Saxony after an unsuccessful audition at the Prague National Theatre. The contract with Dresden does not lead to any performances, but three of her dramas are put on in various Prague theatres. First love affair with Jindřich Vodílek, which ends a year later.
1898	Alice Masaryková enrols in the Czech section of Charles-Ferdinand University to study medicine and history. After one year, she quits medicine and focuses on history and philosophy. In her spare time, she is active in the Czech abstinence movement.

Conclusion

19 July	Stage debut of Ema Kittlová at the Court Opera House in Berlin. She performs under the stage name Ema Destinn in honour of her former teacher Marie Loewe, whose stage name, Destinn, she has adopted. She is prima donna in Berlin for the next ten years and performs in fifty roles.
1899, 4 April	Ema Destinn attempts suicide in her Prague apartment. She returns to Berlin the same night and has her first disk recorded on 12 April, singing the role of Agathe in Carl Maria von Weber's (1786–1826) The Marksman.
1900	First performance by Ema Destinn in her native Prague; she sings in three concerts organized by several Czech cultural associations. Signs an eight-year contract with the Vienna Court Opera House, which makes her the highest paid female opera singer of her times.
1 September	Premiere of Bedřich Smetana's (1824–1884) The Bartered Bride in Berlin with the young conductor Bruno Walter (1876–1962) and Ema Destinn in the role of Mařenka; Destinn has translated the opera's Czech text into German. Cosima Wagner (1837–1930), Richard Wagner's (1813–1883) second wife and daughter of Franz Liszt (1811–1886), invites Ema Destinn to Bayreuth. Destinn starts to write her autobiographical novel *Dr Casanova*, which she completes in 1915.
1901, 25 February	Ema Destinn performs for the first time at the Prague National Theatre; three guest appearances as Carmen and Mignon. She has translated the text of Carmen into Czech. On 31 March she attends the premiere of

	Antonín Dvořák's (1841–1904) Rusalka. Until the end of the year, she performs in Frankfurt am Main, Paris, Bayreuth, Munich, and Darmstadt.
1901, 25 December	Milada Králová (later Horaková) born in Prague to Čeněk Král (1869–1955) and Anna Králová, née Velišková (1875–1933). They have four children: Marta (1899–1914), Milada, Jiří (1908–1914) and Věra (*1915). Marta and Jiří die of scarlet fever in the first year of WWI. Milada's father is an admirer of Masaryk.
1902	Ema Destinn performs for the first time in London in the Wagner cycle; guest appearances in Zurich and Bayreuth. Sings the role of Alice at the premiere of Giacomo Meyerbeer's (1791–1864) Robert le Diable on 3 May and Diemut at the premiere of Richards Strauss's (1864–1949) Feuersnot on 28 October.
1903	Alice Masaryková graduates in philosophy with the final thesis "Magna Charta Libertatum", which receives the highest grade, but she is less successful in the history exam, which she just passes. First unhappy love affair with the Viennese physician Richard Fröhlich.
February	The general manager of the New York Metropolitan Opera Heinrich Conried (1855–1909) offers Ema Destinn a guest appearance. After touring Europe's most prestigious opera houses with great success, the Prague National Theatre issues a three-year stage ban on her in September for her letter of protest. Ema criticizes the Berlin Theatre of

	the West for the bad perfomance of her drama *Dalibor* (1901).
18 November	Ema Destinn attends the performance of Smetana's Libuše at the 20th anniversary of the Prague National Theatre.
1903-04	In the winter term, Alice Masaryková enrols at Leipzig University for postgraduate studies in economics.
1904, 19 May	First performance of Ema Destinn with the Italian tenor Enrico Caruso (1873–1921) at the Royal Opera House Covent Garden in London. She will perform at Covent Garden until 1914, making 150 appearances in 17 roles.
1904-1905	Alice Masaryková is in Chicago, USA, where she studies sociology and modern methods of social work. Activities on behalf of the Czech exile communities in the USA.
1905, 10 July	Ema Destinn and Enrico Caruso sing the leading roles at the London premiere of Giacomo Puccini's (1858–1924) Madame Butterfly. Meeting with Puccini.
1906	Alice Masaryková finds a teaching position at the high school for girls (*lyceum*) in České Budějovice (*Tschechisch Budweis*); translates foreign literature and writes her own studies and texts.
1907, 6 May	Premiere of Strauss's Salome with Ema Destinn in the leading role at the Paris Theatre du Châtelet; the famous actress Sarah Bernhardt (1844–1923) congratulates Destinn on her receiving the title of *officier de l'instruction publique*, the highest accolade bestowed on Destinn by the French Ministry

	of Public Instruction (*Ministère de l'instruction publique*).
1908, 1 November	Ema Destinn's last performance in Berlin; on 15 November, she arrives in New York in the company of her sister and her brother-in-law. On 16 November, she makes her New York debut in Giuseppe Verdi's (1813–1901) Aida.
1910	Alice Masaryková returns to Prague and teaches at the high school for girls in Prague Holešovice. Steps up her public activities for the abstinence movement and publishes her texts.
1911	Alice Masaryková founds the "Section of Sociology", a non-governmental association whose purpose is to support and propagate sociology as a new science. Charles-Ferdinand University has not yet included it in its curriculum. Alice is chairwoman; among her colleagues is the young lawyer Edvard Beneš (1884–1948), the future associate of her father's.
1913	Milada Králová enrols at the high school for girls in Prague Vinohrady in the 1913/14 school year. She is an attentive, ambitious and intellectually gifted pupil and famous for her temperament in discussions. Early plans for higher education at Charles-Ferdinand University.
1914, 10 January	Ema Destinn buys the castle and domain Stráž nad Nežárkou in Southern Bohemia. She performs in her sixth season at the New York Met. Spends the spring and summer months in Prague, avoiding appearances in

	German opera houses after the beginning of WWI.
28 June	Gavrilo Princip (1894–1918) shoots archduke Franz Ferdinand (1875–1914) and his wife Sophie Chotek (1868–1914) in Sarajevo; beginning of WWI. Masaryk and his youngest daughter Olga leave for Switzerland in December; Alice Masaryková supports her mother with her teacher's salary, their only source of income.
1915	Jan Masaryk drafted into the Austrian army; Herbert Masaryk, Alice Masaryková's closest sibling, dies of typhus in January. On 28 October, the Austrian authorities arrest her in Prague; she is suspected of high treason for hiding anti-Austrian texts written by her father. On 7 November, she is transferred to Neudorf women's prison, a section of the Landesgerichtliches Gefangenenhaus (county prison). First signs of mental problems, caused by imprisonment.
1916, 3 July	Owing to international pressure and diplomatic intervention by the USA, the authorities release Alice Masaryková from prison; she spends the remainder of WWI in Prague, caring for her ill mother. They are in financial distress, since Alice has lost her teaching position. She earns a meagre income giving English lessons; friends from the *maffie*, the Czech underground resistance organization, support the two women.
mid-July	The Austrian authorities confiscate Ema Destinn's passport; she is put under house arrest at her castle Stráž.

1917, 4 April	The US Senate declares war on Germany.
November	Ema Destinn performs the female roles in operas by Smetana and Dvořák at the Prague National Theatre, demonstrating her support for Czechoslovak independence.
7 December	The USA declares war on Germany's ally Austria-Hungary.
1918, 31 May	Pittsburgh Agreement signed by Czech and Slovak émigré communities in Pittsburgh, expressing their support for the building of the Czechoslovak Republic.
Autumn	Milada Králová enrols at the high schools for girls in Slezská Street in Prague after having been expelled from the Vinohrady high school. The reason: she has participated in a demonstration on 1 May showing solidarity with Czech soldiers sent to the front by giving them a rose.
18 October	In Paris, Masaryk, Milan Rastislav Štefánik (1880–1919), the Slovak astronomer and General of the French Army, and Beneš sign the Declaration of Washington. The exile troika represents the provisional Czechoslovak government with Masaryk as President, Štefánik as Minister of Defence and Beneš as Minister of the Interior. Negotiations between Beneš and a delegation from the Prague National Committee (*národní výbor*) in Geneva; the two parties agree on a Republican constitution and the personnel that will head the ministries and state institutions before the first parliamentary elections.

27 October	Austrian Foreign Minister Gyula Andrássy Jr. (1860–1929) seeks a separate peace with the allies.
28 October	Czechoslovak Declaration of Independence signed in Prague by Czech politicians and the physician Vavro Šrobár (1867–1950) as representative of the Slovaks.
21 December	Masaryk returns to Prague in triumph after four years of unwavering dedication to the cause of the Republic.
22 December	To honour Masaryk, Ema Destinn sings the Libuše at the Prague National Theatre. This is the last time she performs this role.
1919	For brief months, Alice Masaryková is delegate of the Revolutionary National Assembly for the Social Democrats. In February, her father appoints her chairwoman of the newly founded Czechoslovak Red Cross (ČSČK).
14 May	Ema Destinn's thirteenth and last season at Covent Garden; she leaves in the autumn for the season at the New York Met.
1920	Alice Masaryková's second unhappy love affair with the Slovenian Jože Plečnik (1872–1957), the chief architect engaged in the reconstruction of the Prague Castle.
1921, January	Ema Destinn tours Canada and the USA for the third and last time. On 27 January she has her last performance at the Met performing Aida. From October to December she appears at various concert halls touring the USA: Boston, New York, Urbana in Illinois, Omaha in Nebraska, Denver in Colorado, Tacoma in

	Washington State, Portland in Oregon and San Francisco and Berkeley in California.
7 June	Milada Králová finishes high school with the *maturita*. She decides to study medicine: this plan is most probably a result of the early death of her siblings. Her father who deeply mistrusts doctors convinces her to study a different subject. She chooses law.
27 November	Eva 'Mimi' Zimmerová (later Jiránková) born in Prague.
5 December	Milada Králová accepted as student at the Faculty of Law of Charles University.
1923	Ema Destinn on tour in Czechoslovakia; performs in Czech, Moravian and Slovak concert halls.
19 September	Ema Destinn marries a younger man, Josef Halbach. The marriage is not a happy one, as he is often away.
13 May	Charlotte Garrigue Masaryková dies.
1924	Milada Králová makes the acquaintance of Senator Františka F. Plamínková (1875–1942), who founded the Czechoslovak National Women's Council (ŽNR) in 1922. Plamínková invites the young student to join the Council and remains a close friend until the Germans execute her in 1942.
1925, May	In November, the Prague Conservatory and the conservatory in Brno reject Ema Destinn's application for a professorship.
1926, 22 October	Milada Králova completes her studies with a doctorate in law.

Conclusion 231

1927, 15 February	Milada Králova and Bohuslav Horák (1899–1976), a doctor of civil engineering and scientific editor and presenter with Czech Radio, marry in Prague Vinohrady. Milada, educated in the Catholic faith, accepts the Evangelical confession of her husband. She finds employment at the Main Social Services Department of Prague (*Ústřední sociální úřad hlavního města Prahy*), where she works until 1940.
6 April	President Masaryk invites Ema Destinn for an audience to the Castle.
1928, 16 October	Ema Destinn's last concert in the Royal Albert Hall in London in honour of the tenth anniversary of the founding of Czechoslovakia.
1929	To support herself, Ema Destinn gives singing lesson. On 8 May, she appears in the break between two film shows at a Prague cinema, singing songs by Dvořák, her last public appearance. President Masaryk and Prime Minister František Udržal pay her a visit at her castle in Stráž on their way back to Prague from an exhibition in Southern Bohemia.
	Milada Horáková joins the Czechoslovak National Socialist Party (ČSNS), led by Beneš. She is a close friend of the Foreign Minister and his wife Hana.
1930, 28 January	Ema Destinn dies from a stroke in a hospital in České Budějovice. The greatest Czech opera diva is buried in the National Cemetery in Prague Vyšehrad.

1932, March	Milada Horáková broadcasts for the first time on Czech Radio, addressing current problems of women's emancipation. Her broadcasts are very popular. From 1932 until 1938 and then again in 1939, she broadcasts mainly about women's rights, embodying the ideal of female equality with men, as enshrined in the Czechoslovak constitution.
1933	Jana Horáková born to Milada and Bohuslav. She is their only child.
1935	Milan Hodža (1878–1944) elected Prime Minister of Czechoslovakia. He holds this position until 22 September 1938.
1937, 14 Sept.	President Masaryk dies in Lány.
1938, 30 Sept.	Munich Agreement. Czechoslovakia loses the Sudetenland and Silesia to Germany. Beneš, Hodža and the Czechoslovak government go into exile in October.
1939, 9-10 March	Czechoslovak President Emil Hácha (1872–1945) orders the occupation of Slovakia, referred to as the Homola putsch (*Homolov puč*).
14 March	Under German pressure, Jozef Tiso (1887–1947) declares Slovakia's sovereignty; the state becomes a satellite of Nazi Germany.
15 March	Hácha signs the Czech capitulation. German troops occupy Bohemia and Moravia, which are subsequently referred to as the Protectorate. Milada Horáková joins the Czech resistance movement; active for the "Political Centre" (*Politické ústředí*) group, the "Petition

	Committee Faithful We Remain" (*Petiční výbor Věrni zůstaneme*) and the "For Freedom and Towards a New Czechoslovak Republic" (*Za svobodu do nové Československé republiky*) group.
29 March	Alice Masaryková leaves Czechoslovakia. After a few months in Switzerland and the UK, she moves to the USA. Her tireless efforts for a future renewal of Czechoslovakia, lectures, speeches, social activities, result in her physical and psychological exhaustion. She spends the remainder of WWII in hospitals and sanatoria.
1 September	German attack on Poland; start of WWII.
1940, 2 August	Milada and Bohuslav Horák arrested by the Gestapo. Milada is imprisoned in Pankrác and the prison at Charles square.
1941, 21 June	German attack on the Soviet Union.
1942, 3 May	Věra Čáslavská born in the Prague district of Karlín as the third child. Her father owns a little grocery store and her mother takes care of the children. Věra has two sisters and one brother: Hana (*1935), Eva (*1936) and Václav (*1945).
27 May	The Czechoslovak officers Jan Kubiš (Czech) and Jozef Gabčik (Slovak) parachute to the Protectorate from Great Britain and shoot Heydrich in Prague. He dies on 4 June.
9-10 June	The Germans take cruel revenge for Heydrich in Lidice and later, on 24 June, in Ležáky: all male citizens are shot, the female citizens sent to concentration camps. The children with Aryan looks are sent to SS

	families and raised as Germans. The villages are completely destroyed.
15 September	Mimi Zimmerová and Miloš Jiránek marry in Prague. At 3 am on their wedding night, the Gestapo arrests Miloš.
Around Christmas	Miloš Jiránek transferred to the *Kleine Festung* (*Malá pevnost, small fortress*) in Theresienstadt (*Terezín*).
1943	Milada Horáková transferred to the *Kleine Festung* in Teresienstadt where her husband is also detained. She is in cell no. 8, where Gavrilo Princip died in 1918.
March/April	Miloš Jiránek transferred to Gross Rosen camp near Auschwitz.
1944, 6 June	Allied landings in Normandy.
22 June	Milada Horáková transferred to prisons in Leipzig and Dresden; sentenced to eight years of hard labour and transferred to a prison in Aichach in Bavaria.
20 July	Failed attempt on Hitler's life.
27 October	Fall of Banská Bystrica, end of the Slovak National Uprising (SNP) that had begun on 29 August 1944. The Red Army liberates Eastern Slovakia at the end of the year.
1945, 22–29 March	Signing of the Košice Agreement in Moscow. The negotiating parties, hosted by Stalin, are the members of the London exile government, Czech centre-right parties, the Slovak National Council (SNR) and the Communist exiles in Moscow. Beneš and Stalin do not intervene in the negotiations.

Conclusion

5 April	Declaration of the Košice Agreement in Košice in liberated Eastern Slovakia.
9 May	Liberation of Prague by the Red Army.
10 May	Czechoslovak exile government returns to Prague from London.
20 May	Milada Horáková returns to Prague after liberation by the US Army. She is a leading member of the ČSNS, deputy chairwoman of the Union of Political Prisoners and chairwoman of the National Women's Council. She is also a parliamentarian for the ČSNS in the Constitutional Assembly, representing the constituency of České Budejovice.
10 June	Miloš Jiránek returns to Prague after having survived the death march from Gross Rosen to Flossenbürg; he has been liberated by the US Army.
14 September	Alice Masaryková and her brother Jan, the foreign minister of the Czechoslovak exile government, arrive in Prague. In the years before the Communist coup d'état, Alice is not publicly active. Jan is Foreign Minister under President Beneš's government in the National Front.
1946, 15 May	Martina Anna Milada Jiránková born to Mimi and Miloš Jiránek in Prague.
	Věra Čáslavská enrols at the ballet school of Marta Aubrechtová, where she trains ballet, acrobatics and step dance. She stays at the school for three years.
1947, 11 Sept.	Milada Horáková publishes a longer essay in the women's journal *Vlasta* in honour of the

	tenth anniversary of Masaryk's death in 1937.
1948, 22 February	With her sisters Hana and Eva, Věra Čáslavská performs at the Prague Lucerna Hall; the three girls' dance shows are so popular that they are invited to the Castle, performing first for Hana Benešová and later for Marta Gottwaldová.
25 February	Communist coup d'état. President Beneš dissolves the democratically elected government and appoints a new government according to Klement Gottwald's (1896–1953) suggestions. Antonín Zápotocký (1884–1957) appointed Prime Minister.
10 March	Mysterious death of Jan Masaryk. He is found in the courtyard of the Czernin Palais, the seat of the Foreign Ministry, in the early hours. To this day, it remains unclear whether he was murdered by the Soviets or committed suicide.
	Milada Horáková lays down her mandate in protest against the violation of democratic principles by the Communist Party. Contacts with party members in Czechoslovakia and in exile, such as Petr Zenkl and Hubert Ripka.
1 May	Mimi and Miloš Jiránek attempt to flee through the Bohemian Forest (*Šumava*); they are arrested, but released after a couple of weeks.
7 June	Beneš resigns; Gottwald Czechoslovak President.
December	Mimi and Miloš Jiránek leave Czechoslovakia with their daughter.

Conclusion 237

21 December	Alice Masaryková leaves Czechoslovakia and joins her sister Olga in Geneva.
1949, 18 Sept.	Nataša Lišková born in Prague.
27 September	Milada Horáková arrested at her workplace in Prague. Her husband Bohuslav manages to escape arrest and, after an unsuccessful attempt to warn his wife, goes into hiding. He flees the country the same year and learns about the trial of Milada in a refugee camp in Bavaria.
	As a hobby, Věra Čáslavská starts figure skating. In summer, she occupies herself with athletics, running, jumping and sprinting. She is also swimming and cycling on a regular basis.
1950, 31 May	The trial of Milada Horáková and twelve others accused of high treason and conspiracy against the state begins. The trial is a farce for a rule-of-law state, following a script prepared by the StB and Soviet advisers.
8 June	Milada Horáková, Záviš Kalandra (*1902), Jan Buchal (*1913) and Oldřich Pecl (*1903) are sentenced to death. President Gottwald ignores the international appeals to save her life.
26 June	Milada Horáková allowed to see her sister Věra, daughter Jana and brother-in-law Josef for the first and last time during her captivity. Writes a last letter to her family.
27 June	Milada Horáková executed at Pankrác prison as the last of the four sentenced to death. The exact time of her death is 5.35 a.m. Her family does not receive her last remains. In 2004, 27

	June is declared a state holiday in memory of the victims of the Communist regime.
1951	Alice Masaryková is in New York. She does some broadcasts for Radio Free Europe, but in general keeps a low profile. Her sister Olga joins her in the USA in the 1950s.
23 November	Arrest of Rudolf Slánský (1901–1952).
1952, November	Show trial of Rudolf Slánský, Vladimír Clementis (1902–1952) and thirteen other Party members; 11 of the 14 accused are Jewish. Slánský, Clementis and nine fellow accused executed in December.
1953	Stalin dies on 5 March; Gottwald follows ever faithfully on 14 March.
1956, 25 February	Nikita S. Chruščev's (1894–1971) secret speech to the XX Party Congress, intitiating de-Stalinization. Alice Masaryková moves to Masaryktown in Florida, where she stays with her friend Anna Ferjenčiková. She experiences problems with her sight and suffers a stroke.
spring	Věra Čáslavská applies to the conservatory for dance, where her elder sister Hana studies, but she is refused.
1957	Antonín Novotný (1904–1975) Czechoslovak Prime Minister.
13 April	Věra Čáslavská starts to train in artistic gymnastics under the supervision of the famous gymnast Eva Bosáková (1931–1991), who is often absent. In the years prior to her first competition, the fifteen-year-old teenager trains on her own.

Conclusion

July	As a member of the Czechoslovak national team, Věra Čáslavská is abroad for the first time: with her team she participates at a non-competitive gymnastic show in Yugoslavia.
1960	Věra Čáslavská earns her first Olympic medal at the Games in Rome, Italy; the team wins the silver medal in the team competition.
1963	The Kolder and Barnabite commissions publish their reports about the show trials of the 1950s.
8 April	Alexander Dubček (1921–1992) elected general secretary of KSS.
1964	Věra Čáslavská at the Olympic Games in Tokyo, Japan: she wins three gold medals for vault, balance beam and the individual all-round as well as silver in the team competition.
1966, April	Alice Masaryková moves to a retirement home of the Czechoslovak emigré community in Chicago.
November 29	After a heart attack in early November Alice Masaryková dies at her Chicago home.
1967	Nataša Lišková enrols at the London Polytechnic. Nataša's aunt, Mrs Fišerová, is a friend of Mimi and Miloš Jiránek and their daughter Tina.
1968, 3-5 January	The CC of KSČ vote Novotný out and elect Dubček First Secretary. Start of the Prague Spring.
27 June	Ludvík Vaculík publishes his famous manifesto *2000 words,* calling for further reforms and democratization. Věra Čáslavs-

	ká is among those citizens who sign the manifesto, joining criticism of the KSČ's monopoly of power.
Spring	Nataša Lišková returns to her native Prague from London and enrols at the Faculty of Journalism. She volunteers with a student group and leaves for the Soviet Union.
21 August	Invasion of the Warsaw Pact troops. Soviet troops shall occupy the country until 1990.
30 August	Nataša Lišková and her friends arrive in Prague, after having learnt about the invasion while in Siberia.
October, 12-27	At the Olympic Games in Mexico City, Věra Čáslavská wins four gold medals: individual all-round, vault, floor and uneven bars. She wins silver at the balance beam and in the team competiton. On the podium, she looks away and down when the Soviet hymn plays, which is understood by everybody as a clear sign of protest against the occupation of her country. On 26 October, she marries her boyfriend Josef Odložil (1938–1993), a middle-distance runner (1500 m) and Olympic Champion of 1964 and 1968. Thousands of Mexican fans attend their wedding at the Cathedral in Mexico City. Věra and Josef return to Prague on 31 October 1968.
1969, 17 April	Gustáv Husák (1913–1991) replaces Dubček as first secretary. Start of the neo-totalitarian policy referred to euphemistically as 'normalization'.
July	Věra Čáslavská gives birth to her daughter Radka. She is under constant pressure from

Conclusion

	the authorities, but refuses to take back her signature of the *2000 words* manifesto, which results in years of social isolation and unemployment.
1970, December	The CC publishes *Lessons learnt from the critical developments in party and state following the XIII Congress of KSČ*, rendering the normalization legitimate. The country is transformed into a federation (ČSSR), though not a real one as KSČ does not federalize.
1971, 31 July	Věra Čáslavská's maternity leave is over. TJ Rudá Hvězda Strašnice, the sport's club she is employed at and representing, fires her. She enrols at the Faculty of Physical Education and Sport (FTVS) and enjoys her studies.
31 August	Tereza Maxová born in Pardubice.
1972	Věra Čáslavská's memoirs *Cesta na Olymp* (*The Way to the Olymp*) are published, yet in a censored and shortened edition.
1973	Nataša Lišková graduates at the Faculty of Journalism with excellent grades.
1974, August	Martin, Věra Čáslavská's second child, is born. At the end of the year, she finally gets employment after five years of ostracization. She is appointed team coach of the Sparta Praha club at the girl's high school and works at the stadium in Strahov. Her employment, however, has to be kept secret.
1975	Gústav Husák elected president. Start of the CSCE negotiations that are finalized with the signing of the CSCE treaty that all states of the Soviet bloc sign. In exchange for the acknowledgement of East Germany's borders technical and scientific cooperation

	with the West. By signing, the Communist bloc states pledge to respect civil rights.
1977, 1 January	Foundation of *Charter 77*, the Czechoslovak dissident group which speaks out for civil rights that are enshrined in the Czechoslovak constitution as a result of the CSCE treaty. The first three speakers are Václav Havel (1936–2011), the Professor of Philosophy Jan Patočka (1907–1977) and Jiří Hájek (1913–1993), Foreign Minister under Dubček.
1979, April	Vašek, Věra Čáslavská's little brother, who was politically active in 1968 and under surveillance, dies, run over by a car. The accident is not investigated further, which prompts Věra's suspicions that the StB was involved. A few weeks later, she and her family move to Mexico City for a two-year stay. She and Josef are employed as coaches in Mexico's national programme of sports education. Long-term problems in their marriage result in their separation.
1981	Věra Čáslavská's contract in Mexico expires; she returns with her children to Prague in the summer.
1983	As a result of Juan Antonio Samaranch's visit and influence, the authorities allow Věra Čáslavská to make a comeback; she is appointed to the official jury for Olympic gymnastic competitions and coach of Sparta Praha's team.
1985, 15 March	Mikhail S. Gorbacev (*1921) elected general secretary of the Soviet Communist Party. Beginning of Glasnosť and Perestroika.

Conclusion

1987, February	After years of trying to save her marriage, Věra Čáslavská finally files for divorce. A long and exhausting battle about property and the care of the children begins.
1988	Tereza Maxová and Eva Hercigová leave for Paris to embark on their international careers in modelling. Both will become top models in the 1990s. Maxová's delicate and unusually beautiful face will be on countless covers of international fashion magazines.
1989, 18 October	Miloš Jiránek dies of a heart attack at his home in Devon.
17 November	Start of the Velvet Revolution (*Sametová revoluce*). Foundation of the Czech Civic Forum (OF) and the Slovak Society Against Violence (VPN).
1990, 10 January	President Havel invites Věra Čáslavská to his team; she is appointed director of the section of social politics, and her brief includes health, education, youth and physical education. She also becomes involved in Olga Havlová's foundation Good Will, an NGO with a charitable goal. For the next seven years, she is working day and night, taking care of citizens' problems.
23 April	Constitutional amendment: Democratic Czechoslovakia becomes a federation (ČSFR). Václav Havel elected Czechoslovak President.
June	First free elections in Czechoslovakia since 1946.
1991	President Havel awards Milada Horáková the Order of Tomáš Garrigue Masaryk First Class *in memoriam*.

1992, summer	Negotiations between Czech Prime Minister Klaus (*1941) (ODS) and Slovak Premier Mečiar (HZDS) (*1941) about a common course of economic transformation end in failure. They decide to break up the state. Havel steps down.
1993, 1 January	The Czech Republic and the Slovak Republic become sovereign states; the separation is commonly referred to as The Velvet Divorce (*Sametový rozchod*).
10 September	Josef Odložil, Věra Čáslavská's ex-husband, dies after a row in a club with his son Martin. Martin is accused of murdering his estranged father. The popular press attacks Martin and Věra, condemning them in public before the trial begins.
1996	Tereza Maxová founds the NGO Tereza Maxová Foundation for Children.
24 July	After an unfair trial that ignores the forensic evidence of Josef's death, the district court in Prague sentences Martin to four years' imprisonment for criminal assault resulting in death. Věra Čáslavská's does not intervene for fear of being accused by the press of using her influence at the Castle in favour of her son.
1997, 24 January	President Havel grants amnesty to Martin. The press condemns this as an act of nepotism and protectionism, which prompts Věra Čáslavská's long depression. She spends almost a decade in hospitals and hospices.
1999	The Czech Republic is granted NATO membership.

2000	The Czech government creates a symbolic grave for Milada Horáková in the national cemetery on Vyšehrad.
2004	The Czech Republic is accepted as a member of the EU.
2009	Věra Čáslavská's returns to public life after a decade of illness. She gives interviews and attends a few sports galas broadcast by Czech Television. She lives quietly in Prague; her daughter Radka moved to Mexico, and her son Martin lives in his father's native village of Jeseniky in Moravia.
2015, 26 April	Mimi Jiránková dies peacefully at her home in Devon, surrounded by her family.

Bibliography

"Bratislava, 1992, 22 října. Protest iniciativy 'Za spoločný štáť' proti dohodě o rozdělení Československa zaslaný generálnímu tajemníkovi OSN Butrusovi Butrusovi Ghálímu". In *Češi a Slováci ve 20. století. Česko-slovenské vztahy 1945–1992*. Bratislava, Praha: AEP, ústav T. G. Masaryka, 1998.

"Foreword by Dr. A. G. Masaryková". In *Listy do Vězení*. Praha: Vladimír Žikeš, 1947.

"Vždicky jsem hrála s klukama". *Dobrá Adresa 3*, no. 10 (2002): 50-65.

1948. Únor 1948 v Československu: Nástup komunistické totality a proměny společnosti. Praha: Ústav pro soudobé dějiny AV ČR, 2011.

8000 Years of Wisdom. London: Accent Press Ltd, 2010.

Arendt, Hannah. *The Origins of Totalitarianism.* San Diego, New York, London: Harcourt Brace & Company, 1973.

Argent, Angela. "Hatching Feminisms: Czech Feminist Aspirations in the 1990s". *Gender & History 20*, no. 1 (2008): 86-104.

Baer, Josette. "A Man Motivated by Power". Review of Slavomír Michálek, Miroslav Londák a kol. *Gustáv Husák. Moc politiky. Politik moci*. Bratislava: Veda, 2013. *New Eastern Europe 4*, no. 5 (2014): 156-160.

Baer, Josette. "Ján (Johann) Kollár (1793–1852)". In *Preparing Liberty in Central Europe. Political Texts from the Spring of Nations 1848 to the Spring of Prague 1968*. Stuttgart: ibidem, 2006.

Baer, Josette. "Surviving Totalitarian Regimes. An oral history interview with Mimi Jiránková and Nataša Lišková". *New Eastern Europe 4*, no. 1 (2014): 157-170.

Baer, Josette. "The Genesis of Czechoslovakism. An Interdisciplinary Inquiry into the Influence of Rousseau's Réligion Civile". In *East European Faces of Law and Society: Values and Practices*. Leiden: Brill Nijhoff, 2014.

Baer, Josette. "Thomas G. Masaryk and Svetozár Hurban Vajanský. A Czecho-Slovak friendship?" *KOSMAS Czechoslovak and Central European Journal 26,* no. 2 (2013): 50-62.

Baer, Josette. "Vertrauen ist nichts, Macht ist alles. Gustáv Husák (1913–1991) und die tschechoslowakische Normalisierung. Versuch eines politischen Psychogramms". In *Vertrauen*. Basel: Schwabe, 2015.

Baer, Josette. *A Life Dedicated to the Republic. Vavro Šrobár's Slovak Czechoslovakism*. Stuttgart: ibidem, 2014.

Baer, Josette. *Politik als praktizierte Sittlichkeit. Zum Demokratiebegriff von Thomas G. Masaryk und Václav Havel*. Sinzheim: Pro Universitate, 1998.

Baer, Josette. *Seven Slovak Women. Portraits of Courage, Humanism and Enlightenment.* Stuttgart: ibidem, 2015.

Baer, Josette. *Slavic Thinkers or the Creation of Polities. On Intellectual History and Political Thought in Central Europe and the Balkans in the 19th century.* Washington, D.C.: New Academia Publishing, 2007.

Bajerová, Marie. *O Emě Destinnové*. Praha: Vyšehrad, 1979.

Batscha, Zwi. *Eine Philosophie der Demokratie. Thomas G. Masaryks Begründung einer neuzeitlichen Demokratie*. Frankfurt a. Main: Suhrkamp, 1994.

Bažantová, Ilona. "Zapomenutý ekonom Karel Havlíček Borovský". *Politická Ekonomie 5,* no. 2 (1999): 621-629.

Beller, Steven. "The Hilsner Affair: Nationalism, Antisemitism and the Individual in the Habsburg Monarchy at the Turn of the Century". In *T. G. Masaryk (1850–1937). Thinker and Critic*. London: SSEES, 1990.

Bělohradský, Václav. *Krize eschatology neosobnosti.* London: Rozmluvy, 1983.

Beneš, Edvard. *Paměti II. Od Mnichova k nové válce a k novému vítezství.* Praha: Academia, 2008.

Berlin, Isaiah. *Freedom and its Betrayal. Six Enemies of Human Liberty.* London: Pimlico, 2003.

Bílek, Jan, and Luboš Velek (eds.). *Karel Kramář (1860–1937). Život a dílo.* Praha: Masarykův ústav a Archiv Akademie věd ČR, Historický ústav AV ČR, 2009.

Blažek, Petr. "Rekonstrukce. Prameny k proces s Miladou Horákovou a jejími druhy". In *Sborník Archivu ministerstva vnitra, č. 4, Archiv bezpečnostních složek MV.* Praha, 2006.

Brabec, Jiří, Jan Lopatka, Jiří Gruša, Petr Kabeš and Igor Hájek. *Slovník zakázaných autorů 1948–1980.* Praha: Státní pedagogické nakladatelství, 1991.

Bystrický, Valerián, a kol. *Rok 1968 na Slovensku a v Československu.* Bratislava: HÚ SAV, 2008.

Čapek, Karel. *Hovory s T. G. Masarykem.* Praha: František Borovy, 1946.

Černý, František. *Normalizace na Pražské Filosofické fakultě (1968–1989). Vzpomínky.* Praha: Mnemosyne, Filosofická Fakulta Univerzity Karlova, 2009.

Česko-slovenská historická ročenka 2012. *Češi a Slováci 1993–2012. Minulost je bitevním polem současníků.* Bratislava: Veda, 2013.

David, Zdeněk V. *Realism, Tolerance and Liberalism in the Czech National Awakening.* Washington D.C.: Woodrow Wilson Press, 2010.

David, Zdeněk, V. *Johann Gottfried Herder and the Czech National Awakening: A Reassessment.* Pittsburgh, PA: The Carl Beck Papers in Russian & East European Studies, no. 1807, University of Pittsburgh, 2007.

Deset pražských dnů. 17.–27. listopad 1989. Praha: Academia, 1990.

Dopisy Dr. Milady Horákové. Z pankrácké cely smrti 24.-27. 6. 1950. Praha: Nakladatelství Eva Milan Nevole, 2013 (3).

Drtina, Prokop. *Československo, můj osud.* Toronto: Sixty-Eight Publishers, 1982.

Dubček, Alexander. *Hope Dies Last. The Autobiography of Alexander Dubcek.* London: HarperCollins, 1993.

Dubček, Alexander. *Leben für die Freiheit.* München: Bertelsmann, 1993.

Dudeková, Gabriela. *Na ceste k modernej žene. Kapitoly z dejín rodových vzťahov na Slovensku.* Bratislava: Veda, 2011.

Dvořáková, Zora, and Jiří Doležal. *O Miladě Horákové a Milada Horáková o sobě.* Praha: Klub Milady Horákové v nakladatelství Eva Milan Nevole, 2001.

Dvořáková, Zora. *Kdo je ... Milada Horáková.* Praha: Středočeské nakladatelství a knihkupectví, 1991.

Einhorn, Barbara. "Where Have All the Women Gone? Women and the Women's Movement in East Central Europe". *Feminist Review XXXIX* (1991): 16-36.

Ferber, Marianne, A., and Phyllis Hutton Raabe. "Women in the Czech Republic: Feminism, Czech Style". *International Journal of Politics, Culture, and Society 16*, no. 3 (2003): 407-430.

Formánková, Pavlína, and Petr Koura. *Žádáme trest smrti! Propagandistická kampaň provázející proces s Miladou Horákovou a spol. (historická studie a edice dokumentů).* Praha: Ústav pro studium totalitních režímů, 2008.

Funda, Otakar, A. *Tomáš Garrigue Masaryk. Sein philosophisches, religiöses und politisches Denken.* Bern: Peter Lang, 1978.

Fürbach, František. *Ema Destinnová a Bedřich Smetana.* Praha: Nadace pro dějiny ve střední Evrope, Association for Central European Cultural Studies, 2011.

Geaney, Kathleen. "At home among Strangers: The Extraordinary Year 1950 in the Life of an Ordinary American Family in Communist Czechoslovakia". *COMENIUS. Journal of Euro-American Civilization II*, no. 1 (2015): 25-42.

Gebhart, Jan, Barbara Köpplová, Jitka Kryšpinová a kol. *Řízení legálního českého tisku v Protektorátu Čechy a Morava*. Praha: Univerzita Karlova, Nakladatelství Karolinum, 2010.

Gehmacher, Johanna, and Natascha Vittorelli (eds.). *Wie Frauenbewegung geschrieben wird. Historiographie, Dokumentation, Stellungnahmen, Bibliographien*. Wien: Erhart Locker, 2009.

Hain, Radan. *Staatstheorie und Staatsrecht in T. G. Masaryks Ideenwelt*. Zürich: Schulthess, 1999.

Hanák, Harry (ed.). *T. G. Masaryk (1850–1937). Statesman and Cultural Force*. Basingstoke: MacMillan, SSEES, University of London, 1990.

Hašková, Hana. "The Origins, Institutionalization, and Framing of Gender Studies in the Czech Republic". In *Travelling Gender Studies: Grenzüberschreitende Wissens- und Institutionentransfers*. Münster: Westfälisches Dampboot, 2011.

Havel, Václav. "Anatomie jedné zdrženlivosti (duben 1985)". In *Do různých stran*. Praha: Lidové Noviny, 1989.

Havel, Václav. "Milý pane Ludvíku (25 leden 1979)". In *O lidskou identitu. Úvahy, fejetony, protesty, polemiky, prohlášení a rozhovory z let 1969–1979*. Praha: Rozmluvy, 1990.

Havelka, Miloš. *Spor o smyslu Českých dějin 1895–1938*. Praha: Torst, 1995.

Havelková, Hana, and Libora Oates-Indruchová (eds.). *The Politics of Gender Culture under State Socialism: An Expropriated Voice*. London: Routledge, 2014.

Havelková, Hana. "Dreifache Enteignung und eine unterbrochene Chance: Der 'Prager Frühling' und die Frauen- und Geschlechterdiskussion in der Tschechoslowakei". *L'Homme: Europäische*

Zeitschrift für feministische Geschichtswissenschaft 20, no. 2 (2009): 31-49.

Heitlinger, Alena. "Framing Feminism in Post-Communist Czech Republic". *Communist and Post-Communist Studies 29*, no. 2 (1996): 77-93.

Hoensch, Jörg, K. *Geschichte der Tschechoslowakei.* Stuttgart, Berlin, Köln: Kohlhammer, 1992 (3).

Hoffmann, Roland, J. *Masaryk und die tschechische Frage.* München: Oldenbourg, 1988.

Hronský, Márian, and Miroslav Pekník. *Martinská deklarácia. Cesta slovenskej politiky k vzniku Česko-Slovenska.* Bratislava: Veda, 2008.

Iggers, Wilma A. W*omen of Prague. Ethnic Diversity and Social Change from the Eighteenth Century to the Present.* New York: Berghahn, 1995.

Ivanov, Miroslav. *Justiční vražda aneb smrt Milady Horákové.* Praha: XYZ, 2008.

Ivantyšynová, Tatiana (ed.). *Ján Kollár a slovanská vzájomnosť. Genéza nacionalizmu v strednej Európe.* Bratislava: SDK SVE, 2006.

Kalous, Jan. "KSČ jako iniciátor a vykonavatel politických čistek a procesů". In *Český a slovenský komunismus (1921–2011).* Praha: Ústav pro studium totalitních režímů, 2012.

Kantůrková, Eva. *Jan Hus. Příspěvek k národní identitě.* Praha: Melantrich, 1991.

Kaplan, Karel. *Druhý proces. Milada Horáková a spol. – rehabilitační řízení 1968–1990.* Praha: Univerzita Karlova, Nakladatelství Karolinum, 2012.

Kaplan, Karel. *Největší politický process. "M. Horáková a spol."* Praha, Brno: Ústav pro soudobé dějiny Akademie věd České republiky, Doplněk, 1995.

Kaplan, Karel. *The Short March. The Communist Takeover in Czechoslovakia 1945–1948*. London: C. Hurst & Company, 1987.

Kapusta-Pofahl, Karen. "Who Would Create a Czech Feminism? Challenging Assumptions in Process of Creating Relevant Feminisms in the Czech Republic". *The Anthropology of East Europe Review 20*, no. 2 (2002): 61-68.

Kara, Siddharth. *Sex Trafficking: Inside the Business of Modern Slavery*. New York: Columbia University Press, 2010.

Klíma, Ivan. *Karel Čapek, Life and Work*. North Haven, CT: Catbird Press, 2002.

Kořalka, Jiří. *František Palacký (1798–1876): Životopis*. Praha: Argo, 1998.

Kosatík, Pavel. *Věra Čáslavská. Život na Olympu. Autorizovaný životopis*. Praha: Mladá Fronta, 2012.

Kosta, Jiří. "Systemwandel in der Tschechoslowakei. Ökonomische und politische Aspekte". *Osteuropa 41*, no. 9 (1990): 802-818.

Košťálová, Michaela. *Soukromí Milady Horákové*. Praha: Petrklíč, 2014.

Köstler, Arthur. *Darkness at Noon*. London: Vintage, 2005.

Kováč, Dušan. *Dejiny Slovenska*. Praha: Lidové Noviny, 2007 (2).

Kováč, Dušan. *Slováci. Česi. Dejiny*. Bratislava: Academic Electronic Press AEP, 1997.

Kovtun, Jiří. "Masaryk proti radikalismu a antisemitismu na přelomu století". In *Masarykův sborník VIII*. Praha: Ústav T. G. Masaryka, 1993.

Kozák, Jan, B. *T. G. Masaryk a vznik Washingtonské deklarace v říjnu 1918*. Praha: Melantrich, 1968.

Křesťan, Jiří. *Zdeněk Nejedlý. Politik a vědec v osamění*. Praha: Paseka, 2012.

Kriseová, Eda. *Václav Havel. Životopis*. Praha: Atlantis, 1991.

Langer, Jo. *Convictions. My Life with a Good Communist.* London: Granta, 2011.

London, Artur. *On Trial.* London: MacMillan, 1970.

Lovčí, Radovan. *Alice Garrigue Masaryk. Život ve stínu slavného otce.* Praha: Opera Facultatis philosophicae Universitatis Carolinae Pragensis, 2007.

Luwig, Emil. *Gespräche mit Masaryk.* Amsterdam: Querido Verlag, 1935.

Macho, Peter. *Milan Rastislav Štefánik v hlavach a v srdciach. Fenomén národného hrdinu v historickej pamäti.* Bratislava: HU Prodama, 2011.

Mannová, Elena. "Mužské a ženské svety v spolkoch". In *Na ceste k modernej žene. Kapitoly z dejín rodových vzťahov na Slovensku.* Bratislava: Veda, 2011.

Margolius Kovály, Heda. *Under a Cruel Star. A Life in Prague 1941–1968.* London: Granta, 2012.

Martin, Megan, R. "The growth of Czech feminism: analyzing resistance activities through a gendered lens, 1968–1993". *Gender, rovné příležitosti, výzkum 10,* no. 1 (2009): 37-44.

Marušiak, Juraj. "Slovenská spoločnosť a normalizácia". In *Česká a slovenská společnost v období normalizace. Slovenská a česká spoločnosť v čase normalizácie. Liberecký seminar 2001.* Bratislava: Veda a Ústav politických vied SAV, 2003.

Marzík, Tomas D. "The Slovakophile Relationship of T. G. Masaryk and Karel Kálal prior to 1914". In *T. G. Masaryk (1850–1937), Thinker and Politician.* London: SSEES, 1989.

Masaryk a myšlenka evropské jednoty. Praha: Filosofická Fakulta Univerzity Karlovy FFUK, 1992.

Masaryk, Thomas, G. *The Problem of Small Nations in the European Crisis.* London: Athlone Press, 1966.

Masaryk, Tomáš, G. "Několik poznámek k problému vychování dorostlých". In *Cesta demokracie III. Projevy, články, rozhovory 1924–128*. Praha: Ústav T. G. Masaryka, 1994.

Masaryk, Tomáš, G. "Projev prezidenta Republiky". In *Cesta demokracie III. Projevy, články, rozhovory 1924–28*. Praha: Ústav T. G. Masaryka, 1994.

Masaryk, Tomáš, G. "Proststředky národa malého". In *Ideály humanitní*. Praha: Melantrich, 1991.

Masaryk, Tomáš, G. "Slavjanofilství. Mesianismus právoslavné teokracie. Slavjanofilství a Panslavismus". In *Rusko a Evropa. Studie o důchovních proudech v Rusku*, vol. I. Praha: Ústav T. G. Masaryka, 1995.

Masaryk, Tomáš, G. *Česká otázka.* Praha: Svoboda, 1990.

Masarykova praktická filosofie. Sborník z přednáškového cyklu. Praha: Masarykova společnost, 1993.

Masaryková, Charlotta, G. *Listy do Vězení*. Praha: Vladimír Žikeš, 1947.

Měchýř, Jan. "O lidech v čase normalizace". In *Česká a slovenská společnost v období normalizace. Slovenská a česká spoločnosť v čase normalizácie. Liberecký seminar 2001*. Bratislava: Veda a Ústav politických vied SAV, 2003.

Michálek, Slavomír, Miroslav Londák a kol. *Gustáv Husák. Moc politiky. Politik moci*. Bratislava: Veda, 2013.

Nečasová, Denisa. *Buduj vlast – posílíš mír! Ženské hnutí v českých zemích 1945–1955*. Brno: Matice moravská, 2011.

Neudorflová, Marie, L. "Karel Havlíček, T. G. Masaryk a demokracie". In *Spisovatelé, společnost a noviny v promínách doby*. Praha: Literární Archiv Národného Písemnictví, 2006.

Novák, Jozef (ed.). *On Masaryk. Texts in English and German*. Amsterdam: Rodopi, 1988.

Oates-Indruchová, Libora (ed.). *Tvrdošíjnost myšlenky: od feministické kriminologie k teorii genderu (Publikace na počest Prof. Gerlindy Šmausové)*. Praha: Sociologické nakladatelství, 2011.

Oates-Indruchová, Libora. "The Local and the Global in Czech Gender Studies". *ASEEES Newsnet 53*, no. 4 (2013): 1-3.

Opat, Jaroslav. *Filozof a Politik T. G. Masaryk 1882-1893*. Praha: Melantrich, 1990.

Otáhal, Milan. "Význam bojů o rukopisy". In *Masarykův Sborník VII*. Praha: Academia, 1992.

Padevět, Jiří. *Průvodce protektorátní Prahou. Místa – události – lidé*. Praha: Academia, Archiv hlavního města Prahy, 2014.

Patočka, Jan. "Pokus o českou národní filosofii a jeho nezdar". In *Tři studie o Masarykovi*. Praha: Váhy, Mladá Fronta, 1991.

Pauer, Jan. *Prag 1968. Der Einmarsch des Warschauer Paktes. Hintergründe – Planung – Durchführung*. Bremen: Edition Temmen, 1995.

Paulová, Milada. *Dějiny Maffie. Odboj Čechů a jihoslovanů za světové války 1914-1918*. Praha: Československá grafická unie, 1937.

Pažout, Jaroslav. "Trestněprávní perzekuce odpůrců režimu v období tzv. Normalizace (1969–1989) – faktor stability a indikátor rozkladu kommunistického režimu". In *Český a slovenský komunismus (1921–2011)*. Praha: Ústav pro studium totalitních režimů 2012.

Peroutka, Ferdinand. "O účasti na revoluci (1924)". In *Kdo nás osvobodil?* Praha: Náklad Svazu národního osvobození, Tisk 'Pokrok', 1927.

Pešek, Jan. "Nepriateľ so straníckou legitimáciou. Proces s tzv. Slovenskými buržoáznymi nacionalistami". In *Storočie procesov. Súdy, politika a spoločnosť v moderných dejinách Slovenska*. Bratislava: Veda, 2013.

Pichler, Tibor. "Obavy z politiky: Ján Kollár a myšlienka slovanskej vzájomnosti". In *Národovci a občania. O slovenskom politickom myslení v 19. Storočí*. Bratislava: Veda, 1998.

Plaschka, Richard, G., and Karlheinz Mack (eds.). *Wegenetz europäischen Geistes I. Wissenschaftszentren und geistige Wechselbeziehungen zwischen Mittel- und Südosteuropa vom Ende des 18. Jahrhunderts bis zum ersten Weltkrieg*. Wien: Verlag für Geschichte und Politik, 1983; *Wegenetz europäischen Geistes II. Universitäten und Studenten. Die Bedeutung studentischer Migrationen in Mittel- und Südosteuropa vom 18. bis zum 20. Jahrhundert*. München: Oldenbourg, 1987.

Pospíšil, Miloslav. *Ema Destinnová. Česká pěvecká legenda*. Praha: Nakladatelství Brána, 2008.

Proces s vedením zaškodnického spiknutí proti republice. Horáková a společníci. Praha: Ministerstvo spravedlnosti, 1950.

Pynsent, Robert B. (ed.). *T. G. Masaryk (1850–1937). Thinker and Critic*. Basingstoke: MacMillan, SSEES, University of London, 1989, 1990.

Radzinsky, Edvard. *Stalin*. New York: Anchor Books, 1997.

Reinfeld, Barbara K. *Karel Havlíček (1821–1856). A National Liberation Leader of the Czech Renascence*. New York, NY, Boulder, CO: Columbia University Press, 1982.

Rok Šedesáty Osmý. V usneseních a dokumentech UV KSČ. Praha: Svoboda, 1969.

Rybářová, Petra. "Chiméra rituálnej vraždy. Údajné zločiny Židov v Rakúsko-Uhorsku a ich ohlas na Slovensku". In *Storočie Procesov. Súdy, Politika, a Spločnosť v moderných Dejinách Slovenska*. Bratislava: Veda, 2013.

Rychlík, Jan. *Češi a Slováci ve 20. století. Česko-Slovenské vztahy 1914–1945*. Bratislava: Veda, 1997.

Rychlík, Jan. *Devisové přisliby a cestování do zahraničí v období normalizace*. Praha: Ústav pro soudobé dějiny AV ČR, 2012.

Rychlík, Jan. *Rozdělení Česko-Slovenska 1989–1992*. Praha: Vyšehrad, 2012.

Saurer, Edith, Margareth Lanzinger, and Elisabeth Frysak (eds.). *Women's Movements. Networks and Debates in Post-communist Countries in the 19th and 20th Centuries*. Köln: Böhlau, 2006.

Savelli, Mat, and Sarah Marks (eds.). *Psychiatry in Communist Europe*. London: Palgrave, 2015.

Schmidt-Hartmann, Eva. *Thomas G. Masaryk's Realism*. München: Oldenbourg, 1984.

Šedivý, Ivan. *Češi, České Země a Velká Válka 1914–1918*. Praha: Nakladatelství Lidové Noviny, 2001.

Sedm pražských dnů. 21–27. srpen 1968. Dokumentace. Praha: Academia, 1990.

Šiklová, Jiřina. "Feminism and the Roots of Apathy in the Czech Republic". *Social Research 64*, no. 2 (1997): 258-280.

Sikora, Stanislav. *Po jari krutá zima. Politický vývoj na Slovensku v rokoch 1968–1971*. Bratislava: HÚ SAV, 2013.

Šimková, Dagmar. *Byly jsme tam taky*. Praha: Monika Vadášová-Elšiková, 2011.

Skilling, Gordon, H. *Czechoslovakia's Interrupted Revolution*. Princeton, NJ: Princeton University Press, 1976.

Skilling, Gordon, H. *T. G. Masaryk proti proudu (1882–1914)*. Praha: Práh, 1995.

Škvorecký, Jozef. *The Cowards*. London: Penguin, 2010.

Škvorecký, Jozef. *The Engineer of Human Souls*. London: Vintage, 1994.

Slapnicka, Helmuth. "Die Rechtsstellung des Präsidenten der Republik in der Verfassungsurkunde und in der politischen Wirklichkeit". In *Die Burg. Einflussreiche politische Kräfte um Masaryk und Beneš. Band II*. München, Wien: Oldenbourg, 1974.

Sokolová, Vera. "Getting the Words Right: Transformations of Feminism in Czech Society". *The New Presence 2*, summer (2000): 31-32.

Šolle, Zdeněk (ed.). *Masaryk a Beneš ve svých dopisech z doby pařížských mírových jednání v roce 1919*, vol. I. Praha: Archiv AV ČR, 1993.

Štaif, Jiří. *František Palacký. Život, dílo, mýtus.* Praha: Vyšehrad, 2009.

Štefánek, Anton. *Masaryk a Slovensko*. Praha: Náklad spisovatelový, 1931.

Truhlar, Dalibor. *Thomas G. Masaryk. Philosophie der Demokratie.* Frankfurt a. Main: Peter Lang, 1994.

Unterberger, Betty, M. "The Arrest of Alice Masaryk". *Slavic Review 33*, no. 1 (1974): 91-106.

Urban, Zdeněk. "K Masarykovu vztahu ke Slovensku před první světovou válkou". In *Masaryk a Slovensko (soubor statí)*. Praha: Masarykova společnost a Ústav T. G. Masaryka, 1992.

Vodička, Karel. "Wie der Koalitionsbeschluss zur Auflösung der ČSFR zustande kam". *Osteuropa 45*, no. 2 (1994): 175-186.

Waylen, Georgina. "Women and Democratization: Conceptualizing Gender Relations in Transition Politics". *World Politics XLVI* (1994): 327-354.

Williams, Kieran. *The Prague Spring and its Aftermath. Czechoslovak Politics 1968–1970.* Cambridge: Cambridge University Press, 1997.

Winters, Stanley B. (ed.). *T. G. Masaryk (1850–1937). Thinker and Politician.* Basingstoke: MacMillan, SSEES, University of London, 1989.

Wöhrer, Veronika. "Som feministka, no a čo? Versuche mit einem Schimpfwort politische Arbeit zu machen?" In *Women's Movements. Networks and Debates in Post-communist Countries in the 19th and 20th Centuries.* Köln: Böhlau, 2006.

Internet resources

"Brožová-Polednová návrhla i smrt těhotné žene" on http://www.lidovky.cz/brozova-polednova-navrhla-i-smrt-tehotne-zene-ted-bude-volna-prb-/zpravy-domov.aspx?c=A100301_205502_ln_domov_ani.

"Die ich rief, die Geister, werd ich nun nicht los" on germanstories.vcu.edu/goethe/zauber_dual.html.

"I leave this world without hatred" on http://coldwarradios.blogspot.ch/2010/11/i-leave-this-world-without-hatred.html.

Ilse Koch on https://www.jewishvirtuallibrary.org/jsource/biography/ikoch.html.

Letters of Milada Horáková on http://chnm.gmu.edu/wwh/p/230.html.

Lidice on http://www.lidice-memorial.cz/default_en.aspx.

"Milada Horáková's last speech at court" on https://www.youtube.com/watch?v=Spii_fjdgXs.

Mörike, Eduard. *Mozart's Journey to Prague* (*Mozart auf der Reise nach Prag*). London: John Calder Limited, 1957; on http://www.almaclassics.com/excerpts/mozartsjourney.pdf.

"Olympic Games Mexico 68 Vera Caslavska" on https://www.youtube.com/watch?v=lksI8O8_u7M.

"Pavlik Morozov: Soviet Boy Hero" on http://www.mod-langs.ox.ac.uk/russian/childhood/pavlikmorozov.htm.

"Poučení z krizového vývoje ve straně a společnosti po XIII. sjezdu KSČ" on http://www.totalita.cz/txt/txt_pouceni.php.

"Pri poprávě Horákové mi bylo špatně" on http://www.novinky.cz/domaci/149236-ludmila-brozova-polednova-pri-poprave-horakove-mi-bylo-spatne.html.

Příbeh herečky on http://www.ceskatelevize.cz/porady/10366883725-pribeh-herecky/21156226416.

Rafael Kubelík on http://vagne.free.fr/kubelik/timeline.htm.

"The story of a Czech priest who saw a miracle and was killed for it" on http://www.catholicnewsagency.com/news/the-story-of-a-czech-priest-who-saw-a-miracle-and-was-killed-for-it-66326/.

"Věra Čáslavská at the Olympic Games" on http://www.olympic.org/vera-caslavska.

Villa Bertrámka Mozart museum on http://www.bertramka.eu.

"Vždicky jsem hrála s klukama" on http://www.dobraadresa.cz/old.htm.

Zabíjení soudruha on http://www.ceskatelevize.cz/porady/10362011008-ceske-stoleti/21251212043-zabijeni-soudruha-1951/.

"Zemřela Ludmila Brožová-Polednová, prokuratorka z procesu s Horákovou" on http://www.ceskatelevize.cz/ct24/domaci/299321-zemrela-ludmila-brozova-polednova-prokuratorka-z-procesu-s-horakovou.

"Zemřela Ludmila Brožová-Polednová, prokuratorka z procesu s Horákovou" on http://www.lidovky.cz/ve-veku-93-let-zemrela-ludmila-brozova-polednova-f5k-/lide.aspx?c=A150124_124718_lide_mct.

Kant, Immanuel. *Beantwortung der Frage: Was ist Aufklärung?* (1784) on http://www.gutenberg.org/files/30821/30821-h/30821-h.htm.

Kant, Immanuel. *What is Enlightenment?* on http://www.columbia.edu/acis/ets/CCREAD/etscc/kant.html.

Kýr, Aleš. "Horáková umírala čtvrt hodiny" on http://zpravy.idnes.cz/horakova-umirala-ctvrt-hodiny-zjistili-historici-fs3-/domaci.aspx?c=A050629_090843_domaci_lkr.

Kýr, Aleš. "Pankrácká popraviště z let 1926–1989" on http://www.historickykaleidoskop.cz/1-2006/pankracka-popraviste-z-let-1926-1989.html.

Lukes, Igor. *Rudolf Slansky. His Trial and Trials. Cold War International History Project Working Paper no. 50.* Washington, D.C.: Woodrow

Wilson Center, 2008. On http://www.wilsoncenter.org/sites/default/files/WP50IL.pdf.

Machiavelli. *The Prince* on http://www.constitution.org/mac/prince.pdf.

Operation: Daybreak on http://www.imdb.com/title/tt0075019/.

Proces H on http://www.ceskatelevize.cz/porady/10153697395-proces-h.

Swiss women's right to vote on http://history-switzerland.geschichte-schweiz.ch/chronology-womens-right-vote-switzerland.html.

Tereza Maxová Foundation for Children on http://www.nadaceterezymaxove.cz/en/.

The Czech Institute for the Study of Totalitarian Regimes http://www.ustrcr.cz/en/milada-horakova-en.

The history of the IFRC on http://www.ifrc.org/en/who-we-are/history/.

The Emmy Destinn Foundation, UK on http://www.destinn.com/aims/4523141301.

Totalita on http://www.totalita.cz/vysvetlivky/o_horakovam.php.

What the Czechoslovak Red Cross needs: compiled from official reports on https://archive.org/stream/5926299upenn/5926299#page/n3/mode/2up.

Ždanov, Andrei, A. "Speech at the Soviet Writers' Congress, August 1934" on https://www.marxists.org/subject/art/lit_crit/sovietwritercongress/zdhanov.htm.

Index

'

'black university', 180, 181

"

"small works", 65, 67, 69, 83, 85, 120

A

alcohol, 177
amnesty, 42, 95, 112, 128, 129, 197
Anschluss, 88
anti-Austrian activities, 57, 63, 65
Arendt, Hannah, 132
aristocracy, 4, 19, 20, 23, 68
artist, 22, 26, 28, 34, 213
Austrian monarchy, 4, 21, 34

B

Banášová, Adela, 205
Bartík, Jozef, 105
Bartolomejšska 4, 95
Bass, Eduard, 90
BBC, 91, 92, 216
Beneš, Edvard, 6, 26, 52, 53, 58, 81, 89, 100, 101, 104, 117, 119, 125, 131, 139, 156, 216, 217
Benešová, Hana, 67, 84, 186
Berlin, Isaiah Sir, 135
Biľak, Vasiľ, 174, 175
Bosáková, Eva, 186, 188
bourgeoisie, 144
brainwash, 209
Bratislava Mondays, 205
British VOGUE, 208
Brožová-Polednová, Ludmila, 127, 128, 129, 130
Buchal, Jan, 126
bureaucracy, 4
Bystrička, 61, 79, 80, 84

C

Callas, Maria, 34
Čapek, Karel, 42
Capitalist, 106, 109, 111, 113, 131, 141, 189, 190
Caruso, Enrico, 24, 28, 29
censors, 60
Čepička, Alexej, 140
Černík, Oldřích, 174, 175, 190
Černý, František, 178, 179, 183
Černý, Václav, 179
České Budějovice, 33, 143
České Století, 138
Český Brod, 153, 154
Charity, 75
Charles-Ferdinand University, 6, 13, 36
Charter 77, 14, 47, 176, 179, 181, 196
child mortality, 72
children, 2, 4, 7, 19, 22, 24, 35, 62, 70, 77, 78, 83, 84, 106, 114, 116, 129, 147, 148, 150, 152, 173, 192, 193, 195, 196,

204, 207, 210, 211, 212, 215, 218, 219
Cihosť, 129, 151
civil society, 3, 7, 180, 220
class enemy, 108, 136
Clementis, Vladimír, 110, 138
clergy, 4, 68, 100, 109
Communist coup d'état, 2, 85, 216
Communist Party, 2, 4, 14, 82, 85, 87, 94, 101, 102, 104, 111, 125, 173, 185, 204, 206, 216, 217
Comte, Auguste, 44
concentration camps, 90, 106, 109, 136, 155
Covent Garden, 22, 24, 25
CSCE negotiations, 175
Czech National Theatre, 21
Czechoslovak Association of Physical Education and Sport, 188
Czechoslovak nation, 49
Czechoslovak National Socialist Party, 6
Czechoslovak patriotism, 80, 119
Czechoslovak Red Cross, 6, 36, 65, 69, 71, 72, 74, 77, 79, 83, 119, 214
Czechoslovak Women's Council, 116, 217
Czechoslovakism, 36, 43, 49, 51

D

David, Zdeněk V., 45
Declaration of Independence, 66
democratic procedure, 40, 102
democratization, 46, 48, 53
devisový příslib, 183
Dobrovský, Joseph, 38, 47
Drtina, Prokop, 103

Dubček, Alexander, 5, 174, 175, 178, 181, 190
Dvořák, Antonín, 20, 32, 33

E

eclectic, 7, 44, 46
economic privatization, 9
Einstein, Albert, 155
emigration, 95, 126
engineers of the human soul, 133
Enlightenment, 1, 3, 35, 38, 45, 68, 69
EU, 10, 213
exile *odboj*, 25
Existentialism, 96

F

Fascism, 141
Feminism, 14, 15, 198
feminist approach, 2
First Republic, 2, 6, 8, 9, 10, 14, 36, 40, 87, 102, 106, 107, 111, 113, 116, 117, 119, 125, 131, 152, 213, 216, 217
forces of reaction, 140, 142, 144
foreign currency, 178, 183, 184, 185
freedom of movement, 183
Fröhlich, Richard, 84

G

Gabčik, Jozef, 116, 173
Garrigue, Charlotte, 18
Gebauer, Jan, 39
gender equality, 12
Geneva Convention, 71
German occupation, V, 2, 10, 71
Gestapo, 2, 91, 93, 116
Gilly, Dinh, 28

Gorbačev, Mikhail S., 206
Gottwald, Klement, 79, 95, 104, 125, 126, 135, 136, 137, 138, 139, 152, 154
Great Britain, 6, 25, 26, 78, 82, 85, 87, 89, 91, 92, 94, 95, 96, 117, 217
Great Sweeper operation, 138
Greek tragedy, 196

H

Habsburg monarchy, 11, 40
Havel, Václav, 5, 9, 14, 131, 182, 196, 197
Havlíček, Karel, 48
Herder, Johann Gottfried, 45, 46
Herzigová, Eva, 208
high treason, 30, 56, 59, 62, 124
higher education, 12, 19, 176, 177
Hilsner affair, 36, 37, 40
Hilsneriáda, 37, 40, 42
historic rights of the Bohemian crown, 43, 50
historical context, 7, 17, 35, 36, 173
Hitler, 4, 8, 54, 55, 81, 102, 146
Hodonín, 54, 129
Holan, Vladimír, 91
Hollywood, 193, 209
homosexuality, 28
Humanität, 45
humour, V, 59, 203, 219
Hungary, 40, 50, 53, 66, 185
Hus, Jan, 45, 47
hybrid, 101
hygienic standards, 77

I

individuality, 47, 204
Ingr, Sergei, 151

Intellectuals, 133
invasion, 5, 14, 103, 174, 175, 178, 202, 218
investigation, 7, 153, 154
Israel, 105, 109

J

Jewish ritual murder, 40, 42

K

Kálalová, Vlasta, 152
Kalandra, Záviš, 126
Kant, Immanuel, 68
Kaplan, Karel, 99, 101, 112
Keller, Helen, 57
Klaus, Václav, 9, 128, 130, 176
Kollár, Ján, 45, 47
Köstler, Arthur, 134
Kramář, Karel, 42, 74, 80
Kriseová, Eda, 180
KSČ, 102, 103, 104, 106, 109, 110, 112, 113, 127, 131, 132, 135, 138, 140, 142, 145, 149, 175, 177, 190
Kubelík, Rafael, 91
Kubiš, Jan, 116, 173

L

labour camps, 107, 136
lawyer, 6, 42, 87, 89, 99, 120, 156
legia, 26, 53, 106
Libuše, 21, 38
Lidice, 90
Lidové Noviny, 14, 56, 80, 89, 92, 94, 145, 216
Locke, John, 44
Lucerna, 186

M

Machiavelli, 44, 45, 134
Macpherson, James, 38
maffie, 25, 26, 30, 34, 56, 57, 58, 65, 66, 76, 213
manifesto *2000 Words*, 190
marriage, 19, 22, 23, 24, 25, 26, 27, 29, 89, 197, 213, 214
Marshall plan, 105
Marxák, 203
Marxism-Leninism, 109, 133, 134
Masaryk, Jan, 94, 103, 119
Masaryk, Tomáš, 17, 18, 21, 26, 34, 36, 37, 39, 40, 42, 43, 45, 46, 48, 49, 50, 54, 56, 57, 58, 60, 63, 68, 69, 73, 76, 80, 81, 89, 117, 152
Mečiar, Vladimír, 5, 9
Metropolitan Opera, 6, 19, 24
Mexico City, 6, 174, 198, 218
Minerva, 35
Ministry of Justice, 53, 127, 140, 141, 149
minorities, 102
model, 207
monopoly of power, 127, 132, 190, 217
Moravec, Emanuel, 92
Morozov, Pavlik, 148
Moscow, 2, 105, 110, 131, 137, 190
motherhood, 19
Mozart, Wolfgang Amadeus, 21
Munich Agreement, 4, 55, 81, 90

N

NAM, 105, 184
Napoleon, 23, 27
National Front, 9, 101, 102, 104, 119, 145
nation-building theory, 45, 49, 68
NATO, 10, 213
natural law, 43, 48, 49, 50
Navratilova, Martina, 3, 88
Neruda, Jan, 39
normalization, 2, 5, 7, 14, 174, 175, 176, 177, 178, 183, 192, 196, 201, 203, 204, 205, 218, 219
nuclear war, 146, 147, 150

O

obrození nationalism, 38
Odložil, Josef, 191, 196
odsun, 8, 131
OKAPI, 137, 138
Old Czech manuscripts, 36
Old Czechs, 39
oral history interview, 7, 87
OSS, 137, 138

P

Palacký, František, 39, 48
Patočka, Jan, 47, 179, 180
Pecl, Oldřich, 126
Peroutka, Ferdinand, 51, 89, 92, 93, 94, 216
pětiminutovky, 147
Plamínková, Františka F., 116, 118
Plato, 54, 180
Plečnik, Jože, 84
pledge, 148
political participation, 12, 19, 66
Potemkin villages, 145
poverty, 8, 78, 95, 219
pragmatism, 47, 58, 61, 118
Pragokoncert, 210
Prague Conservatory, 26, 31, 34

Prague Spring, 2, 5, 112, 174, 175, 201, 202, 205, 218
President Wilson, 52, 66
propaganda campaign, 101, 131, 145
propaganda machine, 144
Protectorate, 4, 6, 8, 89, 90, 92
psychological pressure, 132, 143
Puccini, Giacomo, 20

R

Radičová, Iveta, 5
Radio Free Europe, 82, 138, 204
rationalism, 37, 38, 133
Realism, 37, 38, 39, 133
referendum, 10, 11, 55
resolutions, 142, 144, 145
Řevnice, 87
Ripka, Hubert, 95
Roosevelt, Eleanor, 117
Roosevelt, Franklin D., 117
Rubinstein, Arthur, 23, 28, 29
Rudé Právo, 145, 149
rule-of-law state, 3
Ruzyně prison, 122

S

Šámal, Přemysl, 65
samizdat, 176
Samuel, Harold, 25, 26, 29, 213
schizophrenic lifestyle, 203
script, 110, 111, 127, 136, 141, 142, 146, 153
secret service, 103, 104, 132
Seifert, Jaroslav, 90
sexism, 15
show trial, 6, 129, 136, 138, 155
Šimková, Dagmar, 107
Slánský, Rudolf, 110, 113, 135, 136, 137, 138, 139, 155

Slovakia, 6, 8, 9, 40, 43, 49, 50, 52, 53, 54, 55, 70, 71, 76, 78, 79, 84, 85, 88, 103, 132, 174, 177, 205, 216
Smetana, Bedřich, 20, 33
social stigma, 28, 124
Socialist Citizen, 131, 132, 155
sovereignty, 18, 44, 49, 50, 54, 178, 193
Spanish Civil War, 109
Šrobár, Vavro, 13, 53
Stalin, Josef, 101, 105, 109, 110, 126, 133, 136, 137, 138
state-building, 43, 45, 49
statecraft, 44, 45
StB, 104, 107, 108, 137, 138, 153, 179, 182, 204, 206
Štefánik, Milan Rastislav, 13
stengazety, 142
Stránský, Jaroslav, 89, 91, 155, 216
Strauss, Richard, 33
Stráž Castle, 23, 25, 26, 27, 28, 29, 30, 33, 34, 213, 214
Sub-Carpathian Rus, 70, 71, 76
suicide, 24, 27, 76, 179, 182
Sverdlinová, Terezie, 211, 212, 219

T

teenagers, 90, 152, 153, 154
Tereza Maxová Foundation, 7, 211
the Castle, 80, 89, 117, 139, 186, 190, 192, 194, 196, 216
The Czech Question, 36, 45
theories of gender, 1
Theresienstadt, 91, 116
Tito, Josip Broz, 105
Titoism, 109, 136
top model, 3, 7, 210, 219
Toscanini, Arturo, 24, 29

travel, 25, 178, 183, 185, 190, 201
Trianon, 53
Turčianský Sv. Martin, 78

U

unor 1948, 101
USA, 18, 26, 31, 35, 43, 49, 50, 53, 63, 64, 65, 66, 69, 74, 78, 82, 85, 126, 173, 211, 219

V

Vaculík, Ludvík, 190, 192, 218
Vadas, Martin, 126
Vášáryová, Magdaléna, 5
Vatican, 109
Velvet Divorce, 8, 9
Velvet Revolution, 9, 15, 97, 100, 127, 178, 201, 206, 210, 217, 218, 220
Verdi, Giuseppe, 20
Vienna, 21, 35, 58, 59, 63, 64, 68, 88, 215
Vienna University, 18, 37
Villa Bertrámka, 21

výjezdní doložka, 184
vyloučený, 176
Vyšehrad, 8, 22, 33, 48, 214
vyškrtnut, 176

W

War propaganda, 57
Weltgeist, 46
Wild West, 206
witch trials, 146
working among women (*práce mezi ženami*), 14

Y

Young Czechs, 39

Z

Zabíjení soudruha, 138, 139
Zápotocký, Antonín, 79
Zátopek, Emil, 151, 192
Zenkl, Peter, 103
Zídek, Petr, 130
Zionism, 109, 136
Živena, 78
zoon politikon, 174

Josette Baer

Seven Slovak Women

Portraits of Courage, Humanism, and Enlightenment

218 pages, Paperback. 2015
ISBN 978-3-8382-0638-7
€ 24.90

This engaging and insightful book is the first historical study in English portraying the lives and fates of Slovak women. The seven life stories, ranging from the late 19th century to the present day, expose the often cruel political history of Slovakia through the eyes of prominent women whose acts and deeds on behalf of their fellow citizens remain unforgotten in the Slovak collective mind. The four chapters and three oral history interviews offer a captivating insight into how the situation of Slovak women in society has changed during a most eventful period of history.

This book will be complemented by a second volume on Czech women whose lives have been of the same singular importance for the Czech lands as their Slovak counterparts were for their country (ISBN 978-3-8382-0640-0, coming out in fall 2015). The two volumes are separate entities in their own right, but together provide the reader with a comprehensive picture of womens lives in the Czech lands and Slovakia, stressing the distinct political circumstances Czech and Slovak women have faced in recent history.

ibidem-Verlag

Melchiorstr. 15

D-70439 Stuttgart

info@ibidem-verlag.de

www.ibidem-verlag.de
www.ibidem.eu
www.edition-noema.de
www.autorenbetreuung.de

Zeitfracht Medien GmbH
Ferdinand-Jühlke-Straße 7,
99095 - DE, Erfurt
produktsicherheit@zeitfracht.de